T0287774

Dark and Bloody Ground

RICHARD BLACKMON

DARK
AND
BLOODY
GROUND

—The—
American Revolution
Along the
Southern Frontier

WESTHOLME
Yardley

First Westholme Paperback 2013

©2012 Richard D. Blackmon

Maps by Paul Dangel ©2012 Westholme Publishing

All rights reserved under International and Pan-American Copyright Conventions. No part of this book may be reproduced in any form or by any electronic or mechanical means, including information storage and retrieval systems, without permission in writing from the publisher, except by a reviewer who may quote brief passages in a review.

Westholme Publishing, LLC
904 Edgewood Road
Yardley, Pennsylvania 19067
Visit our Web site at www.westholmepublishing.com

ISBN: 978-1-59416-189-6

Also available as an eBook.

Printed in the United States of America.

Contents

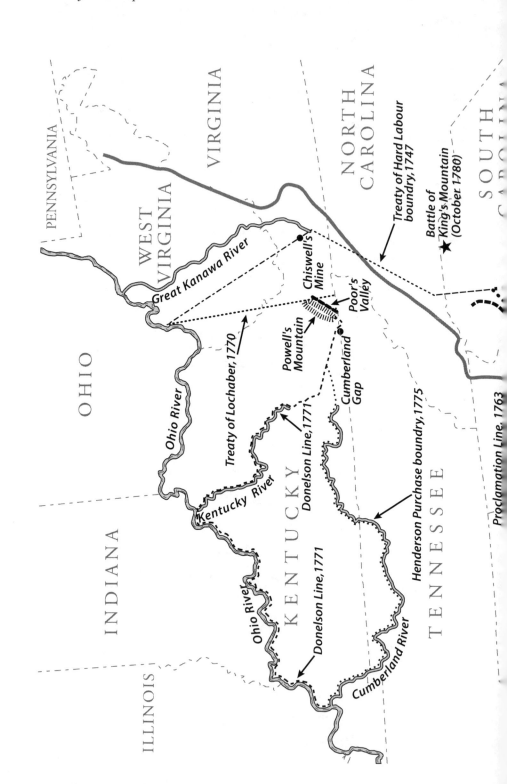

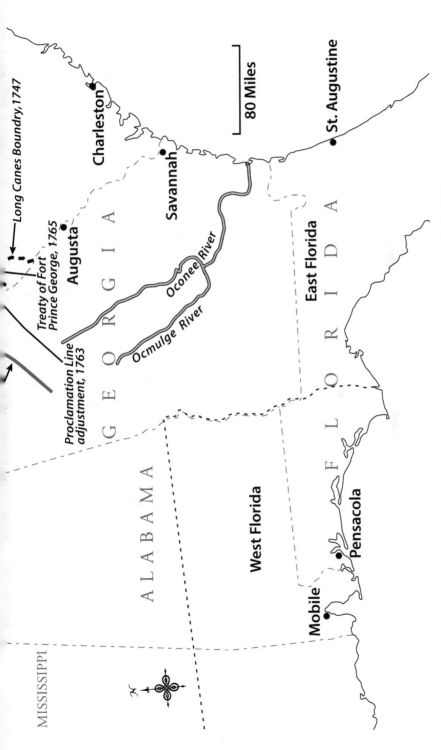

Map 1. Boundaries between Anglo-American settlements and southern American Indian lands, 1747–1775.

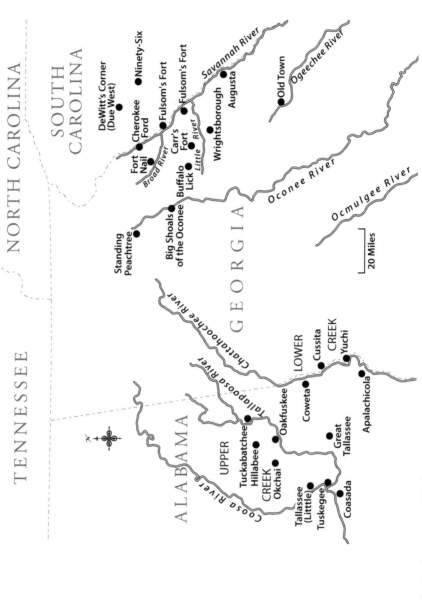

Map 2. Anglo–American and Indian towns in Alabama and Georgia.

Map 3. Anglo-American settlements in Kentucky.

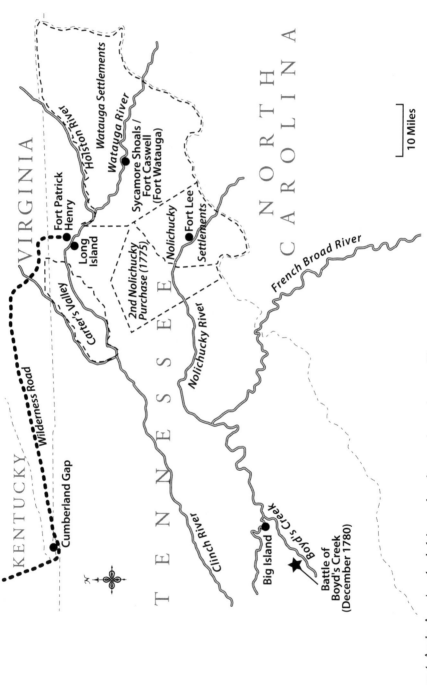

Map 4. Anglo–American land claims and settlements in northeastern Tennessee.

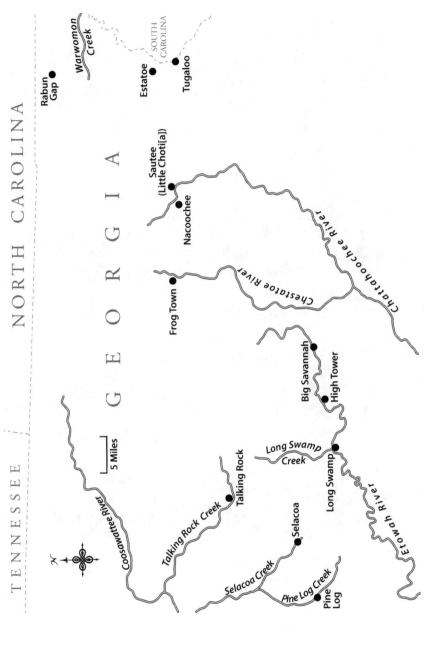

Map 5. American Indian settlements in northern Georgia.

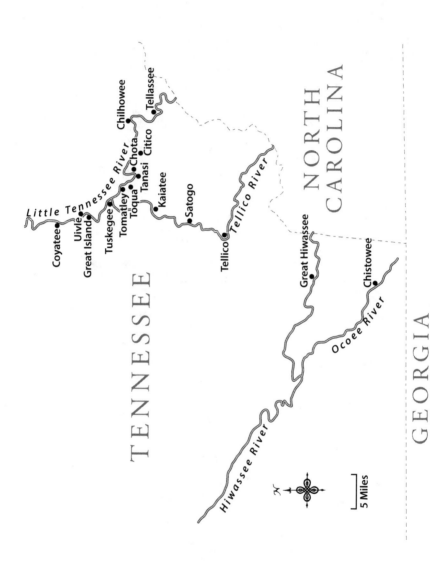

Map 6. American Indian settlements in southeastern Tennessee.

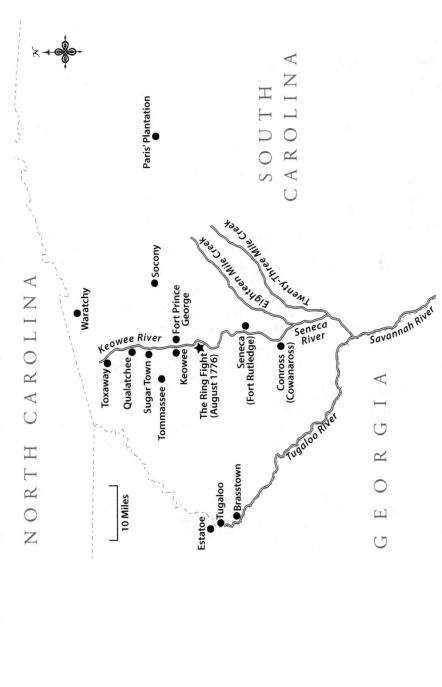

Map 7. Anglo-American and Indian settlements in northwestern South Carolina.

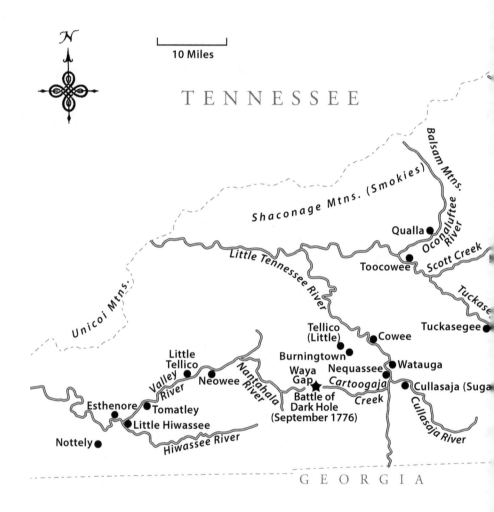

Map 8. Anglo-American and Indian settlements in western North Carolina.

Cathey's Fort

French Broad River

Pigeon River

Catawba River

Davidson's Fort

Swannanoa River

Richland Creek

som Gap

River

own]

NORTH

CAROLINA

Howard's Gap

Round Mtn.

SOUTH

CAROLINA

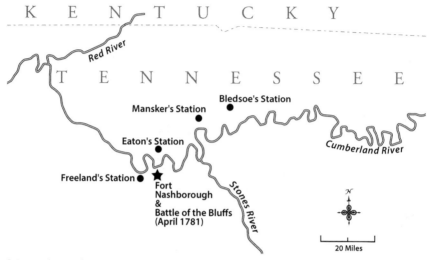

Map 9. Anglo-American settlements in the Cumberland Valley.

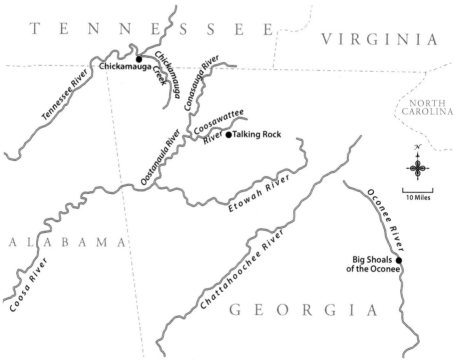

Map 10. American Indian settlements in northwestern Georgia.

Introduction

In May 1769, a man who would become synonymous with the early American frontier first explored the lands west of the Appalachian Mountains. On a ridge overlooking the country, Daniel Boone stood "looking round with astonishing delight, beheld the ample plains, the beauteous tracts below." Indeed, some years later Boone would write of the land that he "esteemed a second paradise." But even at the very beginning, foreboding omens made their appearance. During that first trip west of the Appalachians, American Indians made Boone and his party captives. Though they escaped unharmed and returned to lead their families into the "second paradise," the Indians' presence should have been a warning. Instead of heeding the encounter, Boone determined to emigrate beyond the mountains and live there "at the risk of my life and fortune."[1]

That episode, in many respects, characterizes the years of the American Revolution along the southern frontier. In the 1760s, only a few long hunters—men who would go beyond settlements to hunt for a period of a year or more—had ventured across the mountains. By the early 1770s, a few had settled their families permanently in what would come to be known as the Overmountain region of what was then North Carolina and Virginia. After 1771, the Overmountain settlements experienced a flood of immigrants, due to the demise of the Regulator Movement in North Carolina and burgeoning population.

From 1765 to 1771, colonists in western North Carolina rose up against the corrupt colonial government in Halifax. These colonists, called regulators, primarily occupied themselves with disrupting courts for a lack of unbiased justice and driving off surveyors hired by government officials. In May

1771, however, over two thousand regulators met the governor and one thousand of his militiamen at Alamance, near present-day Burlington, North Carolina. The governor's troops defeated the regulators, hanging seven on the battlefield for treason. A vast majority fled the scene and subsequently escaped with their families to the Overmountain region, beyond the reach of the colonial governor and royal authority.

With the onset of the Revolution, Whig (Patriot) and Loyalist militias ravaged the southern states, forcing thousands of residents to seek refuge across the mountains. The southern Indian tribes directly affected by these American settlers initially included the Cherokees and Creeks, and soon the Shawnees north of the Ohio River. Then the Chickamaugas, an amalgamation of tribes throughout the south and north, established themselves and also became targets. The Shawnees and their various allies are included in this book only insofar as their operations against the Kentucky settlements are concerned. Likewise, the Chickasaws are only included regarding their operations against the Cumberland settlements.

On the eve of the American Revolution, the southern frontiers extended from present-day southwest Virginia and eastern Tennessee (the Overmountain settlements), to the area in western North Carolina east of the Blue Ridge Mountains, down into the northwest part of South Carolina, and into northern Georgia (the Ceded Lands). Expansion from these areas during the Revolution included the area known then, and now, as Kentucky, as well as the Cumberland settlements of present-day middle Tennessee. All of these areas experienced an influx of American settlers as well as almost continuous attacks by various militant factions of Indians. Though the areas except the Cumberland could claim a substantial settlement population before 1775, they experienced geometric population growth from immigration during the Revolution. Whether it was to escape the economic uncertainty of the east, the rigors of the conflict, or the depredations of troops and militias on both sides, settlers flooded west. Their migration put them on a collision course with some southern Indian tribes.

During the conflict, the southern tribes struggled to stem the tide of white settlers and maintain as much of their hunting ground as possible. Hunting had always been vital to sustaining Indian lifeways. Foremost, it provided the major source of sustenance for Indian diets. By the time of the American Revolution, it provided the currency of Indian economies: deerskins. Only by bartering deerskins could native peoples obtain the goods they had become dependent on in recent decades. Also, it provided the means to obtain firearms and ammunition to continue hunting and to defend themselves against enemies, whatever race they happened to be.

American Indian loyalty initially depended largely on the politics of the traders who lived in practically every town. A trader supplied the Indians with all the goods and ammunition they desired through the purchase of deerskins obtained from traditional hunts. The trader's importance could not be denied, and both the British and the Whigs well understood the influence of the trader.

At the end of the Seven Years' War, the British Crown issued the Proclamation of 1763, which established a boundary, the Proclamation Line of 1763, to prevent westward immigration by its North American colonial subjects. Immediately, British officials negotiated adjustments to the line so that the actual locations of Indian towns and colonial settlements could be accommodated. Afterward, every few years until just before the Revolution, the British insisted on another adjustment. The Cherokee headmen implemented an ingenious diplomatic stratagem: rather than continue to allow settlers to spread south into their hunting grounds, they allowed whites to settle Kentucky in 1775 with the so-called Henderson Purchase. The wave of settlers would then bypass the Cherokee hunting grounds for Kentucky—a territory they used infrequently for hunting. It is debatable whether the Cherokees had the right to sell the Kentucky lands, and the Shawnees would have much to say about the matter over the next several years. Designed to redirect the flow of settlers to regions away from the Tennessee Valley, the plan only worked to a limited degree; settlers continued pouring into the river valley.

In 1776, diplomacy, which clearly had not thwarted the flood of settlers, broke down. In the summer, thousands of Cherokee warriors gathered into several large formations and struck the Overmountain settlements, including established forts, in an attempt to reclaim the lands they had lost to encroaching settlers over the previous years. Though British agents and traders supplied the Cherokee warriors with all the goods and ammunition they needed, no British troops were sent to support them. The Cherokees struck with unbridled ferocity, but they did not have the numerical strength to occupy the settled territory nor any artillery to reduce fortifications. After their initial attacks, the Cherokees withdrew, providing the opportunity for the settlers to reorganize.

In response to the Cherokee attacks in the summer of 1776, Whigs organized several expeditions of militia that destroyed practically all the Cherokee towns. Undaunted by the combined and somewhat coordinated Whig expeditions of 1776, hundreds of Cherokee warriors seceded from the Cherokee Nation's traditional towns (what remained of them) to continue offensive operations. Rather than rebuild the traditional towns, these warriors relocated along Chickamauga Creek in present-day southeastern Tennessee. Warriors from other tribes above and below the Ohio River joined these Chickamaugas in waging war against the ever-westward-encroaching settlers.

Some of the Creeks had aligned themselves with the British and attacked the Georgia frontier, the Ceded Lands, prior to the Cherokee War of 1776. But with the devastation wrought on the Cherokees, the attacks ceased, and the Creeks remained relatively passive throughout 1778 until 1779. The British placed a regular field army in the southern theater by 1779, and southern Indians felt supported. This created a situation the Whigs had always feared: a two-front war. Indian attacks were followed by punitive Whig expeditions until British fortunes began to wane in 1781. Regular Whig troops in the form of the Southern Continental Army had been brought into the southern theater and dealt crucial blows to the main British field army, eventually driving it out of the south altogether.

By 1782, Continental troops had driven British forces to Charleston, South Carolina, and Savannah, Georgia, where they could no longer support their Indian allies. As a result, attacks on the southern frontiers decreased dramatically, and the Whigs sent repeated expeditions into Indian towns. That year, British Indian allies realized their strategy had not achieved the desired result—the reclamation of their land—and ceased offensive operations; attrition had taken its toll.

After the 1776 Whig expeditions, so disastrous to the Cherokees, tactics changed on both sides. Coordinated Whig expeditions by several states could not be organized effectively between 1776 and 1782 because of the exigencies of the Revolution in the eastern parts of the states, where the main British army operated. All the states' men and materiel had to be focused on meeting the threat in the east, which took precedence over the security of the frontier—the result of the two-front war. As a consequence, Whigs began to utilize small, highly mobile forces—attack units numbering a few hundred, mounted, with each man carrying his own provisions and supplies. The implementation of true eighteenth-century cavalry tactics also increased their effectiveness, with many militiamen wielding swords in mounted charges.

The Indians did not actually devise new tactics. They rarely enjoyed the support of British regular soldiers, and only once the essential support of artillery. If the latter could have been obtained, and artillerymen trained in their use, the frontier war would have been vastly different. As it happened, the Indians continued to use the ambush as best it could be applied. Frequently, an invading Whig force proved superior in numbers, discouraging use of the ambush. The Cherokees only attempted pitched battles once, during the 1776 attacks, and with their failure returned to the traditional mode of warfare, with small units of warriors employing the ambush, whether on the offensive or defensive. They never possessed the numerical strength to adopt tactics other than their traditional methods of warfare.

The Revolution widened existing divisions among some Indian tribes and created new ones among others. The Whigs made it clear that there was no place in the nascent United States for those pro-British Indians who attacked the frontiers. Pro-American, or neutral, factions of tribes enjoyed easier access to trade, but they, too, had no political standing with the new country. Seven years of continued warfare had left the southern American Indian nations so fractionalized that barely any cohesion remained among them. An uncertain political future and even more uncertainty regarding sources of vital trade for supplies only served to further destabilize their polity.

Beyond the military operations of the conflict, the American Revolution along the southern frontiers changed the interaction of American Indian and white culture forever. No longer would Indians be a commonplace presence in American cities and towns, even on the frontier. The tacit alliance of Indians with the British firmly fixed them as enemies of the United States. That is the most tangible result of the conflict and perhaps the real tragedy: the excommunication of Indians from American society. This is a narrative of how that happened during the American Revolution.

ONE

Early Interrelations

1763–1771

He seemed a very likely choice. His position as an officer in the British army gained him experience in exercising authority. In the recent war with the Cherokees, he negotiated the return of British soldiers held as prisoners. The royal governor of South Carolina recommended him to the British military commander of North America for the post. And, one of the most noted leaders of the Cherokees, Attakullakulla, regarded him as a personal friend.

The appointment of John Stuart as superintendant of Indian affairs for the Southern Department met with no opposition in London and was issued before the end of 1761. As superintendant, Stuart directed relations between the British and the American Indians for the southern colonies. The appointment, coming at the end of a war with the Cherokees and at a time of continued strained relations with the Creeks, was not an enviable one. Also, with the end of the Seven Years' War and the expulsion of the French from eastern North America, colonists would be pressing westward, encroaching on the hunting grounds of several Indian tribes.[1]

Settler encroachment led to the outbreak of Pontiac's War in the Great Lakes region in 1763. To prevent a similar conflict from erupting along the southern frontier, Britain issued two key documents. King George III issued his Proclamation of 1763, and the British Board of Trade issued its "Plan for the Future Management of Indian Affairs" in 1764. These two documents would, in theory, address the great majority of frontier tensions caused by the two greatest sources of contention between Indians and whites: encroachment and trading practices.[2]

King George issued the Proclamation of 1763 in the hopes of avoiding future costly conflicts over encroachment. Essentially, the proclamation drew an imaginary line that connected the headwaters of all rivers that flowed into the Atlantic Ocean and forbade colonists to settle west of that line, which legally limited the western advance of colonial settlement. Leading British political figures trusted that this measure would eliminate the spread of colonial settlement and thus preclude future conflicts with American Indians, something the British Empire could ill afford after the expensive Seven Years' War.

Encroachment represented just one problem between the British and American Indians. The conduct of trade represented another source of tension. Between what they regarded as exorbitant prices and the unscrupulous business practices of many traders, the southern Indians had valid reasons for complaint. Trading was essential for the Indians since it was their only source of firearms, ammunition, metalware, and other manufactured goods, but they were often not getting a fair value for their deerskins. The Indians were requesting British officials to regulate the trade and traders in a more equitable manner and thereby relieve some of the economic pressure many southern Indians felt.

Stuart hoped the sources of tension would be resolved at a congress of southern Indians. He invited representatives of all the major southern tribes: the Catawbas, Cherokees, Chickasaws, Choctaws, and Creeks. Stuart called for them to meet at Augusta, Georgia, in early November 1763. Because of the proclamation alone, the British placed great emphasis on this meeting. Evidently the Cherokees did also, as more than ten years later during the American Revolution, Whigs found Stuart's letter requesting their attendance at Augusta and a copy of the proclamation among the "Lost Archives of the Cherokees," the few papers they actually kept.[3]

Stuart knew that a major issue of the congress would be the Proclamation Line in relation to existing Cherokee towns. The Cherokees lived in areas of four present-day states, the groupings of their towns named by the British. Those in the Overhill Towns were scattered along the Little Tennessee River in what is now eastern Tennessee. The Middle Towns lay along the Tuckasegee and Little Tennessee rivers, while the Valley Towns were on the banks of the Hiwassee and Valley rivers in present-day southwestern North Carolina. And the Lower Towns sat astride the Keowee, Tugaloo, and Chattahoochee rivers of northwestern South Carolina and northeastern Georgia.[4]

All except the Lower Towns lay to the west of the Proclamation Line of 1763. Because the Cherokee Lower Towns lay to the east of the line, a new boundary had to be negotiated that would reflect the physical reality. Also, by treaty, an agreement had been reached between the Cherokees and South Carolina that the line of demarcation for white settlement would be about forty miles east of Keowee, their principle Lower Town. These differences would have to be settled amicably through negotiations conducted by John Stuart, colonial representatives, and Cherokee headmen.[5]

At the congress, the Cherokees expressed their grievances to the British. They complained of settlers who had already established themselves west of the previously agreed upon Long Cane boundary of 1747 between the Cherokees and South Carolina. (At this time, North Carolina settlers did not pose a threat, being far east of the Proclamation Line.) The Cherokees also protested the current trade agreements, particularly the inflated prices that the traders charged them. The other major boundary issue involved the Creeks, whose hunting grounds lay east of the Proclamation Line. They agreed to a new boundary beginning about twenty miles up the Savannah River from Augusta, west to the Ogeechee River, and generally along its course south.[6]

In April 1764, Superintendant Stuart determined that one of his deputies should reside among the Cherokees and the Creeks. The practice would serve "to cultivate and strengthen the Friendship of these Indians to gain their affections . . . and attach them to the British Interest." Additionally, in a letter to

Alexander Cameron, the deputy Stuart chose to reside among the Cherokees, Stuart instructed Cameron to foster the "jealousies" that then existed between the Cherokees and the Creeks. The British greatly feared the idea of the two tribes' forming an alliance and then attacking the colonies. Though perhaps a wise strategic move at the time, the tactic of fostering division among the southern Indians would prove to hinder British interests in the future.[7]

Stuart remained concerned that the tribes would not give up their allegiance to the French. The end of the Seven Years' War changed the political and diplomatic landscape drastically. No longer would the southern tribes have two European rivals to manipulate. Only Britain remained east of the Mississippi River. In a step toward reinforcing the allegiance of the southern tribes to Britain, Stuart had the leading headmen from all the southeastern tribes assemble at Mobile, British West Florida, on June 4, 1764, King George III's twenty-sixth birthday. On that day, the headmen surrendered the medals the French had given them as a badge of their status, and in return Stuart issued them a medal from King George.[8]

After the congress at Augusta, colonists had moved onto land west of Dewitt's Corner in South Carolina. The Cherokees had long desired to have a boundary established and marked so that this encroachment from South Carolina would cease. As a result, Alexander Cameron called a conference to be held in October 1765 at Fort Prince George, near Keowee in the Lower Towns. At the conference, the Cherokees and British signed a treaty establishing a new boundary. In a talk by the Cherokee headmen the day after the signing of the treaty, the Cherokees expressed satisfaction with the boundary. They even suggested extending the line north for the boundary of North Carolina and Virginia. They were also concerned about the growing scarcity of game for them to hunt, since they traded the skins for all manner of goods. Because of the importance of the hunting season (fall and winter), the Cherokees requested the boundary not be marked until the following spring, to which the British agreed. The Cherokees then expressed a desire for traders to lower their prices, a sentiment they had expressed the year before to no avail.[9]

The Cherokees' 1765–1766 hunting season was marred by frequent attacks by their enemies, the Iroquois. That season, the Iroquois even found their way down into the Lower Towns and raided the Cherokees in greater numbers than before, and more frequently. As promised, a party of Cherokee headmen accompanied by Cameron and a surveying party marked the boundary, agreed upon at Fort Prince George, in the last week of April and the first week of May 1766. At a conference upon its completion, the Cherokees expressed satisfaction at the work, stating "we can never have any more disputes about Land." They reiterated their desire to have the line extended into North Carolina and Virginia, saying that five moons (months) from then would be a good time for that task. Then, after recounting the warfare during the hunting season, the Cherokees prevailed upon Stuart to negotiate a peace with the Iroquois. The Cherokees knew that the Iroquois obtained their weapons from the British, as did they, and they asked Stuart if a peace could not be negotiated to at least "take their Hatchetts back again."[10]

Marking the boundary was important to the Cherokees, for they knew that without the demarcation, redress for encroachment would be next to impossible. The headmen believed that with the boundary marked, the westward advance of colonists would have to cease, eliminating that source of contention and potential threat. Fortunately for the Cherokees, only a few violations of the agreed upon boundary occurred during the season. The British had already removed settlers who had established themselves west of the line, but others replaced them. Cameron took advantage of the opportunity provided by marking the boundary to advise the violators to remove or he would have them forcibly removed and their livestock given to the Cherokees.[11]

British officials in London understood the importance of maintaining the integrity of the boundary lines with Indian tribes. In a letter received in the colonies toward the end of 1766, the British secretary of state for the Southern Department, the Earl of Shelburne, impressed upon North Carolina governor William Tryon the importance of implementing and enforcing the Proclamation Line of 1763. This letter, in conjunction with the fact that the Cherokees had long desired to have the boundary marked, spurred Tryon to implement the Proclamation Line the following year. At the end of the letter, the Earl of Shelburne divulged the impetus behind implementing and enforcing the line: to avoid British involvement in an "Indian War." By coincidence, shortly before the earl's letter arrived, the Cherokee headmen sent Stuart a letter written by their trader reiterating their desire to mark the North Carolina and Virginia boundaries. Once again, they pleaded with him to negotiate a peace between them and the Iroquois.[12]

Waiting until their hunting season had passed, Governor Tryon arranged for the purchase of goods as gifts for the Cherokees, an escort of soldiers, a surveying party, and provisions for the entire party. He sent a letter to Stuart advising him of his intended journey from the capital to Salisbury, on the frontier, where he expected to meet the Cherokees. After a month, the Cherokees had still not met with Tryon, who then proceeded west from Salisbury one hundred more miles into the frontier. Finally, in June, the Cherokee headmen met the governor on the banks of the Tyger River. They agreed on the boundary and inquired about the goods. The governor immediately dispatched a squad of troops to retrieve the supplies from Salisbury, and a group of Cherokees accompanied them. A couple of weeks later, the North Carolina commissioners and the principle Cherokee headmen signed an agreement.[13]

As soon as the ink dried on the agreement, the North Carolina commissioners, Alexander Cameron, and the Cherokee headmen prepared to blaze the boundary through the North Carolina countryside. The Cherokee headman Judd's Friend felt confident in the boundary as it followed a line of mountains they called "the long Stone." He impressed upon the British officials the Cherokees' desire that no further encroachments occur, especially since the mountains "stand for a Boundary for ever, as they will never wear out." Another headman, Saluy, reiterated the sentiment when he said "the Line is now run, and not to be altered." The British had already removed settlers from Cherokee lands in South

Carolina, and the Cherokee headmen had no reason to believe that colonial officials would not continue to maintain the integrity of the agreement. The Cherokees wanted the colonists to settle on the lands up to the boundary and voiced this sentiment to Cameron and the other commissioners, the sincerity of their statement reinforced by giving the traditional symbol of truth, a string of white beads.[14]

The commissioners took the opportunity to allay any apprehensions that Judd's Friend, Saluy, and the other Cherokee headmen may have harbored about encroachments. They reassured the headmen that the governor would issue a proclamation forbidding any colonist from settling on Cherokee land and would prescribe a penalty for such a violation. One of the headmen, Young Warrior, mentioned that a colonist had indeed settled on Cherokee land west of the line they had been marking. The commissioners assured them that the first thing they would do upon their return was to have the governor order his removal. Though appreciative of British intentions, Young Warrior then expressed the views of the headmen when he stated that the man had a family and had just planted his crop. For him to move now and not be able to harvest his crop would mean that "his Woman and Children would suffer." The Cherokees allowed the man to stay "and take Care of his Corn for the support of his Wife and Family as we are now all Brothers."[15]

The following month saw the boundary physically marked. Stuart wrote to the Cherokee headmen to state his gladness upon hearing of them marking the boundary with North Carolina and that it would also be done for Virginia. Surely much to their satisfaction, the British had negotiated a peace between the Cherokees and their age-old enemy, the Iroquois. Even the western Indians had agreed to a peace with the Cherokees, making the "dark and bloody ground," as the Cherokees referred to the hunting grounds in present-day Kentucky, not quite so dangerous. In the same letter, Stuart advised the Cherokee headmen that because of the peace that seemed to be settling over the land, Fort Prince George (the only one occupied by British troops along the southern frontier) would be abandoned and destroyed. With colonial migration westward stopped at the boundary and the French threat removed, there would be no need for the British to maintain a fortification on the southern frontiers.[16]

Not before summer 1768 did British officials begin surveying and marking the boundary line between the Cherokees and Creeks in Georgia. By that time, the physical reality had changed drastically from when Indians and the British agreed to a boundary. Many colonists had settled on land west of the line agreed upon during the Augusta conference in 1763.[17]

Later in the year, Stuart met with the Cherokees in Hard Labor, South Carolina, to adjust the boundaries again. Under the Treaty of Hard Labour, in October 1768, the South Carolina boundary remained firm. The boundary for Virginia, however, had been extended from the North Carolina line to Chiswell's Mine, Virginia, and thence along the course of the Kanawha River. Superintendant Stuart proposed a slight variation—that the boundary run from Chiswell's Mine in a straight line to the mouth of the Kanawha River. Because of the harsh winters, the Cherokees did not use the ceded land for hunting, so they would not agree to mark the boundary that winter. They indicated that the terrain in which the boundary would be marked consisted of nothing but mountains. In the winter there would be nothing but snow and ice, and little to provide sustenance for man or beast. They then suggested May 10, 1769, as the day to meet and mark the boundary. Stuart agreed with their reasoning, as well as to meet the following spring.[18]

After the boundary issue had been addressed and agreed upon, the Cherokees expressed a strong desire for the British to enforce the boundary. If they did not, and the Cherokees found colonists settling upon their lands, they would simply tie them up and deliver them to Cameron. There would be no more boundary alterations. The Cherokees then brought up other grievances. They declared that the traders' business practices could only be kept honest by the presence of someone like Cameron. Also, because Fort Prince George had been abandoned, they wanted an honest army officer and thirty soldiers to be stationed at the Cherokee town of Keowee to keep criminals from the colonies away from their towns.

Then the Cherokee headmen thanked the British for negotiating peace with the Iroquois. The Shawnees, however, had not agreed to a truce and continued to make incursions among the Cherokees. Stuart had not allowed the Cherokees to strike back at the Shawnees, but the time had come for them to retaliate, and they requested the blessing of the British.[19]

Stuart responded to the Cherokee headmen directly. He assured them that the governors would vigorously maintain the boundary, with proclamations forbidding encroachment of colonists and delineating punishment for violating the decree. The traders no longer fell under his control, but under that of the governors. Stuart assured the headmen that he would inform the governors about the traders' abuses and that they would be rectified. Whether to station British troops in their territory would also be wholly within the purview of the governors, since they would have to financially support them. Stuart then addressed the matter that troubled the headmen most: the continued attacks of the Shawnees. Because the Shawnees refused to make peace, Stuart could no longer advise the Cherokees to remain passive.[20]

In the discussions that led to the Treaty of Hard Labour, the Cherokee headmen displayed their diplomatic acumen. By 1768, the Cherokees had faced immediate and deadly threats to their existence through prolonged warfare with the Iroquois, and threats to their homeland through westward colonial expansion. The Iroquois threat had been stopped through a British negotiated peace, though the Cherokees remained concerned about the tenuous nature of that peace. The Cherokees themselves had met the challenge of unchecked colonial expansion by negotiating with the British for the boundary. To further ensure a buffer against colonial expansion, the Cherokee headmen informed Stuart of their intention to cede a plot of land of about ten square miles to the son of Alexander Cameron, to be located within Cherokee territory and on their boundary with North Carolina and South Carolina. The headmen told Stuart that they desired that the boy be educated by the British but live among them and take the place of his father, whom they trusted implicitly. The elder Cameron had married a Cherokee woman and ensured the tribe's well-being in all things. They even called him "Brother Scotchie," a reference to his Scottish heritage.[21]

The cession was ingenious because the land would most certainly not be settled by colonists, since the boy could claim white lineage. Yet he could legally hold the property because he could also claim his mother's Cherokee heritage and therefore not be in violation of the Proclamation of 1763. In a legal sense, the land could never be ceded to the British in the future if it had already been designated for an individual who could claim British heritage. Since the boy would not use the land for years to come, and then only a small portion of it, the Cherokees could continue to hunt upon the land.

As soon as the Cherokees thought they had stopped the encroachment to the south, another loomed in the north. Almost immediately after the Treaty of Hard Labour, settlers began to trespass onto Cherokee land along the Watauga, Nolichucky, and Holston rivers into present-day southwestern Virginia and northeastern Tennessee. First a settler would explore the region, then construct a cabin and plant a crop. Then he would return to North Carolina or Virginia and come back with his family and several neighbors. Almost immediately, the Cherokees complained to Stuart of the encroachments, informing him that by summer 1769, white hunters had trekked throughout the area and the Indians' settlements far south of the agreed-upon boundary. Once the colonists had settled, however, there was little Stuart could do to remove them, because he had no military or police force at his disposal.[22]

It is no wonder that the Cherokees and Anglo-American settlers both found the region desirable. According to one visitor to the area:

> Their [the Cherokees'] vallies are of the richest soil, equal to manure itself, impossible in appearance ever to wear out ... [decomposed plant matter and soil] ... are washed down into the vallies, by this means (besides being well watered with rivulets) is become a real

matrice to receive from phlogiston the impregnation of niter, so that there is present a perpetual renewal of what encourages vegitation. Should this country once come into the hands of the Europeans, they may with propriety call it the American Canaan, for it will fully answer their industry, and all methods of European culture and do as well for European produce . . . for provisions of all kinds.[23]

Attention shifted to the north when, on November 5, 1768, headmen from the Iroquois Confederacy, also known as the Six Nations, as well as the Shawnees, Delawares, Mingos, and other tribes in the Northern Department of Indian Affairs, met with the British superintendent, Sir William Johnson, at Fort Stanwix in New York. For the southern tribes, the important part of the treaty that came out of this meeting was a claim by the northern Indians that their lands extended south to the Cherokee (headwaters of the Holston) River. This claim is a crucial feature in relations between the northern and southern Indians. The Six Nations claimed as theirs essentially the watersheds of the Green and New rivers down to the headwaters of the Cherokee River. The problem with this was that the Six Nations did not control the territory that far south—the Cherokees did. Only after Virginia had paid the Six Nations for the land back in the 1740s did colonial officials discover that the Cherokees actually claimed ownership. When British officials confronted the Six Nations with the fact, the latter conceded their deceit, but they kept the goods that had been given them for the land.[24]

After the ownership issue had been clarified, Virginia wanted the Hard Labor boundary adjusted legally. As it stood, the boundary did not include settlements that had been established in Cherokee territory on the headwaters of the Holston River. Virginia wanted the boundary changed to include this land, which it had paid the Iroquois for, even though they did not control it. The governor of Virginia sent two commissioners to consult with John Stuart and wrote to him personally. Stuart, in reply, advised the governor that he could not change the boundary now that it had been agreed upon and confirmed by the king. The two Virginia commis-

sioners met with a few Cherokee headmen at the North
Carolina capital in January 1769, and broached the idea of a
new boundary line. Surprisingly, the Cherokee leaders seemed
amenable to the idea and said they would bring up the subject
at the next meeting of all the headmen.[25]

By December 1769, George III had given his consent for
Virginia to seek another boundary between itself and the
Cherokees. In justifying its conception of where the line
should be drawn, Virginia cited the military force that would
be necessary to guard the surveying party in mountainous terrain and the isolated position of the land sold by the Iroquois.
Virginia, therefore, proposed to include all the land north of
a line made by extending the boundary separating that colony
and North Carolina all the way to the Mississippi River, that
is, all of present-day Kentucky. Fortunately for the Cherokees,
Stuart balked at such a grandiose land grab, citing the facts
that the line would not even intersect the Ohio River and
would preclude the Cherokees and Chickasaws from entering
prime hunting ground, something to which neither would
ever consent.[26]

By spring 1770, the Cherokee-Virginia boundary line took
a back seat to a more pressing issue. Stuart called a congress
of the Cherokees at the Congarees in South Carolina during
April and inquired whether they had formed an alliance with
the northern tribes to war against the western tribes and
Choctaws. The Choctaws had been one of the many traditional enemies of the Cherokees, but at that time only the
Creeks engaged in war against them. After the Cherokees
denied they had any such intentions, the discussions moved
on to the boundary line. The famous Cherokee orator
Oconostota, known as the Great Warrior, advised Stuart that
the tribe had no desire to cede more land to the Virginians,
contrary to what it had earlier intimated. Stuart conveyed his
disappointment at the reversal, and Oconostota revealed the
true reason for the Cherokees' apprehension. Virginia had not
formally agreed to pay the Cherokees for the land they
sought, and if they did not pay before that year's hunting season in the fall, the Cherokees would never again entertain
such a cession. With the Cherokee position plainly stated, the
congress ended.[27]

Throughout the summer, Virginia's governor, Baron Botetourt, hounded Stuart about negotiating a new boundary line between the Cherokees and the colony. The colony had adjusted its preferred boundary to run from the headwaters of the Holston River to the Great Kanawha River, essentially taking in most of present-day southwestern Virginia east of Kingsport. With this more pragmatic approach, the House of Burgesses charged Governor Botetourt with having Stuart call a meeting for the purpose of getting the Cherokees to agree to the land cession, and arranging for it to be marked.[28]

Finally, in mid-October 1770, Stuart and a representative of Botetourt's met with the principle headmen and about one thousand other Cherokees, along with many inhabitants of the frontier, at Lochaber, Alexander Cameron's home in present-day northwestern South Carolina. After traditional ceremonies, Stuart opened the treaty proceedings by introducing the governor's representative, Colonel John Donelson. Then Stuart proceeded to the business of the meeting: establishing the boundary between the Cherokees and Virginia. He explained to the Cherokees the need to move the predetermined line farther west to include settlers between the Kanawha and Holston rivers. To justify such an adjustment, Stuart reminded the Cherokees that the land in question had not been a part of their hunting grounds, so at least they would not be losing land valuable to them. Oconostota replied that the young warriors were out hunting and would question the older headmen for giving up land they did consider hunting grounds. Without Stuart actually conceding that the lands were Cherokee hunting grounds, the Lochaber conference ended with an agreement to extend the boundary between North Carolina and Virginia to the Holston River, thence northeast to the Kanawha River. Since the hunting season was about to begin, Oconostota suggested the boundary be marked the following spring.[29]

In February 1771, the Cherokees ceded another tract of land, in Georgia north of the Broad River, to their traders. Their intention was to exchange the land for clearing up the trade debt they had accumulated over the previous several years. The Cherokees had been preoccupied with warfare against the western Indians and could not hunt enough deer to repay the debt in deerskins, the basis of their economy. They then appealed to the governor of Georgia, Sir William Wright, to use his influence to persuade London to sanction the deal. They also advised Wright that the Creeks probably would lay claim to the land as well. Again the Cherokees displayed shrewd diplomacy in dealing with Anglo-Americans, since they knew that the Creeks had gained control over that tract of land some years earlier.[30]

Soon another problem arose involving the Virginia boundary line. In March 1771, Oconostota advised Alexander Cameron in a conference at Chota, the most important of the Cherokee towns, that the young warriors would not consent to the land cession. Rather, the old Hard Labor treaty line that ran by Chiswell's Mine must be observed. Cameron did not believe that Oconostota had really rescinded his word; he knew the headman could not go against the young warriors and their right to the land. The Cherokees said they could see the smoke of settlers' cabins from their towns and felt they had no choice but to either take what was offered or war against the settlers. Oconostota assured Cameron that he would work diligently to avoid war. Attakullakulla then arrived at the conference and argued that the land the Cherokee has ceded to the Georgia traders in exchange for debt should be officially recognized. Cameron reminded the Cherokee headmen that the agreement at the Lochaber conference had been sanctioned by the king but any deal with the traders had not. Cameron implored the headmen to make the young warriors agree to the Lochaber line, and the conference ended.[31]

By the end of the 1770 Lochaber conference, the amicable days of 1763 had faded forever. The period began with occasional encroachments, followed by the British removing the offenders. It ended with a flood of squatters, and the British negotiating land cessions from the Cherokees. Anglo-American refusal, or inability, to remove trespassers and instead altering boundaries to include them would become an all-too-familiar pattern.

TWO

Mounting Tensions

1771–1775

In 1771, the Cherokees faced two grave problems that had to be resolved as quickly as possible. Often, when the Cherokees returned from a hunt, traders would ply them with alcohol and then take their deerskins to pay for the drink rather than give the Cherokees even minimum value in return, such as guns, ammunition, or kettles. This only served to increase the debt of practically every male Cherokee, since they then had to take necessary goods on credit. Additionally, warriors of the Iroquois Six Nations frequently visited Cherokee towns, imploring them the join in a war against either the colonists, or the Choctaw and Chickasaw to the west. Oconostota told the Iroquois warriors that he considered the colonists his friends, and if they wanted to make war against them they might as well make war against the Cherokees—quite a strong statement considering that John Stuart of the Southern Department of Indian Affairs and William Johnson the Northern Department had recently brokered a peace between the Cherokees and Iroquois.[1]

Virginia, meanwhile, had its own priorities. On May 26, 1771, its representative, John Donelson, met with Attakullakulla and a group of other Cherokees to physically mark the boundary between the colony and the tribe. The line began where the line separating Virginia and North Carolina

ended at that time, on the Great Kanawha River. It then ran
due west until the surveying party struck the Holston River.
Rather than continuing in a due western course as prescribed
by the Lochaber Treaty, the party mutually agreed to merely
follow the course of the Holston until a point six miles above
the Long Island, at present-day Kingsport, Tennessee. Once
around the island, the line should have struck in a northeast-
erly course until the mouth of the Great Kanawha River.
Instead, the party marked the boundary northwest to the
North Fork of the Kentucky River, creating a much larger
land cession than had been agreed upon in the Lochaber
Treaty.[2]

It is unknown why the surveying party deviated from the
agreed upon boundary. Attakullakulla explained the deviation
in terms of Cherokee generosity, saying, "my brothers were
settled upon it and I pittied them," referring to the Anglo-
Americans already settled along the headwaters of the
Holston River. Lord Dunmore, the new royal governor of
Virginia, explained the deviation to London by saying that
the line as run incurred far less expense than the treaty boundary. As delineated, the treaty boundary ran through very
rugged terrain and would have required more time to survey,
which would have cost the state much more in salaries, provisions, and supplies.[3]

In fact, the Cherokees had done exactly what the Iroquois
had done a couple of years earlier at Fort Stanwix: cede land
they did not own or control. And Attakullakulla actually bar-
gained with Donelson until he agreed that Virginia would pay
the Cherokees an additional £500. But the real reason for the
land cession was probably its location. The extra land included in the Donelson survey is the present-day eastern third of
Kentucky, the "dark and bloody ground." What better location to divert Anglo-American expansion away from
Cherokee towns? The Cherokee did not warn the colonials
that the Shawnees would have a serious problem with them
settling in the middle of their hunting ground.[4]

Meanwhile, the Cherokees' Georgia traders had become so
elated about the prospect of reaping the proceeds from the
land given to them by the Cherokee in exchange for debt—
even though the deal had yet to be sanctioned by the crown—

that they had a "cession" drafted and persuaded the Cherokee headmen to sign the sham agreement. The traders' plan was to sell the land to settlers. The "Ceded Lands" encompassed territory north of the Little River to just above the Broad River, bounded on the east by the Savannah River and on the west by the Oconee River. The only problem was that the Creeks also claimed this land. Once the Creeks heard about the Cherokee plan, they naturally became irate and refused any involvement. The Georgia traders, however, solicited their counterparts trading with the Creeks in the scheme with proposed profits from the sale of the Ceded Lands. The Creeks had also accumulated a tremendous debt to their traders in much the same way as the Cherokees. Once the Creek traders supported the scheme, the Creek headmen reluctantly agreed to the cession in exchange for clearing their trade debt. In July, Cherokee headmen and their traders marked out the unofficial cession.[5]

Amid all these land deals, a trader named Richard Pearis attempted to secure for himself and his partner, Jacob Hite, a parcel three miles square from the Cherokee. The deceitful manner in which Pearis and Hite attempted to force the land grab angered everyone. After getting the Cherokee headmen intoxicated, the traders made them sign a paper they claimed was a letter to the Virginia governor concerning trade. Actually, the documents stated the Cherokees had ceded a large parcel of land to both men. After the Cherokees denied the validity of the cession, Pearis embarked on an effort to cajole and coerce the headmen into condoning the transaction. He began referring to the headmen involved using disparaging terms designed to lessen their status among Cherokees—a dangerous tactic at best. In 1772, colonial officials of Virginia sanctioned Pearis and Hite by revoking their trading license.[6]

With stunts such as the Pearis-Hite "cession" and William Drayton's attempting to "lease" the entire Catawba reservation, London officials found it difficult to distinguish between scams and legitimate attempts at land cession, such as that proposed by the Cherokees to traders in Georgia. London denied the legitimate petition of Edward Wilkinson, another Cherokee trader who had complained about Pearis and Hite, and suggested he seek reimbursement from the sales of the land cession proposed in Georgia. Finally, Superintendent John Stuart wrote directly to the secretary of the colonies, the Lord of Dartmouth, arguing against any land deals not brokered through his office.[7] Stuart's action, along with complaints from wealthy colonists about other private land deals, probably provided the impetus for the Royal Order against Indian Land Grants, issued in April 1773, which forbade any private land deals being approved by any royal official other than King George III, on pain of the official's incurring "His Majestys highest Displeasure" and being removed from office.[8]

On June 4, 1773, Georgia governor William Wright, Superintendent Stuart, and many of the Cherokee and Creek headmen met at Augusta in order for the Indians to finalize the land cession and clear their debts with their traders. The Upper Creek headmen opposed the land cession and attempted to prevent the Lower Creek headmen from attending the meeting, but they failed. Many of the young Creek warriors also opposed the land cession, but they could not stop the transaction. Even some of the Lower Creek headmen, who had resigned themselves to the deal, denounced the Cherokee headmen present for instigating the deal for land that they no longer controlled. Regardless of the animosity surrounding the Ceded Lands, the transaction became binding.

From the Augusta conference, a party of some eighty or ninety people, including about a dozen Cherokees and Creeks, immediately set off to blaze the new boundary. With them rode the intrepid naturalist William Bartram, who kept an account of the journey and documented an interesting episode. At one point in the surveying, the colonist using the compass announced the next intended leg of the survey. One of the accompanying Creeks disagreed vehemently with the orientation of the heading taken by the surveyor. When explained to the Creek that the compass did not lie, the Creek sarcastically retorted that this time it did, and he threatened to end the surveying on the spot. After taking the heading provided by the Creek, their arrival at the desired destination proved him correct: the compass had lied. The maps the surveyor had available to him were not as accurate as the Creek's intimate knowledge of his own territory. The rest of the survey proceeded without further incident.[9]

Issues other than boundary lines plagued the frontiers. Cameron had heard rumors of talk among the Cherokee Overhill Towns of warring against the frontier settlers. The venerable Oconostota blamed such talk on Cold Weather, a Cherokee from Chillhowie. But Cameron did not have to worry about Cold Weather stirring up trouble among the Overhill Cherokees, for he had attacked and bludgeoned War Woman in Citico, for which her relations hunted him down and executed him in Chillhowie.[10] Indeed, frontier settlers had little to fear from the Cherokees by late 1773, as the Cherokees went off to war against the northern Indians who had been constantly attacking them.

The cession and boundary marking created even more tension in American Indian and Anglo-American interrelations. Even after some murders of Cherokees and whites along the new border near Broad River, Oconostota refused to join Emistiseguo and the Shawnees in attacking the settlers. Then, in December 1773, a Creek murdered a fellow Creek near the headwaters of the Ogeechee River in Georgia and blamed a nearby settler named White. On Christmas Day, the real murderer led a party of Lower Creeks against the White homestead, slaying everyone. On January 14, 1774, another party of Lower Creek warriors attacked a neighboring settler named Sherrill. In all, some thirteen settlers died and about five Creeks. A unit of Georgia militia set off in pursuit of the second war party, but after being attacked, it retreated. With that, settlers evacuated the frontier in droves, while Governor Wright requested British regular troops for support and the defense of Georgia.

Perhaps all-out war could somehow be avoided. In case it could not, John Stuart directed his brother and deputy, Charles Stuart, to incite the Choctaws to greater war efforts against the Creeks. That, at least, would preclude a combined effort against the colonies. To discover the true nature of the attacks and those involved, Stuart's deputies met with Cherokee and Creek headmen while Wright called upon all the Upper and Lower Creek headmen to meet with him in the colonial capital, Savannah, at the earliest practical date.[11]

Stuart's deputy to the Cherokees, Alexander Cameron, met with headmen of the Cherokee Lower Towns on February 4, 1774. At that meeting, the headmen remembered what Oconostota had told them about listening to "bad talks" that urged attacking the white settlers. They reassured Cameron that they desired peace and wanted him to tell the settlers. The Lower Cherokees especially wanted peace, since Stuart had negotiated a successful end to hostilities between them and the northern tribes. As soon as their warriors returned from hunting, they would meet with Cameron and reaffirm their peaceful intentions.[12]

Before their meeting with Cameron, the headmen of the Lower and Middle Towns gathered to give instructions to a messenger they sent to the Creek town of Coweta. The Creeks who had committed the murders on the frontier lived in Coweta, and that town had sent a messenger to ask the Cherokees to join them in a war against Georgia. The Cherokee response was adamant and unfaltering. They instructed the messenger to tell the Creeks that if they went to war against the whites, they should not bring their war to Cherokee towns, because, "We know our Oldest Brothers have men enough to fight them . . . they are kindling up fires [to burn the Creek houses]." To reinforce their message, the Cherokee headmen included one string of blue wampum (signifying that times had been bad between them previously) and four strings of white wampum (signifying a desire for peace between the Cherokees and Creeks).[13]

The Cherokee Beloved Woman even sent a speech to the Creek Beloved Woman, saying the Cherokees preferred to stay at home and raise their children, but the Creek Beloved Woman evidently preferred to throw hers away—strong words from one mother to another. Bag of Toxaway, a Cherokee headman whom the Creeks had named a "beloved man," rejected that status with them by sending a string of white beads with one black bead. The Cherokees then told their interpreter that the recent killings of white settlers were committed by the Creeks of Coweta, not them, and that they would not join the Cowetas.[14]

Just four days later, on February 25, 1774, Cameron met with the Lower and Middle Cherokees. The headmen advised Cameron that a runner had come to them from the Creeks with a string of white beads that included three red beads, the symbol for peace between them and an invitation for the Cherokees to join the Creeks in war against Georgia. Cherokee spokesman Chinisto told Cameron that he had taken the red beads off and discarded them, indicating their unwillingness to go to war against Georgia. Cameron then asked the Cherokees about the intelligence he obtained that indicated some Cherokees had been with the Cowetas when they attacked the Georgia frontier. Chinisto could neither confirm nor deny the accusation. He added that if some of the perpetrators proved to be Cherokees, they had participated without the knowledge or consent of their towns and headmen. Cameron and the headmen of the Lower and Middle Cherokee towns then sent the messengers, one of whom was Kenitah of Seneca, to Coweta with their messages and strings of wampum and beads.[15]

After the meeting, Cameron sent a report to John Stuart. During his visit, Cameron confirmed much of the information he had received from Kenitah of Seneca prior to his arrival in the Cherokee Lower Towns. When Cameron confronted the Raven of Tugaloo about participating in the murders, he claimed he had been drinking rum and fell asleep. When he awoke he "threw the hatchet away," meaning he had rejected the offer to go to war against the settlers. He warned Cameron that some of his young warriors may have gone while he was asleep but that he did not know. Cameron then inquired of the Raven about a scalp that had been brought into the Lower Towns, apparently from a settler. When Cameron showed the Raven the scalp, which was actually a toupee, and explained what it was, all present had a hearty laugh.[16]

The Cherokees had little inclination to join the Creeks, or anyone else, in a war by 1774. Nor would they purposely do anything that would embroil them in a war with the British, which they knew would be protracted and devastating. Attacks had started again by Iroquois war parties from the north. They even had intelligence that the northern superintendent of Indian affairs, Sir William Johnson, was inciting the Iroquois to war upon the Cherokees, which they told Stuart.[17]

By June the Cherokee messengers to the Creeks had returned with the intelligence that persuaded Cameron to believe that Emistiseguo and Second Man of Tallassee would do all they could to calm the unstable relations between the Creeks and the government. Sadly, neither they nor any single headman in Creek society had enough influence to have the murderers delivered to Cameron, even though the Creeks as a whole would have much preferred that solution to ceding more lands. Evidently Kenitah of Seneca had talked to their young warriors, telling them that if they wanted to attack Georgia they must not be in their right minds, because the British were so numerous they could not be counted, and they would attack the Creeks from every direction. One of the messengers, Creek Pigeon, who used to live among the Creeks, said they were definitely hostile, even keeping some ammunition stores specifically to use in war against Georgia. When that ran out, they said they could get more from the Spanish, join the northern tribes, and drive the "Virginians" "as far as the English down to the Sea Side."[18]

Toward the end of April, only a small contingent of Upper Creek headmen ventured to Savannah to meet with Governor Wright. Though he had guaranteed their safe conduct, given the agitated state of affairs, Wright could hardly blame them. He charged the Upper Creek headmen present with faithfully recounting what he said. Wright was uncharacteristically blunt when he warned the Creek that their trade would be cut off from all sectors, including the illicit trade with the Spanish in Cuba. "Can you make guns, gun powder, Bullets, Glasses, paint and Cloathing etc. etc." he asked them. Wright then demanded that the murderers of the settlers be executed, in fulfillment of previous treaty agreements.[19]

Actually, British officials had already taken steps to cut off the trade to the Creeks, including ammunition. That immediately began to have its intended effects, especially with the Choctaws increasing their attacks on the Creeks. This serious lack of ammunition and other goods began to turn the Upper Creeks and some of the Lower Creek towns toward reconciliation with Georgia.[20]

After suffering the effects of no trade, the Upper and Lower Creeks met in a grand council on May 26, 1774, to discuss the explosive situation that had developed between the Creeks and Georgia. Something had to be done to reinstitute trade so that the Creeks, both Lower and Upper, could obtain goods of every kind, but most importantly weapons and ammunition. All the Creeks were suffering from a lack of goods they could not manufacture, as Wright pointedly indicated. The Creek headmen came to the conclusion that Wright must be appeased and the perpetrators of the White-Sherrill murders executed. That represented the lesser of two evils, the other being to cede land. The only dissenting voices came from Coweta, the town where Oligichy and his fellow murderers lived.

The Creeks executed two of the ringleaders in the White-Sherrill murders and requested that trade be resumed. Wright remained adamant and demanded that the three other executions take place as agreed upon. He continued to ask for British troops, but with the growing crisis of rebellion in the New England colonies over Parliament, it seemed doubtful his request would be met. By October, Governor Wright could at last report to Lord Dartmouth that stopping the Creek trade had produced the desired results. Three of the five executions demanded had been performed, while the other two murderers had fled Creek territory.[21]

Support for the rebel cause had not flourished in the southern colonies by the beginning of 1775. Considering the critical situation between the Creeks and Georgia, the colony did not send a delegate to the First Continental Congress in January 1775. Instead, a Provincial Congress was called for by Whig leaders, but only five of the colony's twelve parishes sent representatives. To make matters worse for the Whigs, the royal governor of South Carolina dissolved the colonial Assembly. The rebel cause would have to await further developments to gain popular support.

Along the frontier, fomenting revolution took a back seat to other activities as well. In January 1775, prominent merchant Richard Henderson traveled to the Cherokee Overhill Towns to negotiate a land deal. The land he wanted essentially stretched from the Cumberland River to the Ohio River and comprised parts of present-day middle Kentucky and Tennessee. It is unknown what terms Henderson negotiated with the Cherokees, but he concluded an agreement with them and arranged a meeting with all the headmen the following March.[22]

Colonial officials were concerned that they would not be able to bring settlers in those lands "to due obedience" if that became necessary. And in the current rebellious climate, that seemed like a distinct possibility. The fact that those lands probably fell within the theoretical boundaries of the colony of Virginia was another major concern. Henderson's obtaining the lands, whether illegally or not, and selling them to settlers would preclude the colony of Virginia from reaping any pecuniary benefit.[23]

Henderson did not concern himself with such matters and proceeded with his land speculation. In fact, he did not even wait for the confirmation meeting in March with the Cherokee headmen. Before the meeting, he sent Daniel Boone and other long hunters familiar with the region to lead groups of settlers and establish themselves in the Kentucky lands he intended to obtain. For Henderson and his associates, a lot was riding on the March confirmation meetings.

One can easily see why the Kentucky lands would be attractive to white settlers and valuable to Cherokee hunters. Felix Walker, a companion of Daniel Boone's, described the explorer's first impression of Kentucky. "We felt ourselves as passengers through a wilderness just arrived at the fields of Elysium, or at a garden where there was no forbidden fruit." He became filled with such an emotion, not unlike Columbus upon reaching the Bahamas, that he fell to his knees and bent over to kiss the earth beneath him. With such descriptions driven by ardent emotions, it is little wonder that Anglo-American settlers began to cross the Cumberland Mountains to reside on a piece of "Elysium" on Earth.[24]

As agreed, the Cherokee headmen met Henderson at Sycamore Shoals on March 15, 1775. By that time, an estimated one thousand Cherokees had assembled, including most of the principle headmen of the Overhill Towns. Only Judd's Friend had not made the journey to the Shoals, but he advised the other headmen he would agree with any deal they entered into. It fell to Henderson to supply provisions for all the Cherokees assembled.[25]

On the first day of talks, the headmen met with Henderson and his business partners, along with many curious settlers, traders, and others. Henderson asked the headmen if, indeed, the Cherokees claimed the land between the Kanawha and the Cherokee (Tennessee) rivers. This caused some discussion among the headmen in voices so low that even those who understood the Cherokee language could not discern what was said. After a lengthy discussion, they announced their claim to the land south of the Kanawha. With the main issue settled to the satisfaction of Henderson and his associates, the business of the day ended with an agreement to continue the talks the next day.

The Cherokee headmen began the second day of talks by offering Henderson the lands on the north side of the New River. Henderson knew that Virginia had already purchased those lands and reminded the Cherokees of the Donelson purchase four years earlier. Then the headmen offered Henderson the lands between the New and Louisa (Kentucky) rivers, which also lay in the Donelson tract of 1771. Again Henderson refused to negotiate for those lands, citing the same reason. The headmen countered with the fact that the deal was for £500 worth of goods, which Virginia had yet to pay. To the Cherokees, the land was still theirs because they had not received their payment.[26]

The talks then began to break down. Henderson reminded the headmen that the lands he wanted lay to the south of the Louisa River. He then became adamant and declared that if he did not get the lands he desired, he would leave and take his goods with him. Also, he noted all the cattle and provisions he had provided to sustain them during the talks. The headmen stated that the white people wanted too much of Cherokee hunting grounds.

One of the headmen, Tsiyugunsini (also Chincanacina), or Dragging Canoe, became so incensed that he walked out of the conference in protest. Some witnesses suggested he did this because of the location of the lands Henderson wanted, while others said Dragging Canoe left because Henderson wanted too much Cherokee land. And still others indicated Dragging Canoe was displeased with Henderson for threatening to leave with all the goods. For whatever reason, Dragging

Canoe did indeed become angry enough to leave the meeting, at which point many of the young warriors followed him. With that, the second day of the conference ended.

The third day of meetings convened with the headmen, including Dragging Canoe, Henderson, and his associates. Henderson took the initiative and delineated the lands they wanted for the goods they brought, said to be worth £10,000 (over $2 million today). The lands Henderson and his associates wanted were bounded by the Ohio, Louisa, and Cumberland rivers, with the eastern boundary being Powell's Mountain—essentially what is today central Kentucky and Tennessee, amounting to about twenty-three million acres.

By this time the Cherokees seemed inclined to acquiesce, but they did complain that "the goods were too few for the number of people [Cherokees] there." In a ploy to obtain more goods, they expressed their hope that Henderson would consider the deal at another time. They told him to return home, and they would seek the payment owed them from Virginia. Henderson became incensed and told the headmen directly that the goods then present was all he would ever offer, and that he would not ask at any other time. Either he would get the lands he wanted or he would take his goods and they would remain friends.

The headmen had another discussion among themselves and finally told Henderson they agreed to give him the lands he wanted. They again mentioned that the lands were a substantial part of their hunting grounds and added that when their children became hunters, they might reproach them for giving Henderson the land.

Whether or not the Cherokees had a legitimate claim to all the lands Henderson had in mind, they issued a warning to the whites regarding the land to the south of the Louisa River in present-day central Kentucky. Some accounts say Dragging Canoe issued the warning. Whether he did or not (most evidence suggests he did not), the headmen told Henderson they considered it a "bloody country," and said there was a "dark cloud over that country." If he insisted on settling in Kentucky, the Cherokees "would not hold him by the hand any longer and [he] must do it at his own risque." That is, he should not blame them later for anything that happened to him in Kentucky.

Further, the headmen said they did not want to see anything happen to him at the hands of the northern and western Indians, those "bad people." They told him not to settle in Kentucky. But Henderson would have none of it. He disregarded Cherokee warnings that the Shawnees used Kentucky as their hunting ground and would not suffer having whites settle there for any reason.

On the fourth day of meetings, Henderson produced eight pieces of paper for the headmen to sign. He called all the Cherokees to the table where he had laid out the documents. There was a great crowding around the table before the headmen put their marks on the documents. At first, the headmen balked at signing so many documents. Henderson explained that they were exactly the same, one each for him and his associates.

Just before the headmen signed the documents, their interpreter, Joseph Vann, gave a cryptic warning to Oconostota and the Raven. Vann, the Overhill Towns interpreter for the British Southern Department of Indian Affairs, told them to be fully aware of what the documents meant and not to later hold him responsible. Henderson then stopped Vann and told him not to be the reason for ending the conference. Vann responded that he had desired to faithfully serve the headmen so they could exonerate him when they conveyed the events to John Stuart.

At that point, a conference attendee named John Reid pushed Henderson to have one of the documents read before the headmen signed. Henderson refused Reid's request until the latter noted it would be "not generous" to have someone sign a document when they did not know what it contained. Henderson allowed one to be read, but only after the headmen had signed the first one. Henderson quieted Reid by reminding him of all the expense and trouble it took to prepare for this conference. Heeding Henderson's warning, Reid made no further objections. The headmen present signed the documents Henderson had laid out.

After Henderson had completed his negotiations, John Carter, the pioneering settler of Carter's Valley, approached the headmen, desirous of obtaining the entire valley in which he resided (and through which the Holston River flowed) and offering about £600 or £700 worth of goods. The headmen refused.

Henderson then noted that the Kentucky lands lay separated from the Watauga lands. He mentioned that he did not want to pass over Cherokee land to reach his land and asked the headmen to allow him a path from Sycamore Shoals to the Kentucky lands. Dragging Canoe became upset and, stamping his foot, exclaimed that the Cherokees had already allowed him the lands from where they sat to the Kentucky tract. But Henderson offered the additional enticement of destroying Carter's account books, effectually eliminating their debt to him, plus an additional two thousand pounds of deerskins in trade goods. The headmen discussed the matter and then agreed to allow Henderson a path to the Kentucky lands.[27]

Once the headmen had signed the documents, Henderson turned over the goods to them. The Cherokee leaders, by virtue of their position, distributed the goods to all the people who had gathered there at Sycamore Shoals. There has always been some question whether Henderson actually had £10,000 worth of goods present. It is known he had a cabin full of goods and that it took a train of wagons to bring them. Whether the Cherokees correctly estimated the goods being too few for the number of people present or they merely wanted more goods is unknown. But one warrior "received only one shirt" and lamented how "he could have killed more deer in one day upon [the land] than would have bought such a shirt." Many of the young Cherokees denounced the division of the goods and returned toward the Overhill Towns that night.

Having already subverted two attempts to defeat the negotiations, Henderson had one more crisis to face. With the distribution of the goods came plenty of rum, an integral part of accepted hospitality at frontier conferences. During the evening, Richard Pearis and Joseph Reid found out that the Cherokee headmen had actually signed deeds of sale to Henderson. They repaired to the Cherokees' camp to advise them of their discovery but found the headmen too intoxicated. The two then decided to inform Oconostota's wife, who became very anxious and tried to inform some of the headmen, but to no avail.

Pearis and Reid waited until the next morning to approach the headmen. The two found them in Oconostota's tent drawing out a map of different rivers. Reid recognized the main one to be the Holston with its branches and the Great Island. Pearis asked the headmen if they had actually sold Henderson the lands bordering the Holston. The headmen responded that they had not, nor would they. When Pearis informed them that was exactly what they had done, they immediately went to confront Henderson. They advised Henderson in no uncertain terms that they had only allowed him a path and had not sold the lands on the Holston River. Henderson then asked the headmen for a small distance on either side of the path so that people going to and from Kentucky could hunt and sustain themselves on their journey, and the headmen agreed.

Henderson had previously met with the Cherokee headmen about the land deal and considered the meeting at Sycamore Shoals as mere finalization of the transaction. He had already determined to have the Kentucky lands settled. Even while the Cherokee headmen met with Henderson and his associates, white settlers arrived in Kentucky and began establishing what would become Harrodstown, while Daniel Boone and a group of settlers established Boonesborough by the beginning of April.[28]

On the heels of settlers pouring into the Kentucky lands came events to the east that would push the colonies further toward violent revolution. In April 1775, North Carolina Whigs drove the royal governor out of that colony. The following month, Whig leaders gathered in Mecklenburg and adopted the Mecklenburg Resolves, which essentially declared North Carolina independent.

The Whig cause then received some disturbing information that required a radical reevaluation of its strategy. The South Carolina Committee of Intelligence, composed of Whigs who corresponded with other revolutionaries throughout the colonies, intercepted a letter believed to have been written by John Stuart. In the letter, he is said to have encouraged the Cherokees and Creeks to organize and attack the western frontier settlements. They would be assisted by a strong column of British regulars coming up from Pensacola in West Florida. The greatest fears of rebellious Whigs seemed about to be realized: a two-front war. To negate the threat in the west, the Whigs wrote Stuart, advising him that his estate in South Carolina would be held by them and "stands security for behaviour of Indians." The South Carolina provincial congress demanded Stuart put up his estate as bond and defend himself against the charges of inciting the Indians against the frontiers, which Stuart refused to do. In response, the Whigs appointed commissioners of their own to try to counter Stuart's influence and keep the Cherokees and Creeks out of any future conflict with Great Britain.[29]

South Carolina appointed three commissioners to the Cherokees and three to the Creeks to counteract the influence of Stuart and his deputies. Other members of the Intelligence Committee wrote directly to British Indian affairs agents and traders to determine their loyalties. A South Carolina committeeman who knew Alexander Cameron even wrote to him, suggesting he should resign and retire, admired by those who knew him. Cameron responded by saying he had not received instructions to incite the Cherokees against the frontier colonists, only to keep the Cherokees "firmly attached to His Majesty." Another wrote to a militia officer in the backcountry, Colonel Thomas Fletchall, directly asking him if he had agitated the Cherokees to attack the state. South Carolina Whigs seemed intent on finding out exactly whom they had to contend with.[30]

The letter Stuart supposedly wrote inciting the Indians to attack the frontier had actually been forged by some residents in the Overmountain settlements who desired a frontier war as a means of wresting more land from the Cherokees. Stuart wrote to the Intelligence Committee at Charleston and quite naturally denied the accusations. He also denied having received orders to enlist the Indians as active participants in the British cause. While in Charleston, he barely escaped an angry mob and boarded a British ship bound for Savannah. That is the last John Stuart ever saw of his home in Charleston.[31]

In June, Georgia Whigs created a Council of Safety to communicate with other Whigs throughout the colonies. Simultaneously, South Carolina formed a provincial congress to counter the influence of royal authority. Cherokees readied themselves to fend off parties of rebels whom they heard were intent on entering their towns to capture Loyalists, the prize being Alexander Cameron himself. The Whigs had a legitimate concern about Loyalists in the backcountry. When given the opportunity to sign the allegiance to South Carolina, none of Colonel Fletchall's Upper Saluda militia regiment in the backcountry signed.[32]

The issue of whether the Cherokees or Creeks would support the British seemed to hinge on the matter of trade, especially their access to ammunition. Ammunition provided the means for Cherokees and Creeks to hunt, obtain deerskins, and trade the deerskins for the goods they could not manufacture. The only problem in summer 1775, from a Whig perspective, was that additional ammunition could be used in attacks against frontier settlements. Whigs attempted to walk a fine line between providing Cherokees and Creeks with enough ammunition for hunting, but not so much that they could use it to attack the frontier. If the Whigs did not provide them with ammunition, the British certainly intended to, which would induce the Cherokees and Creeks to support them. George Galphin, the primary Whig commissioner and long-standing trader to the Creeks, stated that opinion rather forcefully.[33]

Toward the end of June, the South Carolina Committee of Safety voided John Stuart's appointment as superintendent of Indian affairs on the grounds of correspondence that purportedly showed he had urged the Cherokees and Creeks to attack the southern frontiers. They urged him to appear before the committee, but they could hardly expect him to, given the fact that he had already fled to Charleston. Immediately after Stuart left his position, the Committee of Safety appointed a Committee of Inquiry, whose members would in effect serve as Whig deputies to the Cherokees and Creeks.[34]

One of those deputies, George Galphin, had already become indispensible to the Whigs for maintaining amicable relations with the Lower Creeks. The Whigs hoped to supplant the influence of John Stuart with equally influential traders, like Galphin, who supported their cause in the struggle. Galphin advised Henry Laurens, of the South Carolina Committee of Safety, that he would have his employees do all they could "to counteract anything he [John Stuart] might say." Galphin also keenly understood that goods, particularly ammunition, marked the path to peaceful relations with the Creeks and he emphasized that point to Laurens.[35]

By August 1775, John Stuart had to maintain at least two primary, and divergent, strategies of interrelations within his department. He knew that goods and ammunition provided the key to peaceful relations, or possibly an alliance, with the Cherokees and the Creeks. His immediate lack of goods to supply both placed him in an awkward and critical predicament. Stuart countered his lack of ammunition for the Cherokees by advising them that the Whigs had captured the supply intended for them. He also knew full well that the rebels could not provide the southern Indians with anything but a modicum of ammunition.

The Creeks posed a different problem. While they also required supplies of ammunition, Stuart did not believe that ending the Choctaw-Creek War "would be convenient to us." Supplying both with ammunition, as Britain had been doing since he assumed the office of superintendent, still seemed the best strategy. Too little ammunition might incite the Creeks to attack the British. Too much ammunition could tip the balance of power toward the Creeks and entice them to attack the British if they were also under the influence of the Whigs. With the escalation of revolutionary fervor in the southern colonies, Stuart's strategy was no doubt to maintain the status quo.[36]

And revolutionary fervor was growing in the southern colonies in late summer and early fall 1775. In Savannah, Whigs had dismissed Loyalist militia officers and replaced them with men of Whig convictions. They also closed the port of Savannah to British shipping, not allowing a single vessel designated "His Majesty's Ship" to anchor in the bay.

South Carolina Whigs had forced the royal governor to flee Charleston and find sanctuary aboard a British man-of-war in the harbor. In the South Carolina backcountry, Loyalist sentiment seemed to prevail in isolated locations, and the Council of Safety decided to send Chief Justice and fellow Whig William Drayton, among others, to that region in order to suppress that sentiment.

During his mission to the backcountry of South Carolina, Drayton invited the Cherokees to meet with him. The concern about the Cherokees arose from intelligence received that Cameron would gather three thousand warriors from the Overhill Towns and fight for the king. Though the Lower Towns would not participate, Drayton thought it prudent to attempt a diplomatic mission with them. Further intelligence he received stated Cameron requested that the Overhill Town warriors attack the Overmountain settlements, but the warriors indicated they could not without ammunition. Cameron assured them he would furnish them with ammunition. For this reason, state assemblyman William Tennent advised the South Carolina Council of Safety to carefully guard the gunpowder just acquired.[37]

On September 25, 1775, the Cherokee Good Warrior and an entourage came down to the Congaree River to meet with Drayton. It is no wonder that Drayton had much to say, considering the urgency of keeping neutral a potential enemy so numerous and skillful. Drayton began by impressing upon the Cherokees that the Americans desired peace with them. To reinforce that notion, Drayton explained why the Americans had begun to prepare themselves militarily. Essentially, Drayton gave them a history of the English people and their colonization of North America. No doubt his rendition differed somewhat from the oral history of the Cherokees. Drayton concluded his history lesson, ironically, with a lamentation of how the measures of Parliament had been "like so many hatchets, chopping our agreement to pieces." Considering that the Cherokees had been experiencing the same scenario for years, perhaps they drew a parallel between themselves and the Whigs.[38]

The most important aspect of Drayton's speech may have come when he addressed the Whig seizure of gunpowder intended for the Cherokees. He explained that the revolutionaries had captured a British ship bearing ammunition intended for them. The Whigs intercepted the ammunition out of necessity because the British intended to cut off their supply. But to show good faith and that the Americans considered the Cherokees their "brothers," some would be sent as a gift, not sold to them as the British would have done. The Americans needed most of the captured gunpowder to fight the British, and in so doing would actually be defending the Cherokees. Drayton further explained that to leave the Whigs without sufficient powder would be to leave them exposed to their enemies, who "cannot hurt us, without hurting you also." Throughout his talk, Drayton implied the American cause would protect the Cherokees from economic abuses by the British.[39]

When he broached the subject of trade, Drayton must have at least been familiar with diplomatic nuances when meeting with Cherokees. Because the colonies had agreed not to trade with Great Britain, goods and supplies could become scarce for a while, harming the Americans and the Cherokees. But to show that the Americans intended to supply the Cherokees as best they could, Drayton took off his coat and gave it to Good Warrior, donning an Osnaburg split shirt in its stead. He then mentioned the recent murder of a warrior, assured them the matter would be investigated, and said that if a white man was found to be guilty of the unprovoked act, he would be punished. In the meantime, Drayton offered a quantity of goods for the widow and children of the slain warrior.[40]

Before he left the backcountry, Drayton took the time to write a letter to Cameron urging him to leave the Cherokee territory. Drayton intimated that if Cameron stayed, he would somehow not be safe, though Drayton did not specify that he himself had created the threat to his safety by offering a reward for the British deputy. Cameron politely declined. That would hardly be the end of the matter, or the extent of duplicity as a weapon.[41]

THREE

The Breaking Point

Fall 1775–Spring 1776

The Whigs understood American Indian diplomacy and conducted it effectively. But they did not have the resources to supply the commodity most valued by the Cherokees and Creeks: ammunition. British superintendant John Stuart knew that his government did. Stuart realized that the intense diplomatic struggle he waged against the American rebels was for no less than the assistance of the southeastern American Indians. The race to provide ammunition continued as British supply ships sought safe passage and a friendly port, while rebel privateers cruised the shores of the southern colonies for those ships. But Stuart held one distinct advantage in the diplomatic war.

By the middle of September 1775, the Creeks complained openly to their British agents about the lack of supplies. The hunting season would soon be upon them, and they had no ammunition. Evidently, Whigs in the low country greatly interfered with the British ability to supply the Creeks. Even though the Whigs could not supply the Cherokees and Creeks with ammunition, they continued pressuring the Indians to remain neutral. George Galphin managed to obtain some ammunition and sent it to his traders in the Lower Creek towns. Both the British and the Whigs knew that the Cherokees and Creeks would comply with the wishes of whoever supplied them with goods and ammunition. In case any doubt existed among the Whig leaders, Galphin wrote to the South Carolina Council of Safety, reiterating the fact that it exerted no influence among the Creek Upper Towns for that very reason.[1]

Stuart realized that before the Creeks could take to the warpath against the southern rebels, he would have to end their current conflict with the Choctaws. Fortunately for Stuart, the Indians had grown weary of fighting each other, and toward the end of October, the Creeks asked him to broker a peace. The Creeks found themselves in the same position as the southern colonies: trying desperately to avoid a two-front war. The Creeks knew that Georgia Whigs had already seized two British forts near Augusta and had sent out patrols to recapture stolen horses, as well as to apprehend the Creek warriors responsible. With this unrest to their east, the Creeks needed to eliminate the threat to their towns from the Choctaws to the west, especially if they were to resist effectively any attacks by the Georgia settlers.[2]

The Whig southern Indian commissioners sent a message to the Creeks in mid-November, stating their position on matters. They did not want the Creeks to take sides "in the disputes of whites." Further, all British agents and deputies should be expelled from their towns. The commissioners invited the Creeks to a May 1 congress in Augusta; wrote disparagingly of Stuart; and promised to provide the Creeks with supplies. To counter the rebels, Stuart sent a message to the Creeks, reminding them that they could only obtain ammunition from the "King's faithful subjects."[3]

It must have been a little confusing for the Cherokees and Creeks when, though a little late for the start of hunting season, Galphin did manage to send five hundred pounds of gunpowder and an equal amount of ball to the Overhill Cherokees by December. He also sent four hundred pounds to the Lower Cherokees. He realized the necessity in also supplying rum, and requested some from the South Carolina Council of Safety, along with an additional two thousand pounds of gunpowder for the Cherokees and Creeks. The council replied that it had ships out looking for British vessels carrying gunpowder, but at that time a British fleet threatened the southern coastline and it would be "imprudent" to release any gunpowder. The council essentially told Galphin "rum and good words will have to suffice." It was an unfortunate predicament for the Whigs, especially since at the end of December, John Stuart's brother, Henry Stuart, arrived in Pensacola with a supply of ammunition for the Indians. He would soon be departing for the Cherokees with his valuable commodity.[4]

Also in December, John Stuart received instructions from the British military commander in North America, Sir Thomas Gage, instructions that Whigs believed had already been issued. Gage charged Stuart to have the Indians in his department "distress the rebels by all means in their power when occasion offers." The British minister of war, Lord Dartmouth, had finally instructed General Gage to utilize Indians throughout North America. In case Stuart needed any justification, Gage advised him, "The Rebels themselves have done this."[5]

When Stuart received the letter, he immediately ended his efforts to keep the southern American Indians peaceful. But he did not construe Gage's instructions to be direct orders with any definitive purpose. Stuart did not want to stir the American Indians in his department to war without the clear support of regular troops in the southern colonies. More importantly, he did not want the Indians attacking the frontiers indiscriminately, killing Whig and Loyalist alike, but rather acting under the direction of his deputies so they could distinguish between the two. Otherwise, Stuart feared, Loyalists and Whigs would rally together to defend against the Indians.[6]

Stuart instructed his deputies and agents to apprehend Whig traders and agents "if possible." His instructions purposely allowed the British agents to exercise their own discretion in attempting to capture Whig traders. Stuart knew that interfering with a trader who supplies an Indian town with the means to hunt created a delicate situation. The influential role of the trader in American Indian life is precisely why the Continental Congress selected traders to the Cherokees and Creeks as their agents.[7]

Though American vessels looked for British ships loaded with supplies and gunpowder, they acted as privateers. If they captured a British ship, the cargo would not be given to the rebel governments, but rather sold at auction. Because the Whigs might not have captured enough ammunition and goods for the Indian commissioners, the South Carolina Council of Safety requested $10,000 from the Continental Treasury to cover the expenses of supplies and congresses with the American Indians, as the commissioners who met in Salisbury suggested. The next day, January 1, 1776, Loyalists who reorganized in the backcountry captured a supply of powder and lead meant for the Cherokees.[8]

Since receiving instructions from General Gage to prepare the American Indians in his department for war, Stuart did everything possible to accomplish his mission. In early January, Stuart wrote several times to Lord Dartmouth for authorization to broker a peace between the Choctaws and Creeks. The superintendant also implored Lord Dartmouth to establish a depot at Pensacola from which he could supply all the American Indians in his department. Stuart had even persuaded some traders to relocate from Augusta to Pensacola and requested five thousand weight of gunpowder and ten thousand weight of lead for them to supply the Indians. To show Lord Dartmouth the Indians' level of devotion to the British, Stuart related that a group of more than sixty Cherokees had traveled all the way to Saint Augustine to meet with him, though they were "naked and hungry."[9]

In February, Galphin wrote to Henry Laurens, a member of the South Carolina Council of Safety, fully briefing him on the state of Indian affairs. Galphin warned that the nonexportation of deer skins would end the Whigs' ability to supply the Indians, contrary to what they had been telling the Indians. If that happened, the Indians would never again listen to the Whigs. In such a case, Galphin advised Laurens, he would resign his commission as Indian agent. Meanwhile, the British agents were doing all they could to establish trade through West Florida and to mediate a peace between the Choctaws and the Creeks.[10]

In a reply to Galphin, Laurens suggested that South Carolina's representatives to the Continental Congress in

Philadelphia could only obtain an exemption from the nonexportation and nonimportation laws. Further, South Carolina had one thousand pounds of gunpowder for him and was hoping to obtain more from the West Indies. Laurens ended by imploring Galphin not to resign and offering some words of encouragement, saying "deliverance is coming." No doubt Galphin read the letter from Laurens with some disappointment.[11]

With the forced departure of the royal governor earlier in the year, the provincial congress of Georgia drafted "rules and regulations" in February to govern the province. Also that month, Loyalists had organized in the North Carolina low country and marched toward the coast in the hopes of meeting up with a British fleet. Whig militia met and stopped them at the Battle of Moore's Creek Bridge and ended the planned British offensive in the southern colonies. Encouraged in their cause, the Whigs of South Carolina declared its independence and established a government by forming a general assembly and electing John Rutledge president of the new state.

It took the Lower Creeks until late March 1776 to respond to Stuart's message of December 1775. They complained of no longer being able to trade through Augusta and wanted to trade in Pensacola, as did the Upper Creeks and Cherokees. Essentially, they lamented the conflict between the "English," if for no other reason than the interruption to their trade. Regarding peace with the Choctaws, the Lower Creeks told Stuart it mattered more to the Upper Creeks than to them, but they would agree to such a peace.[12]

In mid-April 1776, a large party of Cherokees met at Fort Charlotte along the Savannah River in South Carolina, with Indian commissioners appointed by the Continental Congress. The main point the commissioners wanted to convey was that they wanted the Cherokees to stay neutral in the conflict between "us and old England." Curiously, they tried to show an affinity with the Cherokees, saying, "We live upon the same ground with you, the same land is our common birthplace." Then the commissioners told the Cherokees that if the British troops came to take their property and destroy them, "What can you who are Indians expect from them afterwards?"[13]

Yeththenno, of the Valley Towns, and Ekoonee (Good Warrior) responded to the commissioners very sincerely. Yeththenno pledged to remain peaceful with the Americans. Continual encroachments on Lower Cherokee lands jeopardized that peace, he warned. Further, the recent conflict between the king and his colonies disrupted Cherokee trade. He then smoked tobacco with the commissioners, a symbol of truth in speech and goodness of thought, and stated that he acted on behalf of the Valley and Middle Towns.[14]

The next day, a warrior named Double-head spoke. He did not hide his disdain for the commissioners. Other headmen had told him not to come, for he would receive no goods for his trouble. Disbelieving, he came, trusting that the commissioners would supply them bountifully, but they could not. In a society where the amount of goods a headman commands indicates his status, Double-head said, "I am ashamed to go home again." To persuade his followers to make the journey, he told them they would be plentifully supplied. The commissioners had made him a liar. Without ample goods, the commissioners would have been better off not meeting with the Cherokees.[15]

In stark contrast, Henry Stuart and Alexander Cameron arrived in the Overhill Towns with a packhorse train of goods in April. The Cherokees received them like distinguished guests:

> Five Colors were displayed on the Town House, a party Naked and painted was Detached from the main body with two Drums and Twelve Eagle Tails to meet him at the End of the Square where they danced and Told their War Exploits by Turns. Five Great Guns were then discharged, after which we were taken hold of and Supported with a Beloved man under each arm to the Town house, and Seated on Cane Cabins Covered with Deer Skins, &tc.[16]

By the time Henry Stuart arrived in Toqua, tensions along the frontier had already resulted in violence, but only in isolated, individual encounters. Frontier colonial settlers had constructed "forts" (stockaded cabins) within fifteen miles of the Cherokee Lower Towns. Patriotic rebels attempted to apprehend Loyalists, who then fled into the Lower Cherokee Towns. In their zeal, the rebels would enter the Cherokee towns and attempt to kill or capture the Loyalists. The Cherokees considered the Loyalists "brothers" and defended them against the rampaging rebels.[17]

On May 1, 1776, Indian commissioners appointed by the Continental Congress met with the Creeks at Augusta as planned. The Creeks who went to the meeting consisted of Upper Creek Okfuskees following Handsome Fellow and a group of Lower Creek Cowetas with Ishenpoaphe leading them. Handsome Fellow enjoyed a long-standing trade association with George Galphin, and one of the Cowetas, Escochabey, had a similar relationship with Robert Rae, both traders appointed as commissioners by the Continental Congress.

The commissioners told the Creeks they had no goods to give them because the king had cut off the colonies in an effort to prevent them from rebelling. Then they blustered about their ability to otherwise supply the Creeks soon and their military capability to defeat the king's troops and capture all the British ports. Further, they said, because the Whigs would control all goods and avenues of supplies reaching Creek towns, the Creeks should expel all British deputies and not allow any British troops to pass through their territory. The commissioners ended by restating their true desire for the Creeks to remain neutral.

Chewakly Warrior responded that he wanted to "keep the path between the Whigs and Creeks white," but he needed justice (in accordance with Creek law and custom) for a relative of his who had recently been killed by whites. Galphin replied that justice would be served, and if a couple of warriors stayed after the conference, they could see the culprits hanged. Unfortunately for the Whigs, the Creeks who witnessed the hanging discovered that only one man was executed, and he had actually been convicted of killing his wife, not killing a Creek Indian. Fellow Whig Indian commissioner Willie Jones thought that the southern colonies, particularly

Georgia, would be fortunate if the incident resulted in the death of only one or two settlers, in reprisal.[18]

Though they thought further efforts would produce no significant effect, Whig leaders continued to try to persuade the Cherokees and Creeks not to become active in the coming conflict. Even after the talks at Fort Charlotte, Willie Jones, an Indian commissioner, believed it was clear that the Lower Cherokees (and those in the Middle and Valley Towns, for that matter) would follow whatever course of action the Overhill Towns pursued. That course seemed to be on the warpath straight for the Overmountain settlements. Confirmation of his beliefs came just after the talks, when Cherokee trader Edward Wilkinson accompanied the Lower Cherokees back to their respective homes in Keowee. Wilkinson advised that a party of Overhill Cherokees brought a white man's scalp into Keowee, where they received it at the council house and a dance was held. The reception and the dance indicated approval of the deed and a declaration of war. Further, Loyalists well acquainted with the Cherokees and the frontiers began to gather in the Cherokee towns. Jones predicted that if the Overhill Cherokees had not already initiated hostilities, they soon would. His warning would prove prophetic.[19]

At the beginning of May 1776, Cameron wrote to John Stuart to apprise him of the situation among the Overhill Cherokees. He informed the superintendant that his brother, Henry Stuart, had arrived with ammunition, but they did not intend to send the Cherokees against the frontiers until British troops arrived in the southern department. As for the Cherokees who had met the Whigs at Augusta, they returned not very satisfied: the Whigs had few goods to give them. A few warriors from Toqua had attacked the Overmountain settlements, but obtained only one or two scalps. Cameron succeeded in calming the warriors, and he waited for directions from Stuart.[20]

On May 7, 1776, Henry Stuart and Alexander Cameron sent the settlers of the Overmountain settlement of Watauga a letter, warning them of the agitated state of many Cherokee warriors. They advised the settlers that if they remained on land west of the boundary, they would invite attack by the

Cherokees for their encroachment. They offered the settlers the opportunity to settle in West Florida and have certificates verifying their land grant. The Cherokees would allow them safe passage through their territory. They had twenty days to leave.[21]

Almost a week later, the Watauga settlers returned an amicable response. John Carter, on behalf of all the settlers, stated that they desired to continue living in peace with their neighbors the Cherokees. If a contract the Wataugans had made with the Cherokees to buy their lands at the Henderson Purchase was not legally binding, they would be willing to give up the land. Carter stated that the settlers intended to "Obey Their Sovereign" in the conflict between the king and his American subjects. The Wataugans asked only for more time to move and a location to serve as "an Asylum for We . . . are determined to support His Majesty's Crown & Dignity."[22]

Overall, the letter seemed quite conciliatory, and it appeared that the Cherokees would not have to engage in war. The Wataugans seemed to be under the impression that Cameron and Stuart had stirred the Cherokees into threatening an attack because of the rebellious tendencies of the Watauga and Nolichucky settlers. Hence, the professions of loyalty to king and country expressed by Carter and supposedly endorsed by the vast majority of settlers. If they professed loyalty, then perhaps Cameron and Stuart would allow them to remain.

But as Stuart mentions foremost in his response to the Wataugans on May 23, the dispute between "Great Britain and the Provinces" did not influence the Cherokees in their determination to drive off the settlers. Stuart meant that he and Cameron had absolutely no effect on the young Cherokee warriors, but that "they seem unanimously resolved to recover their lands." He continued with a warning to any other settlement west of the boundary, as the Cherokees intended to recover those lands. Furthermore, some Cherokees at the Fort Charlotte meeting repeated what the Indian commissioners had said about having trespassers removed.[23]

Apparently, along with the Watauga reply, the settlers of Nolichucky also sent a letter to Stuart and Cameron. It seems, though, that Jacob Brown—a man who supposedly purchased the Nolichucky lands in March 1775 as part of the Henderson Purchase—wrote both letters. He also sent a message to the Raven of Chota, in which he expressed surprise at the Cherokees' laying claim to the Nolichucky land, especially because Attakullakulla and the Raven himself had established the boundaries to the property. The writer then delineated the numerous goods given as payment for the Nolichucky lands.[24]

Stuart's reply to the Nolichucky letter was markedly different from his second letter to Watauga, which was dated the same day. To prevent any misunderstanding, Stuart stated that the initial letter to the Watauga settlers was sent "without any regard to their Political Principles." He and Cameron had merely wanted to warn the settlers of a possible attack. Stuart extended the same offer to the Nolichucky settlers, and even expanded it to include the opportunity for herding stock down to West Florida. The Cherokees would even barter with them for goods they needed.[25]

As before, the Cherokees' trader Isaac Thomas again carried the letters of May 23, 1776, to Watauga and Nolichucky. By that time, the young warriors distrusted any correspondence and planned to waylay all couriers. When Thomas refused to go without a Cherokee escort, Oconostota offered to escort him and to kill anyone who tried to interfere. The young warriors allowed Thomas sixteen days to return before they would attack the settlements.

About this time, Stuart and Cameron received information that the Whigs intended to capture all the Loyalists in the Cherokee towns and either capture or kill Cameron. (Most of the Whigs and Loyalists in Cherokee towns were traders, but as the conflict intensified, Loyalists sought refuge in Cherokee towns to avoid Whig aggression.) Whigs considered the British deputy a serious threat for supposedly urging the Cherokees to attack the frontiers. The information about the Whigs' intentions toward Cameron proved correct when he and Stuart learned that a Whig trader in the Valley Towns had just returned from the settlements with other rebels, threatening Loyalists and Cameron. The fact that these rebels wore the unofficial insignia of the Whigs, a deer tail in their hats, confirmed their allegiance.[26]

In light of such developments, Stuart and Cameron thought it best to administer an oath of allegiance. All of the non-Cherokees in the Overhill Towns took the oath, and fifteen of them, with Willanawaw and three other Cherokees, set out the next day for the Lower Towns to apprehend all Whigs. The Loyalists and Cherokees seized the Whigs and returned to Toqua with them.[27]

The Cherokees had more to be concerned with than groups of Whigs coming blithely into their towns after Loyalists. They had heard rumors of an army coming from the settlements to the Overhill Towns, as well as the Whigs offering more bounties for Cameron. In response, some young warriors sallied out from the Great Island and waylaid some whites from the Kentucky lands. They brought back a scalp and some letters found on one of the victims encouraging his friends in North Carolina to join him. Even facing a greater onrush of white settlers, not all of the Cherokee headmen approved of their action. To make matters worse, Isaac Thomas's sixteen-day deadline had passed, and the young warriors grew impatient. Rumors of a Whig army from the settlements advancing against them still circulated.[28]

At such a critical time, John Stuart was off the coast of North Carolina meeting with General Sir Henry Clinton. While developments unfolded rapidly on the frontier, propelling the Cherokees toward full-scale conflict, Stuart indicated his request for British troops to operate in the southern department before he could ensure the Indians would commit to active military operations. Clinton, however, could not devise a pragmatic plan for British troops to operate in the department; Stuart, therefore, decided to merely keep the Indians "in good favor."[29]

During this highly agitated state, a delegation of northern and western Indians visited the Cherokees. Some Cherokee headmen at Chota sent for Cameron and Henry Stuart to be on hand when the delegation arrived. The fourteen emissaries entered Chota all in black. They gave a stirring account of their journey to Chota from the Mohawk lands; it took seventy days to pass from Pittsburgh to Chota. Those lands used to be Shawnee and Delaware hunting grounds, but settlements, forts, and large bodies of armed militia currently filled

the country. Because of the white populations and fortifications, the delegation had to make a three-hundred-mile
detour to avoid being detected.[30]

More to the point, the delegation recounted how a force of
whites living around the Mohawks had entered one of their
towns, killed several, captured the son of the northern superintendant of Indian affairs, and subsequently tortured and
killed him. The whites had attempted to enter their town
twice afterward, but the Mohawks met them and drove them
off. Surely, this account sounded eerily familiar to all
Cherokees present.[31]

The delegation members noted that they had come representing all American Indians. Soon the British would attack
the Whigs on the coast, and if the tribes united and attacked
from the west, they said, "they would find them nothing." The
delegation meant that if united, the Whig forces would be no
match for them. The Cherokees should not be concerned
about previous wars they had had with any other tribe, the
delegates said, because the delegates' tribes had sent out messages to the Wabash Indians and "they would not trouble the
Cherokees any more." The Wabash, like the Shawnees and
other tribes north of the Ohio, had clashed with the
Cherokees in Kentucky and even made incursions farther
south.[32]

With that, the delegation said it would give a speech
explaining their mission in ten days, in order to allow
Cherokees from all the other towns to arrive. Cameron and
Henry Stuart returned to Toqua for the interim. Those ten
days proved to be a precarious time for the Cherokees and the
king's officers. Practically every young warrior in the Overhill
Towns painted his face black. The topic of war against the
frontiers seemed to consume them. Still, Cameron and Stuart
endeavored to dissuade them from plunging the Cherokee
people into war.[33]

Cameron and Stuart emphasized the "dangerous consequences" of their proposed assault on the frontiers. They
warned that an attack on all whites on the frontier, Loyalist as
well as Whig, would not only attract "the King's displeasure,"
but would also galvanize the two factions against the Indians.
Cameron and Stuart most feared an alliance between

Loyalists and Whigs. They implored the Cherokees to await the return of Isaac Thomas. They held out hope that he would return with the news that the settlers had moved off the Watauga and Nolichucky lands.[34]

The young warriors became impatient with Cameron and Stuart's placating attitude. Even now that the Cherokees faced invasion, Cameron and Stuart did not want them to take the warpath. The young warriors accused Cameron and Stuart of collusion with the frontier settlers. From that moment on, the young warriors decided that no more letters would be written, and that no one would cross the Cherokee lands and warn settlers of Cherokee attacks.[35]

Cameron and Stuart resolutely defended their actions, particularly the letters they had sent to the Wataugans. Stuart said that if the settlers moved, there would be no reason for the Cherokees to attack them. On the other hand, if the settlers raised and sent an army, as had been rumored, then the scouts Stuart and Cameron advised the Cherokees to send out would give plenty of warning. The demeanor of the young warriors did not improve, but the British deputies concluded to merely "go about our business."[36]

Events throughout the Cherokee nation only served to further strain already heightened tensions. In Seneca, Edward Wilkinson, an Indian commissioner, sent four men to apprehend a Captain York from Sugar Town in the Middle Towns. Other rebels captured two Loyalists near Keowee who had been sent out by Cameron to bring in cattle. And a Lower Town trader sent word that Virginia had raised an army of nine hundred to attack the Cherokees. The headmen of Chota invited Cameron and Stuart to hear the main speech from the northern delegation. When they arrived, Cameron and Stuart noticed that the Cherokees had raised the standard of war and the Town House poles had been painted black and red—the war colors.[37]

The principal delegate for the Six Nations, a Mohawk, rose to give the opening speech. He offered a belt of white and purple wampum with strings of white beads and purple wampum attached. In reference to the rebels' entering a Mohawk town, capturing the son of the northern superintendant of Indian affairs and then torturing and killing him, the

Mohawk delegate warned the Cherokees present that "what was their [Mohawk] case one day might be the case of another Nation another day." He continued, saying that the Indians' interests had now become one and that all other quarrels should be forgotten so that all can "turn their eyes and their thoughts one way." He delivered the belt to Chincanacina (Dragging Canoe). Several other delegates from the northern tribes followed with speeches exactly like the Mohawk's. Each had a belt of wampum, which they gave to Chincanacina.[38]

The other delegates made speeches and offered belts of wampum, after which the Shawnee delegate finished with the main speech. He produced a war belt about nine feet long and six inches wide, made of purple wampum, on which he had thrown vermilion powder, indicating a call to war. He primarily spoke of the loss of Mohawk lands and how all other American Indians had had the same experience, so that they all "hardly possessed ground enough to stand on." The lost land made up part of their hunting grounds, and settlements and forts now covered those grounds. Obviously, the whites wanted to eliminate the Indians, and the Shawnee delegate thought it "better to die like men [fighting the encroachment] than to diminish away by inches." If they fought hard, perhaps they could not only recoup their lands but enlarge them. He ended with a stern warning that any Indian nation that did not join them would become the target of their wrath after they ended the war against the settlers. Again, Chincanacina accepted the belt.[39]

It was an intense session. The gravity of the words spoken and the belts given as punctuation of those words weighed heavily on all Cherokees present. Some minutes passed after the Shawnee delegate finished without any response from the Cherokees. Finally, after some time, a headman of Chilhowie arose, took the Shawnee's war belt from Chincanacina, and began to sing the war song, with the delegates joining in the chorus. At that point, practically all the young warriors took up the song while the leading headmen "sat down dejected and silent."[40]

All of the delegates had been powerful speakers and said many things of great importance to contemplate. The belts carried tremendous cultural and diplomatic meaning, and the symbolism weighed heavily on all Cherokees present. In their euphoria at being on the verge of recuperating their lands, the Cherokees wanted Cameron and Stuart to share in the moment and accept the belt, but they would not. Even now, they felt the Cherokees stood on the brink of destruction, and they could not condone such a decision.[41]

Cameron and Stuart delineated their apprehensions about the Cherokees' going to war against the settlers. The numbers alone created a foreboding scenario, especially when they considered the Seven Years' War, when the settlers had numbered half as many as they then did and still withstood the combined efforts of the French and united northern tribes. Now that the settlers had doubled in number while the Cherokees had diminished, the figures seemed even more ominous. Further, if the Cherokees should go over the boundary or attack indiscriminately, killing women, children, and Loyalists, they would provoke the wrath of Loyalist and Whig alike. Not unless the Whigs had an army in the field ready to invade Cherokee territory did the British deputies believe an attack should be made. To ensure clarity, Cameron and Stuart emphasized that the interpreter needed to "very distinctly" convey their message.[42]

In light of what all the delegates had said, countered by Cameron and Stuart's admonishment, the Raven told the northern delegation that the Cherokees would need to meet and discuss everything before giving an answer. The meeting was to take place the next day at Tellico. Cameron and Stuart accompanied the Cherokees to Tellico, where the young warriors expressed displeasure with the two for not taking up the war belt with them. They accused Stuart of harboring a grudge for the Cherokees' capturing his brother, the superintendant, during the late French and Indian War. They even accused the two men of collusion by bringing ammunition to the Cherokees but not letting them use it, so it would be captured by the settlers.[43]

For the next three days, Chincanacina, the northern delegates, and then all the headmen present attempted to persuade Cameron and Stuart to condone the Cherokees' going to war. Neither deputy acquiesced, and neither wanted anything to do with their machinations. Stuart even got

Chincanacina to confess in front of all the headmen that it was he who had agitated all the young warriors to such a fever pitch about going to war. Because the deputies placed much weight on the return of Isaac Thomas, the Cherokees wanted Stuart to write another letter to the settlements, inquiring about him. Eventually Stuart conceded and wrote what the Cherokees wanted him to say so it could not be misconstrued as a warning of impending Cherokee attack.[44]

On the fourth day after the Tellico meeting of Cherokees, the deputies sent a runner to find Thomas. They soon returned, having found him only a few miles out on his way to Tellico. Thomas had been detained by the settlers and carried with him a letter from the Committee of Fincastle. The threatening tone of the letter, combined with the news of an army six thousand strong on the frontiers of Virginia and North Carolina, was all the Cherokees needed to hear. They decided on war, and the British deputies could do or say nothing to dissuade them.[45]

FOUR

Cherokee Offensive

Summer 1776

Toward the end of June, tensions along the western frontiers of the colonies had already erupted into open violence, but it had not become an all-out war. To preclude such a catastrophe, the Council of Safety in North Carolina advised its commander in the western provinces, General Griffith Rutherford, "to prevent our people from Committing any Hostilities until the Indians make an attack upon them." Because all intelligence indicated that a general Cherokee attack could happen, the council had already sent Rutherford powder and lead. For the rest of the month and most of July, many incidents and clashes occurred along the frontier between the Cherokees and the Carolinas that boded ill for the future.[1]

In late June, Captain James McCall and a portion of his militia company entered the Lower Cherokee Towns in another attempt to capture Alexander Cameron. After a couple of days' searching through several towns unmolested, McCall and his party did not locate Cameron. Then, on the night of June 26, a Cherokee war party attacked McCall's camp, killing four and capturing the captain.

Some Cherokees had attended the Fort Charlotte talks in the hopes of getting back horses that had been stolen, or the value thereof. Because the commissioners did not give them any satisfaction, they stole three horses from Andrew Pickens (cousin of the soon-to-be-famous partisan officer Andrew Pickens) on their return home. Old Skiuka, the headman of Tugaloo (a town on the river of that name), knew Pickens, and he told a trader named Hughes that Pickens could probably reclaim his horses for a couple of kegs of rum. Hughes sent word to Pickens, who traveled with a friend to Tugaloo, a distance of more than forty miles. When Pickens arrived, he learned that Old Skiuka and the warriors of Tugaloo had plundered Hughes's store that very day before heading out to attack the Carolina frontier. Pickens and his friend suddenly found themselves in a very precarious situation. Some warriors left in the town had seen the two white men and inquired about them to Hughes, who said Pickens and his friend were Loyalists come to join them. After meeting and embracing the two, the warriors left, and Hughes helped Pickens and his friend escape the town without further incident.[2]

Another war party ventured into present-day Buncombe County, North Carolina, near the head of the Swannanoa River, killed several settlers, and plundered the cabins of feather beds, blankets, and other items. Militia Captain David Smith and Lieutenant Robert Brown hastily gathered sixteen men and chased the war party from the Upper Fort on the Catawba River. They cut the war party's trail, which had been negligently marked by pillow feathers and other domestic items obviously from a settler's cabin. Smith and his men pursued all that day and night, and all the next day into the night. The second night Smith and his men caught up to the war party asleep around a campfire near a spring. Smith divided his small party into four groups so as to be able to surround the war party, and he gave the order to await daybreak and his shot to commence the engagement. As soon as it became light enough to see, Smith discharged his weapon, and his men did likewise. The Cherokees were taken by surprise. Those not injured fled. In the area, Smith and his men found the bark peeled from a Chestnut tree on which the Cherokees had painted war figures. The spot, near the French Broad River, has since been known as Paint Spring Gap.[3]

The attacking Cherokees targeted a series of fortified positions on the lower Catawba originally constructed during the

French and Indian War. The first location they came to, called the Block House, lay just over the South Carolina line. To prepare for their attack, a Cherokee war party halted their advance on Round Mountain, just a couple of miles north of the Block House. While preparing for their assault, militia Captain Thomas Howard learned of their presence and decided to take the initiative rather than await an attack. Howard maneuvered his men through a gap to the east, now called Howard's Gap, and by daylight gained the rear of the Cherokee camp and attacked, dispersing the war party and thwarting its assault.[4]

In early July, the rebels feared the Lower and Upper Creeks' also going on the warpath. The Council of Safety in Georgia urged the Lower Creeks to disregard what the British agents told them, bolstered with the assurance that trade goods would soon be forthcoming. Timothy Barnard, a trader along the Flint River, though still in the employ of the British government, gave all the assistance he could to the Whig cause. He would receive messages for the Lower Creeks from the council in Savannah and interpret them, but when asked about them by Stuart, he would claim they had been destroyed and he could not remember their content. A few days after the Declaration of Independence was signed, the Handsome Fellow, Beaver Tooth King, Chavaller Warrior, and two hundred other Lower Creeks traveled to Augusta, where they met with Galphin. He sought to placate them, but more importantly, he gave them all the rum they could drink. He also gave them ninety to a hundred kegs of rum to take back to their towns at the end of their meetings. Galphin had no choice but to give them "rum and good words," for he had nothing else to give them. David Taitt, one of Stuart's deputies, told him that only Sempoyaffe and Escochabey had actually listened to Galphin, and that the Lower Creeks "are now pretty well reconciled [to the British], though they would rather be neutral."[5]

During this first week of July, Cherokees from the Overhill Towns expanded their attacks by crossing the spine of the Appalachians into present-day North Carolina. They established a sort of headquarters, or base camp, on the Nolichucky River. From there the warriors ranged along the Tow River, and as far south as Crooked Creek below the Blue Ridge Mountains. Throughout the broad region, the Cherokees attacked settlers, destroying all before them.[6]

General Rutherford knew by early July that only a concerted military effort would fully protect the frontiers. Not only his sizeable force but also simultaneous expeditions from South Carolina and Virginia would be necessary. He also realized that in his absence, the frontiers behind the expedition would have to be protected by mounted militia acting as patrolling rangers. So Rutherford asked the North Carolina Council of Safety for the authority to order rangers out and to pay and supply them while on duty. Additional supplies of gunpowder and lead for his expedition would also be required.[7]

Rather than wait for a response from the council, Rutherford took the initiative as much as he deemed proper and requested Major Andrew Williamson, the commander of South Carolina's Ninety-Six District militia, to proceed against the Lower Towns "until they come to terms." That would take some of the pressure from Cherokee attacks off the frontiers. Rutherford planned to embark on his military campaign within a few days, orders or not. He impressed upon the council of safety the urgent necessity of their authorizing the actions he recommended and appropriating the needed funds by summarizing the situation: the Cherokees had engaged in an all-out war against the colonies, the evidence of which included the capture of patriot leaders, the widespread killing of settlers, and the destruction of their homesteads.[8]

Williamson certainly would have agreed with Rutherford's candid assessment of the frontier situation and the means to alleviate it. However, the South Carolina commander received instructions from the state's president, John Rutledge, to guide the expedition, forcing the Cherokees to deliver all those who had committed murder, robbery, or theft, and to surrender all white Loyalists among them, particularly Cameron. Then, Williamson could negotiate peace and form an alliance with the Cherokees. Fortunately for Williamson, President Rutledge conceded his absolute ignorance of such affairs by allowing the commander complete discretion in all of these matters.[9]

On July 8, 1776, Lord William Campbell, the royal governor of South Carolina, who was on a British warship off Charleston, wrote to Lord Germain, secretary of state for the colonies, advising him that the Loyalists remained ready to assist the British and that the rebels had not gained the friendship of the American Indians. He did not know just how correct he was, for at that very moment, the Cherokees were busy preparing to attack the frontiers. Isaac Thomas, the Cherokee trader, estimated that the Raven could attack with about six hundred warriors, and he believed he would very soon.[10]

To protect Loyalists still in the settlements, Alexander Cameron devised a plan whereby Captain Nathaniel Gist and three traders—William Faulin, Isaac Williams, and Isaac Thomas—would accompany the war parties. When the force reached the outskirts of Nolichucky, Gist and the traders would enter the settlements and advise Loyalists to hold a white signal in their hands or otherwise mark themselves. The war party would then strike the settlements, killing those not so marked and burning their dwellings. They even intended to kill all the livestock, except horses, and supplied themselves with plenty of bows and arrows. As with the best laid plans, things would not go as expected.[11]

By July 11, Thomas, Faulin, Jarot Williams, and one other trader had made their way from the Overhill Towns to Fort Lee in the Watauga settlements. They warned the militia commanders that the Cherokees had been preparing for war and intended to launch an attack against the settlements. Colonel John Sevier, commander of the Washington District militia (the Overmountain settlements), sent a message informing a Fincastle County militia colonel named Russell of the developments, something frontier settlers had been expecting.[12]

The intelligence that Isaac Thomas and his fellow traders brought to the settlements spread like wildfire. Settlers from below the mouth of the North Fork of the Holston River fled their homesteads. Within just a few hours of hearing the news, they were making their way east on horseback, in wagons, and on foot, the children clinging to their parents' clothes. Those west of the Holston waded across the ford about a half mile above its mouth, where it was only about knee deep. The entire region fled, disorganized, to friends in Virginia or to the nearest settlement, that of Amos Eaton.[13]

Though the information received by the North Carolina Council of State indicated there were coordinated attacks on the frontiers of all the southern colonies simultaneously, these reports for the moment came from South Carolina. Within hours, however, the council was notified that Indians had attacked settlements east of the "Cherokee line," the boundary established as the official western limit of North Carolina in the Treaty of Hard Labour in 1768. The council members thought they should travel to Salisbury, on the frontier, in the hopes that their presence would prevent those settlers west of the boundary from conducting retaliatory attacks on the Cherokees merely as a means to acquire more land.[14]

The day after Isaac Thomas arrived at Fort Lee, General Rutherford advised the North Carolina Council of State that some forty Cherokees had attacked settlements on Crooked Creek, inflicting casualties. Other war parties operated farther south on the Catawba River. Clearly, the Cherokees had crossed the boundary line. Rutherford therefore requested one thousand pounds of gunpowder and three hundred pounds of salt, the latter to preserve provisions for the expedition on the march.[15]

Only two days later, Rutherford wrote the council again, requesting more gunpowder and reporting that he had heard many more reports of Cherokee attacks on the western frontier. Thus far, the Cherokees had killed thirty-seven people and surrounded Colonel Joseph McDowell with about 120 men, women, and children at Davidson's Fort, present-day Old Fort, North Carolina. Rutherford set out for the Salisbury District with what militia units had gathered to relieve McDowell and settlers in the area. Rutherford realized that the delay in his messages getting to the council and their responses getting to him allowed further attacks on the frontier. He therefore requested that the council move closer to him on the frontier and relocate to Hillsborough to reduce the delay in communications. It was a sound military request, but one the council would not heed.[16]

In South Carolina, the militia regiment from the New Acquisition District (an area of South Carolina acquired from the Catawba Indians in 1772) and the militia regiment from the Sparta District also began gathering in separate locations east of the Broad River. Colonel Thomas Neel's New Acquisition regiment moved to Prince's Fort and joined Colonel John Thomas's Sparta regiment, then the two forces marched on the house of a known Loyalist. Numbering around three hundred, the militia took up a concealed position in a ravine the night of July 14 and awaited daylight. At dawn, the Whigs surrounded the homestead, but they found only one Cherokee family and some livestock. After taking everything of value, the militia burned the buildings and marched their prisoners back to Prince's Fort, along with the captured livestock.[17]

Far away from North Carolina, the Kentucky region seemed almost insulated from American Indian attacks and depredations. That would quickly change. The diplomatic delegation of northern and western Indians that had visited the Cherokee Overhill Towns began making its way back to the Shawnee towns north of the Ohio River. On the way, they decided to initiate war in Kentucky by capturing three girls from the Boonesborough settlement in the Henderson Purchase.[18]

On Sunday, July 14, three teenagers—Jemima Boone, daughter of Daniel Boone, and Elizabeth (Betsy) and Frances (Fanny) Calloway, daughters of Colonel Richard Calloway, commander of the Kentucky militia—got into a dugout canoe at Boonesborough and paddled somewhat clumsily toward the northern shore of the Louisa (Kentucky) River, considered by the settlers to be Shawnee territory, to pick wildflowers. Some reports say the idea to pick flowers was Jemima's; others say it was the Calloway girls'. In either case, they proceeded until they almost reached the river cane growing in the shallow water by the river's edge. Suddenly, an Indian came out of the cane, grabbed the rope hanging off the bow of the canoe that was used to tie it up, and began pulling them to the shore. Fanny Calloway started vigorously beating the Indian on the head and shoulders with her paddle. Four more Indians came out of the cane to assist their comrade, but not until after Fanny had broken her paddle.[19]

When they were all ashore, the Indians set the canoe adrift and quieted the screaming girls by wielding their knives and tomahawks in threatening gestures. Once they were up the steep hill where the canoe had landed, the Indians cut off the girls' dresses and gave Jemima and Betsy moccasins because they had no shoes. The warriors moved out quickly, following the ridges' rocky terrain as much as possible to lessen the likelihood of leaving tracks. The party pushed on rapidly, the girls attempting to mark a trail by breaking twigs on bushes and dropping strips of cloth, until it had covered about six miles before dark ended their progress. Now the warriors tied the girls' elbows in such a manner that their hands could not touch. Then the kidnappers took the end of the rope that bound the girls together and laid it across one or two of themselves so they would feel any movement of their captives. In the course of securing the girls, one of the warriors, a Cherokee named Hanging Maw, recognized Jemima as one of Daniel Boone's daughters.[20]

The girls' screams had alarmed the settlers at Boonesborough, and several of the men investigated, but all they found was the empty canoe, drifting on the far side of the river. Despite the possibility of a war party lingering on the north shore, a volunteer swam the river and retrieved the canoe. Daniel Boone and five others crossed the river in the canoe while Colonel Calloway and ten or eleven others mounted horses and went to the ford about a mile downstream. Boone and his men split into two parties to find the trail; Calloway and his group joined them shortly thereafter.[21]

Once they found the trail, Boone advised Calloway to take the mounted party directly to the Lower Blue Licks, a favorite crossing point of Indians, fearing they would kill the girls upon hearing the approach of mounted pursuers. Boone would lead the group on foot and follow the trail. Boone and his party traversed about five miles before darkness impeded their progress, so they stopped for the night. The barking of a dog drew Boone and his companions cautiously away from the trail to discover a group of nine men building a cabin. One of the men in Boone's group went back to Boonesborough for ammunition and provisions.[22]

As soon as day broke the Monday morning darkness, the Indians and their captives resumed their course toward the Shawnee towns across the Ohio River. The girls continued to break twigs and drop bits of cloth to mark their trail. Upon discovering their subterfuge, the Indians brandished their knives and tomahawks in violent gestures. In the early afternoon, the group came across a pony, upon which the captors placed Jemima and Fanny, and occasionally Betsy. But the girls managed to keep falling off and shrieking in an effort to delay the party and give away their position. Before long, the warriors abandoned the mount.[23]

The party pushed on as quickly as the warriors could compel the girls to keep up, splitting up and making several trails. As night fell, the party stopped, again refraining from starting a cooking fire. Legend has it that Hanging Maw and several other Indians supposedly spoke English fairly well, and they conversed with the girls, speaking of Cherokee attacks on Watauga and the breaking up of those settlements, among other things. They spoke of a war party numbering some fourteen already on the Louisa River.[24]

Young John Glass, the rider selected to retrieve supplies from Boonesborough during the night, returned to Boone and the small company with ammunition, jerked venison, moccasins, and other supplies before daybreak. As soon as they could find the trail, Boone and his comrades, bolstered by three cabin builders, resumed their pursuit. Despite having been only about a mile from the captors, it took Boone and his party some time to come upon their camping spot of the previous night. After finding the several trails and splitting up to follow them, only to meet again, Boone reckoned their destination to be the Shawnee towns on the Scioto River and suggested they head straight in that direction. In this manner they cut across the girls' trail several times, based on the signs they had made. They continued until darkness impeded their pursuit and they stopped to rest.[25]

As Tuesday dawned, the warriors and their captives resumed their journey to the north. Though moving with alacrity and caution, the Indians did not seem as apprehensive as the previous two days. Eventually they crossed Hinkson's Fork and continued on some eight or nine miles. Their trail now joined the Great War Path between the Cherokee and Shawnee towns, which they occasionally left to follow a buffalo road, then returned to the War Path. The kidnappers then considered it safe enough to shoot a young buffalo and secure some of the savory hump meat. A short distance on, they crossed a stream and decided to halt briefly and cook the meat.

Also at dawn Tuesday, Boone and his party resumed their trek. Within hours they came across Hinkson's Fork, where they picked up the Indians' trail, the water still being muddy from their crossing. They, too, followed the Great War Path and parallel buffalo traces until they came across a buffalo that had been killed for its hump meat. Boone advised extreme caution, figuring that the Indians would stop to cook as soon as they came to a stream. Shortly, the pursuers did come across a stream, but they could find no trail on the other side—the Indians had traveled in the stream to hide their tracks. Boone split the party to find the trail. Only a couple of hundred yards upstream, Boone and his comrades came across the trail at about the same time as they discovered the Indians kindling a fire.[26]

Not heeding Boone's instructions for them all to gather before attacking the Indians, one of the pursuers fired. He was quickly followed by Boone and one other in their party. With at least two of the captors wounded, the Indians only had time to fling one tomahawk in the direction of the girls before all fled the scene. Hanging Maw had gone to the stream for water and evidently fled the area also. Jemima Boone, upon hearing the report of her father's rifle, exclaimed, "That's daddy's!" and the three girls began to run in the direction from where the report came. Once safe, the pursuers and the rescued girls returned to Boonesborough without incident.[27]

Farther south, the struggle for the backcountry of the Carolinas intensified. When the Cherokees began their attacks, settlers along the Saluda River gathered at Lindley's Fort (near present-day Laurens, South Carolina) near Raybon Creek. There, at 1:00 a.m. on July 15, a force of over eighty Cherokees and one hundred Loyalists, many of the latter dressed and painted as Cherokees, attacked the post. Fortunately for the settlers, Whig militia Major Jonathan Downs had arrived the previous evening with 150 men, on their way to join Major Williamson's expedition into the Cherokee territory. The Cherokee and Loyalist force that attacked the fort was unaware of Downs's presence, and it was surprised to receive intense return fire. Undaunted, they maintained their attack until daylight, at which time they withdrew. Downs pursued them and captured thirteen of the Loyalists, whom he sent to the Ninety-Six jail.[28]

Later that day, David Fanning gathered a company of fellow Loyalists and led them to the plantation of a Loyalist named Paris on Reedy River (near present-day Greer, South Carolina). There some Cherokee warriors and other Loyalists joined Fanning, bringing the number to 260. They then attacked the log fort around the plantation for approximately two and a half hours. The Whigs numbered over four hundred, according to Fanning, and they effectively repelled the attackers.[29]

Cherokees attacked the frontier to stem the tide of settler encroachment, but because Superintendent John Stuart and his deputies had been accused of inciting the Cherokees to attack the frontiers, settlers considered the American Indians as being in the service of the Crown; therefore, the settlers believed the Cherokees' motive was the same as the British— to suppress American liberty or rebellion (depending on one's perspective). Further evidence of Cherokees acting at the behest of the British was the number of Loyalists who fled the frontier to Cherokee towns in order to escape persecution. The combined Cherokee and Loyalist forces would then attack their former neighbors in retribution. Their wearing the dress and paint of a Cherokee warrior did not improve matters. Whigs referred to these Loyalists as "Scoffelites." The origin of the term is unclear, but it probably refers to the followers of a Loyalist militia colonel named Scophol (or Scovel) in the Ninety-Six District of South Carolina.[30]

After Francis Salvador, a volunteer aide to Major Williamson, spread the alarm about the Cherokee attacks, the assembling of militia began in the South Carolina backcountry. Salvador eventually arrived at Whitehall, Williamson's home. Williamson began assembling the militia of his regiment as he moved through upper South Carolina, and by July 8 he had mustered more than two hundred men. In another week his force had swelled to over four hundred, and a convoy of wagons loaded with ammunition, weapons, and other supplies had reached him, sent by South Carolina president John Rutledge.[31]

Finally, on July 21, the North Carolina Council of Safety gave General Rutherford the orders he had been waiting for—to advance into the Cherokee Lower Towns, leaving the particulars of the expedition to his discretion. The council empowered him to raise as many militia as he thought necessary to march into Cherokee territory. Further, the council expected Rutherford to coordinate his expedition with that of Major Williamson, which would advance into Cherokee territory out of South Carolina. The council hoped the two expeditions would "effectually . . . put a stop to the future depredations of those merciless savages" and eliminate the threat of a two-front war.[32]

The council advised Rutherford that another shipment of one thousand weight of gunpowder and lead for bullets would be forthcoming from the Chiswell Mines in Virginia. To ensure a more-than-sufficient force to "conquer" the Cherokees, the North Carolina council ordered an additional five hundred militiamen from the Hillsborough district to Rutherford. The gunpowder he requested had also been sent.[33]

After due consideration, it dawned upon Whig leaders in Virginia that the Cherokees might, in the face of a double-pronged attack, evade the Carolina expeditions by crossing the mountains to the Overhill Towns. In that case, the expedition under Colonel William Christian out of Virginia would bear the brunt of Cherokee forces. To help bolster the expedition under Christian, the Virginia Council of Safety asked North Carolina for three hundred militiamen. They would rendezvous at Stalnackers on the Holston River.[34]

Loyalists joining Whigs to combat the Cherokees—something John Stuart feared most—almost became a reality. Late in 1775, Whigs arrested Robert Cunningham and Richard Pearis for loyalism and jailed them in Charleston. They were released after Loyalists and Whigs in South Carolina agreed to a treaty in summer 1776. As South Carolina militia gathered at Williamson's camp for a punitive expedition into Cherokee territory, Cunningham and Pearis arrived at the Whig camp and volunteered their services. Williamson realized that if he accepted their services, much less offered them commissions, most of his militiamen would revolt. Williamson also feared the effects such a move would have in reestablishing their leadership roles in the region. So he politely rejected their offers and advised them to turn their attentions toward their private business at their homes.[35]

Major Williamson, Colonel Neel, and Colonel Thomas continued recruiting their militias and preparing for the expedition into Cherokee territory. Boosting these efforts came the news on July 22 that the British attempt to capture Charleston on June 28 had been defeated. In the next week, militiamen poured into the camps. Williamson's forces nearly doubled to about one thousand one hundred. The regiments of Neel and Thomas combined also swelled to more than one thousand. Riflemen, mounted militia, infantry, even Catawbas joined Williamson, Neel, and Thomas from all over upper South Carolina. Williamson also gathered provisions to supply the army in what he knew would be difficult terrain.

Just before embarking on the expedition, the state of South Carolina commissioned Andrew Williamson a militia colonel. That way no other militia officer would outrank the expedition commander and possibly cause confusion. Sufficiently supplied, Colonel Williamson marched his force to Twenty-Three Mile Creek on July 29, 1776. There he encamped his army and ordered scouts out to gather intelligence. The scouts returned with two Loyalist prisoners who told Williamson that Alexander Cameron had come to the Lower Towns with a dozen or so other Loyalists only a few days before. Cameron had gathered a force of some one hundred Seneca and other Lower Town warriors and encamped on Oconore Creek, about thirty miles from Twenty-Three

Mile Creek. Williamson's scouts also confirmed that the Cherokees had abandoned Seneca, their town on the Keowee River.[36]

By the beginning of August, Rutherford and the North Carolina militia had repelled the Cherokee war parties that had ranged out from the Lower Towns into the southern part of the state. Then he turned his attention northward, to the Overhill Cherokees who had taken up position along the Nolichucky. Rutherford led three hundred to five hundred of his men in an attack on them. They encountered about two hundred warriors some twenty-five miles within the Cherokee line. Once Rutherford forced them back over the mountains, he returned to Salisbury and joined the rest of his army.[37]

After his return from the Nolichucky operation, General Rutherford wrote to the North Carolina council to advise it of the situation. He acknowledged receiving the council's order a week earlier to send three hundred men of the Surry County militia to Virginia to assist the expedition planned under Colonel Christian, but they awaited the arrival of salt to take with them. When reports of Cherokee attacks had first reached Rutherford, he determined to keep in reserve the Surry militia while calling the militias of other counties in the region to stop the attacks. He accomplished that with the forays on the Catawba River and the recent one on the Nolichucky River. Now he had to keep the militias of Tryon and Rowan counties in their respective districts to garrison posts and act as rangers along the frontier. Loyalist activity in the Guilford and Anson districts precluded the use of militia from those counties. So Rutherford had no alternative but to call up five hundred men from the Hillsborough district far to the east for his expedition. Regardless of the time required in gathering them in Salisbury, he had nowhere else from which to draft militiamen.[38]

One hundred fifty miles to the east, some of Williamson's scouts captured two Loyalists who had been sent out to gather cattle for the Cherokees. They informed Williamson that Cameron, twelve Loyalists, and a Cherokee force mostly from Seneca, amounting in all to about 150, were encamped at the Cherokee town of Cowanaross. The women and children had already been removed to the hills outside of the town. Everything seemed ready for combat. Williamson decided to press forward rapidly with a force of 330 mounted men, taking the two Loyalists with them as guides. He planned to leave the horses with a guard about two miles before they reached Cowanaross and move on foot to surround the town in the night and attack at daylight. The Keowee River presented an obstacle before reaching their destination, and the militia could only ford it at Seneca. Though Williamson preferred not crossing there, he did not know of any alternative.[39]

An hour or two after midnight, Williamson and his force reached the outskirts of Seneca on the east bank of the Keowee. He knew the Cherokees had abandoned the town and therefore expected no opposition, particularly that late at night. The Cherokees, however, received intelligence of the column's movement and took up a position at Seneca. While most of the Cherokee dwellings stood on the west bank of the river, some houses lay between the river and a small hill on the east side upon which sat the headman's and trader's houses. The road into Seneca skirted the base of the hill parallel to a log fence, which the Cherokees had covered with brush and corn stalks. Cherokee warriors posted themselves behind the fence and in the houses that formed the outskirts of the town.[40]

As Williamson's column approached Seneca, the guides and advance guard almost reached the outlying houses when the discharge of five or six guns shattered the night, killing one of the guides' horses. Taking the advance guard and the head of the column by the flank, the fence line erupted in gunfire, pouring an enfilade into the column. The Cherokees probably mistook Francis Salvador, dressed in a fine white hunting shirt, for Williamson. Salvador fell at the first fire with several shots through his body. He no doubt made an excellent target in the glow of a near full moon that night. Williamson's horse fell with a shot through the neck, and at least ten others were hit. Williamson dismounted his horse before it fell completely to the ground, and he began hopping around to regain his balance, his sword in hand. He then called to his servant to retrieve Salvador's horse and mounted it.[41]

The column recoiled from the sudden attack and began to withdraw. It obeyed the only order Williamson gave, "to dismount in case of being attacked." In the moonlight, both sides fired at the muzzle flashes of their opponents. The Cherokees and Loyalists came out from Seneca and took up positions behind trees and other cover. As some militiamen rallied and attempted to assault the fence line, they came under fire of their comrades. Captain Andrew Pickens, coming up from behind Williamson, ordered the men to dismount and hitch their horses if they could do so conveniently, and if not, to let them go and dash forward. As a result, the bewildered and loose horses only added to the confusion along the road. Captain Smith noticed a figure beside Salvador but did not molest him, because in the moonlight he thought he was his servant. The figure turned out to be a Cherokee warrior scalping the mortally wounded Salvador.[42]

Though sustaining high casualties, the militia eventually pushed the Cherokees away from the fence line with a charge led by Captain Pickens. After gaining position on the fence line, his men poured about six rounds into the Cherokee position. After gaining an enfilade position, Pickens and his men fought for about twenty minutes. The action was intense, with a continual blaze of musketry coming from the fence and the constant yells of the warriors. Colonel LeRoy Hammond managed to rally a platoon, ordered it to hold its fire, and led it up to the fence: "they delivered their fire through it; and jumping over, they charged the enemy." At this unexpected and emboldened action, the Cherokees and Loyalists began to withdraw.[43]

The whole action lasted about an hour. After the firing died away, Williamson found Salvador, who asked if the battle had been won. Williamson said yes, and according to the colonel, Salvador "said he was glad of it, and shook me by the hand—and bade me farewell—and said, he would die in a few minutes." He did. Williamson had him buried at the foot of an uprooted tree.[44]

With his plan of surprising Cameron in shambles, Williamson held his force at Seneca until daybreak. They fed their horses on corn right off the stalks before setting the torch to the fields and the town. The militiamen tended their wounded and made litters for them by lashing a pole on either side of two horses and securing a blanket between the poles.[45]

Williamson then prepared to cross the Keowee and finish the destruction of the town and fields. The militiamen feared another ambush and refused to cross. A detachment of sixty men went downstream to locate another crossing. After finding another ford, the detachment refused to cross there, so it returned. Frustrated, Colonel Hammond volunteered to cross if someone would point the way. Three militiamen agreed, and the small party crossed without incident, followed by the rest of the column. They ranged for two or three miles along the river and destroyed all the dwellings and fields, but refused to advance any farther. Earlier, Williamson had arranged a meeting with Colonels Neel and Thomas at Twenty-Three Mile Creek and led the column from Seneca back to the encampment. From there, a detachment escorted the wounded on the horse litters back to the settlements.[46]

While the Battle of Seneca raged, Neel and Thomas moved their regiments toward the upper Cherokee Lower Towns with Major Frank Ross commanding the advance guard of 125 men, including a group of twenty-five Catawbas. The Catawbas, acting as guides, checked the bark of trees along the trail for signs of being climbed by Cherokee scouts, who thereby gained warning of their approach. Moving cautiously to avoid being ambushed, the Catawbas spotted trampled wild pea vines and weeds. After stopping to await the arrival of the main body before proceeding, others in the advance guard persuaded the Catawbas to continue pushing forward. Reluctantly, they resumed their advance until they came across additional signs that a large war party had recently passed that way. At this the Catawbas absolutely refused to continue without the main column.[47]

After about a half hour, an impatient man named St. Pierre spoke up, saying he would lead the advance in continuing its pursuit of the war party if the rest would follow. The militiamen agreed and followed St. Pierre up the trail in single file. The trail led up to a bald through a thick, towering entanglement of wild pea vines. They had gone about four hundred yards up the trail, when a single shot dropped the impetuous St. Pierre. Immediately, scores of guns fired on the advancing column, punctuated by the yells of Cherokee warriors. The advance guard had found the war party—or vice versa. Rather than beat a hasty retreat back down the winding path they had trod, the militiamen headed straight down the hillside, through the pea vines, with the Cherokees in hot pursuit. Attempting to run through the vines proved futile until the militiamen unwittingly discovered that somersaulting forward about every thirty feet extricated them from the entanglement.[48]

Because of the difficulty of running through the pea vines, only a few Cherokees continued the pursuit to the bottom of the hillside. One warrior caught up with Ross but only landed a glancing blow of his tomahawk on the major's head before being killed. The remnants of the advance guard collected themselves at the bottom of the hill, injured and disheveled. Shortly, the main column arrived and, learning of the ambush, immediately proceeded up the hill in pursuit of the Cherokees. Unable to catch the swift-moving war party, the column halted on a round hill and encamped for the night. They spent the next several days destroying the houses and crop fields of Estatoe, Qualatchee, and Toxaway before marching back to Keowee.[49]

Not to be dissuaded by the Battle of Seneca, Williamson relocated his base camp from Eighteen Mile Creek to Twenty-Three Mile Creek. On August 4, he sent Captain Benjamin Tutt with four hundred men to burn Keowee. Tutt found Keowee deserted but for a single Cherokee, old and infirm. He told Tutt that the residents had abandoned their towns four days prior, upon hearing of a large army approaching from South Carolina. Evidently, they had learned of Neel's and Thomas's regiments. The Cherokees did not say to where the townspeople had fled. With the area clear, Williamson moved the main body to a camp near Keowee. Williamson spent the next two days destroying nearby Sugar Town and Socony. In the process, he learned that Cameron and a body of Cherokee warriors had reached Oconousee, some dozen miles away. Williamson selected seven hundred men and beat a hasty march to Oconousee, but he found it abandoned as well. After destroying the town and crops, he led the army toward Tugaloo.[50]

As with many Cherokee towns, Tugaloo was divided by a river, in this case, one of the same name. When Williamson and his column reached the town, they discovered that the part of it on their (east) side of the river was intact, while the other (west) side lay in ashes, destroyed by Major Samuel Jack's expedition from Georgia a couple of months earlier. Williamson directed his men to destroy the habitations and crops on their side of the river.[51]

At the crossing of the Tugaloo River, Pickens had command of the advance guard. His troops expressed concern about the possibility of Cherokees lying in wait to ambush them on the other side. Pickens retorted that if they went to the very head of the river, Cherokees would probably be there, so they might as well cross then. Pickens then plunged into the river, and the advance guard followed. What Pickens did not know was that some Cherokees had taken up a position on an elevated point of land, covered with trees, on the opposite bank. From there they opened fire. Pickens, holding his feet up out of the water, narrowly escaped being killed. Instead, he only received a slight wound, his horse receiving a more severe wound. With no other casualties, the guard continued through the river under fire. Once across, Pickens led them around the point of land in an attempt to cut off the Cherokees. After an exchange of shots, the Cherokees withdrew to avoid capture.[52]

On August 8, Neel's and Thomas's regiments marched to Toxaway, where they had a brief firefight in which they killed one warrior and had one man wounded. The column pushed on to Tulpehakin, where the militiamen killed one Cherokee woman and captured another, along with two black men. From their prisoners they learned that the Cherokees of that area had abandoned their homes and encamped some sixteen miles away in the mountains. After they threatened the Cherokee woman with death, she led the militiamen through a narrow defile, extremely rugged for those on foot, much less the packhorses. Because of the difficult terrain, the Cherokees could not field a larger-than-normal war party, but they did manage to harass the column as it eased along the confined trail. Darkness descended before the militiamen could reach the Cherokee camp, so they halted on the trail as best they could. Knowing of the column's approach, the Cherokees abandoned their encampment before the militiamen reached it in the morning, leaving only the corpse of Mrs. Catherine Hite, a woman taken prisoner during the Cherokee offensive of 1776. Her nephew, Edward Hampton, was in Thomas's regiment, and he buried her before the force returned to Keowee.[53]

Before Neel and Thomas arrived at Keowee, Williamson received intelligence about Cameron and a large war party encamped at Oconore. Having waited for Neel and Thomas at Keowee for two days, Williamson led the South Carolinians toward Oconore. They arrived to find it deserted. Williamson then decided to push on for the Cherokee Lower Towns of Estatoe and Tugaloo. Before arriving at Estatoe, he sent Captains Andrew Pickens and Robert Anderson ahead to reconnoiter the area. They returned to report seeing Cherokees on both sides of the Tugaloo and on the surrounding heights. Regardless, Williamson continued the march and reached Estatoe.[54]

The next day, August 10, the army arose and took up the march by 5:00 a.m. in the early morning darkness. After about one mile, the army reached a ford and began crossing the Tugaloo River. By the time the advance guard was halfway across, about twenty yards, the sun had risen, and it afforded ample light for the Cherokees and Loyalists posted on a high hill commanding the ford. The blast of gunfire forced the advance guard to withdraw back across the river, and it began returning fire. The main column rushed to the scene and posted itself along the bank opposite the combined Cherokee and Loyalist force, and the action then became general. Soon, part of the Cherokee and Loyalist force posted itself in a position to pour crossfire on the South Carolinians. The situation became grim as Williamson ordered a strong detachment upriver about half a mile to another crossing point, but the Cherokees had secured that ford as well and prevented the militiamen from crossing. The situation then grew critical and forced Williamson to order another large detachment up a hill that allowed it to lay suppressing fire on the Cherokees and Loyalists across the river. With the enemy thus distracted, some of Williamson's men located the Cherokees' canoes and retrieved them. This allowed about 220 of the South Carolinians to cross the Tugaloo and engage the Cherokees in close quarters. Around 2:00 p.m., the Cherokees began to withdraw. After the battle, the militia destroyed the houses and crops in the vicinity and encamped in the area. The next day, the column marched to Brasstown and destroyed it and its crops.[55]

On the trail again the next day, August 12, Williamson marched his army to Tommassee, a dozen miles away. Upon reaching the town, Williamson noticed fresh tracks and dispatched Captain Pickens again with about fifty or sixty men to reconnoiter the surrounding mountains. About three o'clock in the afternoon, they discovered a Cherokee scout and fired on him. He fled, with part of Pickens's command in hot pursuit until the militiamen found themselves in a dense cane break and almost surrounded by a large Cherokee war party. Pickens ordered his men into a circle and not to fire until the warriors were mere paces away from them. Then they loosed a lethal blast into the faces of the charging Cherokees, who had decided to settle the issue with their tomahawks. Recoiling from the volley, the Cherokees resorted to their muskets at very close quarters. At this point, Pickens and the rest of the advance guard arrived and joined their comrades.

Upon hearing the firing, a relief force of about 150 men set out from Tommassee, and they soon reached the scene of action. By this time, the Cherokees had enveloped Pickens and his men. Even with the arrival of the relief force, the Cherokees continued the engagement for over an hour. The relief force began to surround the Cherokees, and only at that point did the warriors begin to withdraw. Several recorded instances of personal, hand-to-hand combat illustrate the sharp and intense nature of the battle. Though the Cherokees usually removed their dead and wounded from the field of action, they left over a dozen warriors on the ground. The abandoned casualties served as a testament that they remained to the very last possible moment before withdrawing. It is impossible to know the extent of the casualties incurred by either side, but the total could have been close to one hundred. The militiamen encamped on the site for the night, exhausted after this Ring Fight, as it came to be known, and marched back to Keowee the next day, reaching it late in the evening.[56]

At this point, the effective cohesiveness of the South Carolina militia units seems to have completely deteriorated. After the Ring Fight, Williamson stayed in the area of the upper Keowee River and destroyed the towns along it, as indicated by his intelligence information. By the time he returned to Seneca, many of the militia units he had left there had returned home. After only a couple of weeks of marching in rugged, mountainous terrain, the campaign had inflicted a heavy toll on men, clothing, and equipment. The constant sniping by Cherokee war parties had added to the general fatigue and distress, so Williamson granted furloughs for the men remaining at Seneca. He ordered the militiamen to reassemble at Seneca by August 28.[57]

Not surprisingly, Neel's and Thomas's regiments left prior to Williamson's arrival. They had been on constant campaign for almost a month and under daily attack since leaving the South Carolina backcountry. It is no wonder that on August 12, Neel and Thomas decided to return home with their regiments for a well-deserved rest and refit. For the following ten days, while Williamson marched his troops back to Seneca, Neel and Thomas marched their regiments over 150 miles to the backcountry of South Carolina without incident.

After only a few days' respite, Neel and Thomas received word from Williamson to reassemble at Seneca by August 28. On August 23, they formed their regiments again and took up the march to Seneca. Over the next several days, they moved along the upper backcountry of South Carolina, across the Broad, Pacolet, and Tyger rivers. It took a full week for them to cover the more than one hundred miles back to Seneca.[58]

While waiting for Neel and Thomas, Williamson received wagons loaded with provisions of flour and salt. He also received word that President Rutledge had ordered Colonel Thomas Sumter to join him with one thousand pounds of gunpowder and two thousand pounds of lead. After the arrival of Neel and Thomas, Williamson would not necessarily need Colonel Sumter's regiment, but he desperately needed the ammunition. In fact, he could not resume the expedition without the gunpowder and lead. Williamson sent Sumter a message to deposit some of the ammunition at his residence, White Hall, along his march as a reserve and to hurry with the remainder.[59]

Williamson also made the sound military decision to construct a fortified supply depot. Beyond the obvious military advantage, it had the simultaneous effect of occupying his idle troops until Sumter arrived. On August 26, his troops began clearing the ground around a 180-foot-square area laid out for the fort, which removed potential cover for the enemy and provided timber for the structure. Militia continued to arrive at the camp, including a company of about twenty Catawba Indians. Others gathered provisions and packed wagons as they arrived. Neel and Thomas hurried their regiments of militia along, sometimes marching twenty-five miles in a day.[60]

On August 30, Williamson grew impatient and began what active military operations he could while maintaining his base. He sent instructions to the militia units stationed in the various forts along the frontier to protect their communities. Williamson then sent the company of Catawbas and 150 militiamen to the Cherokee towns on the upper Keowee River north of his position to capture prisoners and gather intelligence.[61]

By the end of the month, Neel and Thomas had almost reached Seneca. Thus far, their march had been without incident. On the morning of August 30, as some of the men rounded up their horses that had wandered off during the night, Cherokee warriors fired on them. The militiamen sent a runner back to camp and returned fire but inflicted no casualties. Nevertheless, the war party withdrew from the area, taking some horses. A small squad of militiamen pursued the Cherokees while the rest of the regiments pushed on. The next day, word had reached Neel and Thomas that the pursuit party had ventured almost to the Cherokee town of Soquani, which some Cherokees still occupied. Neel and Thomas dispatched almost fifty men there, but by the time they arrived at the town, it had been abandoned. That day Neel and Thomas arrived at Seneca to join Williamson. On September 1, Lieutenant Colonel John Lisle arrived at Seneca with 150 men of the Spartan regiment.[62]

The scouting parties Williamson sent up the Keowee River on August 30 reported finding some Cherokees about twelve miles above Waratchy, at Socony. Williamson dispatched Colonel Hammond with 210 men, supplies, and ammunition as reinforcement. Impatient, the Catawbas and militiamen attacked the Cherokee encampment. Fortunately for the attackers, their first fire dispersed the Cherokees, who managed a scattering fire, with the Catawbas in hot pursuit. The quick action resulted in a few casualties, including one Catawba who had gone forward to secure a horse as a prize. After their attack, the militia and Catawbas began their return march to Seneca. Chagrined at having been surprised, the Cherokees laid an ambush for the returning detachment and inflicted a few more casualties, including one Catawba.[63]

From the town of Toqua, Alexander Cameron felt confident enough in Cherokee strategy, having participated in some of their actions, that he wrote a letter to John Stuart. He explained that although he had not earlier encouraged the Cherokees to attack, he did so now because they had already gone to war. One of his most experienced subordinates, Captain Nathaniel Gist, was in the field with the war parties trying "to control them." Cameron felt strongly that if the British supplied the Cherokees, the southern colonies would "submit" by the next year. War parties returning from Watauga said that their primary war aim, to drive out all the white settlers from Watauga, had been accomplished, except for the forts. Because of Cherokee attacks, Cameron noted that the South Carolina expedition withdrew to Seneca so a peace conference could be held. Thus far, Cameron stated the situation accurately.[64]

FIVE

Whig Expeditions

Summer & Fall 1776

As Major Andrew Williamson gathered South Carolina militia around Seneca for another expedition, North Carolina's General Griffith Rutherford began his expedition. Almost immediately, the Cherokees dashed Rutherford's hopes to arrive at the Cherokee towns undetected. The second night out, the army encamped on the bank of the Swannanoa River, east of present-day Asheville, North Carolina. Something, probably Cherokee warriors, spooked the dozen or so cattle the army herded along to provide fresh sustenance. The cattle broke through their makeshift corral and stampeded toward the encampment. General Rutherford, hearing the noise, stepped out of his marquee to investigate the excitement. After learning the cause, he said with accustomed authority, "Boys, there's Indians around—the cattle smelled them—to arms!" Great confusion prevailed as the militiamen rushed about the camp. The cattle quieted down, and the encampment became calm again after no Cherokees appeared.

Whether or not the Cherokees hovered around Rutherford's camp at the Swannanoa River, they certainly made their presence known at other times. The following day, despite the possibility of imminent attack, Rutherford continued the march, in line to cross the French Broad and Pigeon rivers. In passing Laurel Hill on the way to the French Broad, a Cherokee war party fired on the column and inflicted a few casualties. They crossed the river on horseback and rafts made for the purpose.[1] Once on the other side, a small, concealed war party of Cherokees again fired on the column, wounding several men.[2]

As Rutherford moved west, Williamson still awaited Colonel Thomas Sumter, who finally arrived at White Hall, over fifty miles away, on September 3. There Sumter halted and requested flour and cattle for the remaining march to Seneca. Exasperated, Williamson sent an express rider to Sumter authorizing the supplies, and he ordered Sumter "to proceed with all speed to the camp" at Seneca with the ammunition.[3]

In the meantime, Williamson did everything possible to prepare the expedition to march. On September 4, Colonel Hammond and his reinforcement, which had been sent to Socony, returned to Seneca. Williamson continued work on the fort and sent out strong detachments to destroy Cherokee towns and fields within a day's return march. Beginning on September 5, Williamson began transporting supplies across the Keowee River, which took a few days. By September 9, Sumter still had not arrived, and Williamson began crossing the army to the west bank of the Keowee while leaving the sick at the fort. He spent the next day making last-minute preparations for continuing the expedition.[4]

Unlike Sumter, Williamson felt the need for quick movement, since he previously had advised General Rutherford that the two would meet on September 5 in the Middle Towns. As the date to meet Rutherford passed and Williamson still awaited Sumter at Seneca, Hammond tried to dissuade Williamson from the expedition. Logically, he pointed out that by the time Sumter arrived and the expedition could resume, Rutherford would have already destroyed the Middle Towns and probably already be in the Valley Towns. In that case, Williamson could not hope to trap the Cherokees of the Middle and Valley Towns between him and Rutherford as planned. Therefore, Williamson should remain at Seneca. The force of Hammond's observations could not be denied, but Williamson felt bound to make the march to the

Middle Towns, since he had advised Rutherford he would. Besides, Williamson said, he would not be able to forgive himself if he did not go and something devastating befell Rutherford.[5]

Rutherford continued his march west toward the Tuckasegee River, crossing branches of rivers along the way. The North Carolinians followed a branch of the Pigeon River south to Balsam Gap near present-day Waynesville. As the advance guard, with an old trader named Brown for a guide, approached the summit of the ridge, they spotted a scouting party of three Cherokees. The Cherokees immediately scattered, and the advance guard galloped after them. One of the Cherokees whom Brown began pursuing injured himself jumping over a fallen tree and could not move. Upon Brown's approach, the two recognized each other, and the Cherokee said, "don't have me killed?" Brown turned around and joined the others.[6]

After crossing the Balsam Mountains, Rutherford divided his force, sending Colonel Francis Lock with one thousand men to a Cherokee town on the Tuckasegee River. Lock preceded his detachment with a scouting party about a half mile in advance. That scouting party was fired on by about twenty Cherokees some seven miles from the town of Watauga. The scouting party returned fire and then waited for the rest of the column, and the entire force continued for five miles before encamping for the night. The next day, September 8, Lock entered Watauga; Rutherford and the remainder of the army followed the day after.[7]

Rutherford had anticipated meeting Williamson in the Little Tennessee River valley, but the South Carolinians could not be found. On September 10, Rutherford sent a scouting party up the Little Tennessee River to locate Williamson and his army. Until the South Carolinians could be located and brought to his camp, Rutherford decided to accomplish the goals of the expedition while waiting for Williamson. He also sent out reconnoitering parties and a detachment of three hundred men to the Cherokee town called Sugartown, up the Sugartown River (now the Cullasaja River).[8]

Sugartown sat at a junction formed by two rivers, occupying the triangular area between them. When the detachment entered the town, it encountered a large party of Cherokees, who fired on the militiamen from the riverbanks and from behind a work they had constructed out of timber and brush. The militiamen took shelter from the withering fire inside the Cherokee dwellings and returned fire as best they could. It took about three hours for Rutherford to hear the sounds of the battle, organize a relief column, and march to the scene about five miles away. Once the relief arrived, the Cherokees withdrew and ended the engagement. Rutherford's forces suffered at least eighteen killed and twenty-two wounded. Cherokee casualties remain unknown.

The militiamen did manage to capture a Cherokee during the action. Only after threatening the warrior with death did he agree to show the North Carolinians where the Indians had secreted their women and children along with some cattle. He led the militiamen up the Sugartown River some seven miles through a narrow defile where the mountainous terrain jutted in from each side as the river twisted its way through the valley. After negotiating the path to the hidden town, the militiamen found it deserted save for a few elderly Cherokee. The militiamen saw Cherokee warriors high above the narrow valley, gazing down at them, but neither side fired. The militiamen burned the town, took the cattle, and returned down the valley.[9]

Finally, on September 11, 1776, Colonel Sumter arrived with 330 men, supplies, and, most importantly, the ammunition Williamson desperately needed. Fortunately, about two thousand South Carolina militiamen had already assembled at Seneca for the expedition. Many of Sumter's men could not continue because of fatigue, so Williamson ordered them to join the other sick in the fort. Although Williamson had already delayed his march so long, the next day required mounting cattle guards, distributing the ammunition, and other last-minute affairs. These included designating the newly constructed fortification Fort Rutledge and assigning Captain Tutt as its commander with a garrison of 250 men. Williamson charged Tutt with gathering intelligence through scouting parties and maintaining communications with officers on the line of frontier forts to the east.[10]

Undaunted by the Sugartown ambush, on September 11,

Rutherford marched his army to Cowee. The next day he sent a detachment to Allejoy, about seven miles away, and a party to Nequassee, about ten miles away. Both days saw brief skirmishes and ambushes with the Cherokees resulting in a few casualties. After the return of the two detachments, Rutherford moved the army up to Nequassee. An unfortunate incident occurred on the march when the lock on a soldier's musket got caught in a burl and the weapon accidently discharged, killing another soldier. The Reverend James Hall held a ceremony at the old mound in Nequassee for the soldier. The sermon, probably the first one in that part of North Carolina, was from 2 Corinthians 13: 5, "Examine yourselves, whether ye be in the faith, prove your own selves. Know ye not your own selves how that Jesus Christ is in you, except ye be reprobates."[11]

At 7:00 a.m. on September 14, Williamson and his army moved out of its encampment on the west bank of the Keowee and crossed the Oconee Mountains. Scouts found horse tracks on the west side of the mountains, and Williamson concluded that messengers from Rutherford had made them. The North Carolina general had sent out riders to try to locate Williamson. Unfortunately, Rutherford did not tell the messengers that Williamson would be coming from Keowee, and they turned around before making contact. With the two commanders out of communication with each other, the opportunity to entrap the Cherokees near Little Chota (or Choti) evaporated, and Williamson steadily proceeded up the Tugaloo toward the Middle Towns.[12]

Before continuing the advance at 10:00 a.m. on September 15, Williamson distributed the remainder of the ammunition. The army marched through a "very hilly and broken ground," and Williamson encamped it on three hills facing west. That evening, he sent a lieutenant and thirty men three miles west to establish an ambush and prevent Cherokee scouts from locating the army.[13]

On September 15, Rutherford held a council of war with his officers to determine their next course of action, because Williamson and his army had not yet arrived, being ten days late. The council decided to give Williamson one more day, and if the South Carolinians did not appear, Rutherford and his officers would continue with their mission of destroying Cherokee towns. When Williamson and his army did not show up on the sixteenth, Rutherford left his wounded and sick at Nequassee under Colonel James Martin and led twelve hundred men down the trail west toward the Valley Towns.[14]

September 16 was a typical day for Williamson's column. By 10:00 a.m., the army had marched three miles, arriving where Williamson had sent the ambush the previous evening. They reported no contact with the Cherokees, and the army continued to Warwoman Creek. Williamson sent out strong flanking parties to secure the heights that commanded the ford. The army crossed and continued its march toward Stickoe Mountain. About 4:00 p.m., the army halted and encamped. Williamson sent a detachment of fifty men under a Major Watson to establish ambushes on the roads leading to the Middle and Valley Towns.[15]

On September 17, Rutherford led his army some eight miles to Neowee, consisting of about seventy houses and other structures. As had been almost a daily occurrence during the expedition, a small war party fired on the column and quickly withdrew. Rutherford made it to Neowee and continued the policy of destroying everything in the town and the surrounding fields of crops. He then led the column another mile up the Hiwassee River and made a dry camp. Next day they advanced "over two very steep mountains" and encamped at a creek on the Hiwassee. Between the terrain and the constant sniping, physical fatigue and psychological stress became acute.[16]

For almost a week, Rutherford and his militiamen methodically destroyed the towns along the Hiwassee River, then they turned north up the Valley River. They burned Quanassee and Chowa, and detached units of several hundred mounted militia to destroy nearby towns. The North Carolinians captured about a dozen prisoners, including Loyalists, with their Cherokee wives and children, and their slaves. More importantly for the expedition, they captured seventy or eighty horses and a number of cattle—allowing for desperately needed remounts in the rugged terrain and fresh beef for the troops. They found corn in the fields plentiful before putting them to the torch.[17]

Williamson established contact with Rutherford's force after crossing through Rabun's Gap and heading down the Little Tennessee River to Nequassee. There he met up with Colonel Martin and the North Carolinians' baggage train guard. Martin informed Williamson that Rutherford had left three days earlier for the Valley Towns, taking the well-known trail to the west. Williamson decided to encamp and rest his army until the following day, when he would resume the march in an effort to catch up with Rutherford.[18]

On September 19, Williamson started his army in pursuit of Rutherford's column. He led his militiamen west out of Nequassee up the Sugartown River. Williamson had several traders as guides and therefore knew the trails and locations of many towns. After about an hour, the column swung to the north, taking the main trail to the Valley Towns over the Nantahala Mountains. The trail led up the Waya Creek valley, called "the Dark Hole," directly to Waya Gap. Steep mountainsides covered with a dense forest formed the valley, limiting the amount of sunlight that came through. At about 10:30 a.m., Catawba scouts reported signs of Cherokee warriors, and Williamson halted the head of the column so the rest could close up ranks; then the whole proceeded cautiously. The advance guard of one hundred men had just about reached the steepest part of the trail leading up to the gap when the valley erupted with musketry fire.[19]

Williamson and his men did not realize that Oconostota led the Cherokees in person. The Great Warrior had positioned his force below Waya Gap and along the sides of the valley so that when the battle began they almost completely enveloped Williamson's column. The initial volley killed almost twenty militiamen as the column recoiled under the galling fire. After that, the Cherokees poured a steady fire into the militiamen, causing great confusion and fear of being cut off. The advance guard fell back to the rest of the column, which had halted in the floor of the valley, an open area of about forty or fifty acres. Oconostota maintained pressure on the enemy by alternating rather than coordinating attacks. Cherokee warriors first charged down one side of the valley; then, after they had withdrawn back up the mountainside, more Cherokees would attack down the other side of the valley. The militiamen beat back the Cherokee assaults only through the firepower and range of five wall guns—heavy, large caliber smoothbore muskets.[20]

Oconostota had the South Carolinians pinned in a most unenviable position. Williamson had to rally his troops and keep them on the field while simultaneously ensuring the safety of the packhorses. Not only did the Cherokees have firearms, but also their traditional weapons of bows and arrows, as well as spears. And they used tomahawks and knives in hand-to-hand combat.

Finally, Colonel Samuel Hammond gathered about twenty militiamen and began moving toward Waya Gap. Seeing Hammond set off, Edward Hampton gathered some thirty militiamen and joined him. Passing the advance guard, Hammond gave the command, "Loaded guns advance! Empty guns fall down and load!" He and Hampton moved toward the gap. With extreme difficulty negotiating the rugged terrain, and withstanding the withering musket fire, spears, and arrows of the Cherokees, Hammond managed to reach his objective. From this position and with a body of fifty troops, Hammond had flanked the Cherokees, who began to withdraw. Fearing the capture of their great warrior, a group of Cherokees surrounded Oconostota while others laid down fire on Hammond's troops to clear an escape route.[21]

Around four o'clock in the afternoon, the flanking troops had been sufficiently advanced up the mountainsides, and Hammond gained and occupied Waya Gap, forcing a general Cherokee withdrawal. The Cherokee retreat was not precipitous, and scattered firing continued throughout the last hours of light. After such a lengthy and exhausting fight, with Cherokee warriors still lurking about, Williamson decided to encamp his army on the battlefield, posting pickets along the mountainsides. One of these sentinels discovered a Cherokee behind a tree. Not only had the Indian been wounded through the thigh, rendering flight impossible, but the warrior proved to be a woman armed with a bow.[22]

The Battle of the Dark Hole continued for approximately six hours and involved some of the most desperate fighting of the entire campaign. Williamson lost over sixty men killed, including several Catawbas. The wounded South Carolinians amounted to "a considerable number," perhaps well over two hundred. Hardly a man on the field did not feel the effects of extreme fatigue and exhaustion that night. Colonel Martin, back in Nequassee, heard the battle and sent about 150 men under Colonel Benjamin Cleveland to Williamson's aid. Unfortunately for the militiamen, he arrived as the Cherokees began their withdrawal.[23]

The next morning, the army resumed its march to the Valley Towns, a distance of some twenty-five miles. After collecting their wounded and sending them back to Colonel Martin at Nequassee under a guard of one hundred men, Williamson and his column continued west. On September 20, the column marched only about five miles because of the steep mountains. The terrain did not improve over the next several days. Williamson kept out an advance guard and flankers, though the latter had to march along the mountain-tops somewhat separated from the main column, which plodded down into the Nantahala Valley, "Where we had not the happiness of the sun to shine on us." Though the militiamen expected an attack every day, none came, and except for one woman, the column did not see another Cherokee.

The sole Cherokee prisoner informed them that a camp of warriors lay four miles ahead; the column pushed forward but did not encounter them. The entire route lay through deep ravines that, "abounding with laurel thickets and sidling swamps," slowed the march to a crawl. Because the terrain was so rugged and mountainous, Williamson progressed only about five or six miles a day. Since the beginning, much of the expedition traversed terrain similarly rugged, but this stretch was (and still is) noted for being particularly so. William Drayton described it as a route that, "Penetrated through woody bottoms, full of thick laurel swamps, covered with dense thickets of bushes, vines, and briars: and some of these, so completely embosomed by the height of adjacent mountains, that the rays of the sun scarcely ever reached them." Even today, the Nantahala Gorge is called "the land of the midday sun."[24]

Drayton continued, "In addition to these difficulties, the baggage, ammo, and provisions, were carried solely on pack-horses; which, sometimes stumbling in their march, were hurled down and torn in pieces, before they reached the base of the mountains." After three days of extremely rough marching through narrow defiles, the South Carolinians emerged from the mountains and descended into a savanna whereupon they encountered their first of the Cherokee Valley Towns.[25]

Rutherford's men had also faced their share of hardships. Before daylight on September 22, a trader named Robert Brown led Rutherford's column to the outskirts of Hiwassee Town. There the militiamen waited until just before sunrise, when they attacked the town. They surprised the few Cherokees in the town, who fled in all directions. The mounted militiamen broke up into groups of a half dozen or so and chased the Cherokees into the woods bordering the town. Sometimes they chased a solitary Cherokee and shot him down. Other times the Cherokees gathered and lay in ambush for the pursuing militiamen, inflicting several casualties. The militiamen experienced such ambushes throughout the expedition. Even when they achieved total surprise, they knew the Cherokees to be deadly and cunning foes.[26]

In Hiwassee, Rutherford's men found an elderly Cherokee woman who threw up her hands upon their entry. Out of the twenty or thirty dwellings in the town, they did not burn hers. The militiamen found a great quantity of corn, some in cribs, some on the stalk, along with cattle, hogs, peas, nuts, and other sustenance. Because of the bountiful provisions, Rutherford rested his army there for several days, refitting and recuperating. Considering the fatiguing nature of the expedition thus far, the militiamen desperately needed the respite.[27]

About that same time, Williamson and his army encountered their first Valley Town, called Burning Town, consisting of some 110 dwellings. The South Carolinians surrounded the town before descending on it, but they found no residents. The next day, September 24, the militiamen burned all the structures and cornfields, totaling about 250 acres. The column then headed down the valley to the next town, Tomatley, only two miles distant.[28]

On September 25, Williamson's column continued its systematic destruction of the Valley Towns. Tomatley boasted not only fields of crops but also orchards of peach and apple trees, all of which the militiamen cut down and destroyed. Moving two more miles down the valley, they entered the deserted town of Neowee. As with previous Cherokee towns, all dwellings and crops were destroyed. The column continued to the next town, Takliwa (Tellico), and again destroyed all dwellings and crops before moving on to yet another town, Canosti. In this one day, Williamson's army had destroyed four Cherokee towns. The exhausted militiamen encamped for the night.[29]

Continuing the next day for a few miles, Williamson's column reached the town of Canuce, or Little Hiwassee, and destroyed everything. Resuming the march for eight more miles, the militiamen reached the main Cherokee Valley Town of Hiwassee. Here they finally met Rutherford and the North Carolina militia army, who greeted them with a salute of thirteen salvos from their swivel guns. The two commanders held a council of war to determine their next course of action.[30]

Because Williamson had come down the Valley River and Rutherford had come up from the Hiwassee River, both concurred that they had destroyed all the Cherokee Middle Towns. They contemplated their next course of action, discussing whether they should attempt crossing what the Cherokees called the Shaconage Mountains (today's Great Smoky Mountains) to attack the Overhill Towns. The conversation surely included their recent difficulties in crossing the extremely rugged terrain as well as the incessant sniping. No doubt neither commander relished continuing farther into Cherokee territory. After two months of endless slogging through narrow defiles in treacherous mountain terrain and being constantly ambushed, their armies had sustained hundreds of casualties, while hundreds more were made physically unfit for action. The two commanders decided to end their campaigns and return whence they came. On September 27, after Rutherford handed over to Williamson some eighteen prisoners consisting of blacks, Loyalists, and an assortment of Cherokee men, women, and children, the two commands marched together for about a half a mile before taking their separate paths home.[31]

After leaving Rutherford, Williamson's army marched to Great Ecochee, which the North Carolinians had already destroyed. Moving on through the smoldering remains, the South Carolinians reached Chowwee. Chowwee and Casqutetheheh, adjacent to each other, combined for some five miles in length and were at places two miles wide. Rutherford had not destroyed these towns, so Williamson had his army encamp to spend the rest of the day destroying the habitations and extensive fields. As they continued their work the next day, some Cherokees ambushed two militiamen who had ventured from the main body. This tactic—surprise attacks on small, isolated groups of militiamen—is the foremost characteristic of the expedition recounted by participants.[32]

As the militiamen continued their work of destruction, an observer estimated the extent of the cornfields to be about nine hundred acres. Once all the corn and dwellings in both towns had been destroyed, the column buried the militiamen killed, made litters for the wounded, and resumed the march south. In a couple of miles, the South Carolinians came to Theatugdueah and made camp. The next morning, September 29, the column took up the march at seven o'clock, crossed the Hiwassee, and marched about fourteen miles to Nacuchey before making camp. At this point, Williamson directed Sumter and his regiment to take up the right wing, Hammond and his regiment the left, and Neel the center with the main column. Williamson knew the headwaters of the Hiwassee River lay ahead, and they had encountered too many ambushes in just such places to be caught off guard. To the happy surprise of the South Carolinians, they passed unmolested, though they crossed the river over twenty times.[33]

Once Williamson and his army crossed the mountains separating the headwaters of the Hiwassee, they entered present-day north Georgia, to the west of the route they took into the Cherokee Middle Towns. Several Cherokee Lower Towns remained in this region, and the South Carolinians destroyed them. Little Chota, one of the largest Cherokee towns, consisted of over one hundred dwellings and such vast fields of corn that an observer could not accurately estimate their extent. September 30 and October 1 were spent destroying the town and fields. Williamson then ordered a detachment to another Cherokee town, Frogtown, about sixteen miles farther east, but before proceeding too far, the guide declared the detachment too small to attack the town. They returned for reinforcements, but the day being advanced, they encamped at Little Chota for the night. The next day a body of three hundred horsemen marched to Frogtown and on arrival found no cornfields and only a couple of dwellings, whereupon the detachment returned to the main body.[34]

Once out of the rugged terrains of the Appalachian and Blue Ridge Mountains, the North Carolinians began making longer marches. On September 30, Rutherford had his men up and on the march before daylight, traveling some twenty-five miles before reaching the Pigeon River and halting. Then the rains began. For two days the North Carolinians slogged through the hilly terrain, crossing rivers and enduring rain throughout the nights. The rain stopped by October 4, but the trail continued to be treacherous and slippery. That evening the column reached Cathey's Fort, and the officers treated their men to brandy. Another few days saw most of the North Carolina militiamen back at their homes.[35]

While General Rutherford had been on his expedition against the Cherokees, some of the tribe had infiltrated behind him and attacked frontier settlements. In light of such activity, the North Carolina Council of Safety thought it wise to construct and garrison forts along the frontier, in the counties of Tryon, Rowan, and Surry. These would be properly supported and connected by forts to be constructed by Rutherford in the Cherokee towns (like Fort Rutledge in Seneca).[36]

On October 3, Williamson's army advanced only two miles, to Little Chota, in present-day northeastern Georgia, and destroyed the fifty or sixty houses and about two hundred acres of cornfields there. The next morning, the column proceeded to Soquee, a Cherokee town on the Sautee River.

Because of an ambush by Cherokees, a packhorse loaded with flour was lost while fording the river. Once everyone was across, Williamson released a prisoner who had been their guide: an elderly Cherokee woman taken early in the expedition. She accurately guided the column from town to town, and at Soquee, Williamson gave her a horse and sent her back unmolested. In another week, Williamson and his army reached the settlements in South Carolina without further incident, and he discharged his army.[37]

The last leg of the journey, if not the entire expedition, could have been worse for Williamson and his army. Because the Creeks did not join the Cherokees, the South Carolinians faced only Cherokee warriors and Loyalists. From the Hiwassee River on, they did not face any determined resistance, which they probably would have if the Creeks had joined the Cherokees. Williamson's men also could not have received any assistance from the Georgians because of the activity of two Creek war parties from Cussita that attacked their western frontier near Augusta.[38]

The instructions given to Williamson concerning his campaign proved totally impractical and illustrate the extent to which political leaders in the east did not understand life on the frontier, much less the Cherokees. President Rutledge instructed Williamson to have the Cherokees "deliver up all who have committed any Murders, Thefts, or Robberies." By the time Williamson embarked on his campaign, the Cherokees who fell into that category probably included over half the male population of the Lower, Middle, and Valley Towns. Another of Rutledge's instructions was to have the Cherokees "deliver up all whites, particularly Cameren." This too was an unrealistic order. Though Williamson tried several times to capture Cameron, he was staunchly protected by Indians and Loyalists alike, and Williamson's army paid the price of severe casualties inflicted by Cherokee ambushes. To capture the hundreds of white Loyalists who then resided among the Cherokees was simply impossible.[39]

The standard interpretation of the 1776 Carolina expeditions and the Cherokee response has been that the expeditions swept through the Cherokee Lower, Middle, and Valley Towns forcing all the inhabitants to flee and leaving nothing but desolation in their wake. This perspective was perpetuated by nineteenth-century historians such as John Haywood and J. G. M. Ramsey. Since then, their interpretation has become standard, in that very little has changed from the patriotic perspective of the eighteenth century. Though technically not incorrect, this interpretation certainly does not include the whole context of circumstances and events. A more comprehensive narrative produces a somewhat different account, and a better evaluation of the operations becomes possible.

The strategy employed by the Cherokees against the Carolinian expeditions reflects a change in American Indian warfare. Perhaps with the reduction of the Tuscarora fort at Neoheroka in 1712, the Cherokees learned the weakness of fortified towns against a Euro-American military force by participating in that siege. The traditional strategy of repelling an attack from within the fortified walls of their towns may work when fighting other American Indians, but obviously not against Euro-American military forces, especially ones with artillery. By the 1720s, the likelihood of facing Euro-American forces grew, and Cherokees apparently stopped fortifying their towns. Invasion by Euro-American military expeditions called for a change in strategy.[40]

The new strategy involved a defense with a limited offense in which the Cherokees would evacuate their towns targeted by invading enemy forces, drawing them into extremely rugged and difficult terrain, and ambush the enemy whenever the opportunity presented itself. With complete success, the Cherokees would inflict enough casualties for the enemy to withdraw. If only partially successful, the Cherokees would inflict enough casualties to deter the enemy from penetrating all the way through their territory, or shorten its time in Cherokee territory. It is the same logic as that famously employed by the Roman general Quintus Fabius Maximus

Verrucosus, by which he avoided pitched battles against the Carthaginian general Hannibal during the Second Punic War. It later came to be called the "Fabian strategy" in military parlance.[41]

When first implemented, the new strategy produced highly effective results. Twice in 1760, during the French and Indian War, the strategy initially succeeded in repelling invading Euro-American armies. In 1776, Cherokees employed the strategy, again with a measure of success. Neither Rutherford nor Williamson withdrew after being ambushed, but their casualties resulted in several negative consequences for the invaders. Whether they collected their wounded in a designated location or sent them directly back to the settlements, both actions required able-bodied troops to guard the invalid militiamen and horses to carry them, detracting from those available to carry supplies for the main armies. Cherokee ambushes exacerbated what Carl von Clausewitz would later call "friction" in the military operations of Rutherford and Williamson, making them increasingly difficult the farther they advanced.

The ambush had long been a favorite Cherokee tactic, and it became an integral part of the Cherokee strategy in combating Euro-American invasions. It had usually been employed to inflict enemy casualties while minimizing their own. The terrain dictated an invading force to be strung out in a long column, precluding its ability to amass in strength at any given point. Cherokee warriors would be positioned in a half-moon formation, preferably on ground higher than that of their enemy. The formation allowed Cherokees to envelop the flanks of a foe that had been halted by sudden and point-blank fire. The clearest example of this during the Whig expeditions was the Battle of the Black Hole.[42]

The Cherokees did not just utilize the ambush tactic on a large scale during the 1776 expeditions. At every opportunity, small war parties would attack straggling or separated militiamen. Almost daily throughout Rutherford's and Williamson's expeditions, Cherokees inflicted casualties. The "terrifying brutality" of being ambushed in terrain that dictated close confinement by an unseen foe who disappeared before a counterattack could be mounted took its toll on the South and North Carolinians in the form of psychological stress and combat fatigue (what today is termed posttraumatic stress disorder). Indeed, the terror of ambush is the most common and striking feature recorded in first-hand accounts of the expeditions.[43]

In Western military terms, the Cherokees waged a highly effective *petite guerre*, or guerrilla war. When historian Ian Steele made his observation that American Indians "learned the hard way that they must defend nothing, not even stockaded settlements or cornfields," he could have been referring to the Cherokees in 1776. With such a strategy, the Cherokees embraced the harsh reality that mere survival would be an achievement.[44]

In North America, Euro-American military forces began a return to older military traditions in that an engagement, or war, would not cease before an enemy had been destroyed. If a leader's military forces remained on the field of battle after the engagement ended, they assumed themselves to be the victor. Frequently, however, these victories could easily be Pyrrhic in nature. Such was the case with the many engagements during the Rutherford and Williamson campaigns. Cherokees did not feel the need to occupy the battlefield to obtain victory—inflicting severe casualties while minimizing their own served as more of a genuine victory.[45]

An extremely rugged terrain that forces formations into disjointed groups lacking cohesion and making them susceptible to ambush at any moment; the constant sniping at individuals or small, isolated groups of militiamen; the frequent lack of supplies; the breakdown of equipment—all these factors produced a nightmarish experience for over two months. Additional casualties occurred after the return of the expeditions, as the participants "died after their arrival at home in consequence of their exposure, privations and fatigue." It is no wonder that many survivors of the Rutherford and Williamson expeditions did not actively participate in any military service for several years after 1776.[46]

Euro-American military forces discovered an effective offensive strategy in waging war against American Indians from their first contact: deploy a force big enough to numerically overpower any the Indians could field; adequately supply for extensive operations away from a base; and destroy every dwelling, structure, and crop field the expedition encountered. Needless to say, the killing or capturing of every individual, regardless of age or gender, was equally important as a concomitant goal. As historian Colin Calloway noted, war against villages and crops could be quite devastating to traditional life ways. Indeed, an unintended effect of the expeditions was the disruption of the ceremonial culture shared by the Lower, Middle, and Valley Towns. The expeditions destroyed all corn used not only for sustenance, but also seed. Without a corn crop, the annual Green Corn Ceremony could not be held. The most important celebration in Cherokee life, the ceremony symbolically swept away the previous year and allowed a fresh beginning to a new year. But such a "food fight," as historian Wayne E. Lee calls it, though inflicting widespread devastation on towns and crops, and disrupting an important cultural event, did not render the Cherokees militarily impotent.[47]

As in previous wars pitting Euro-Americans against American Indians, Rutherford and Williamson both utilized the services of other Indians against the Cherokees, primarily the Catawbas, an ancient enemy of the Cherokees. Though the Catawbas were used to advantage as scouts in advance guards, troops and commanders did not heed the information they obtained. If they had, casualties would not have been so great, and the expeditions might have been more effective.

By 1776, the Cherokees had learned to yield before an invading force that had numerical strength. Their primary goal was to maintain a fighting force, and in that they succeeded admirably. Though Rutherford and Williamson reduced many of the Lower, Middle, and Valley Towns to ash throughout the Hiwassee, Little Tennessee, and Keowee river valleys, they did not eliminate the Cherokees as a viable military force. Thus, the Whigs did not accomplish their primary goal, which Rutherford called the "Finel Destruction of the Cherroce Nation."[48] Along almost the entire extent of the Whig militia expeditions, Cherokee warriors challenged their advance at every opportunity, while not allowing the Carolina militiamen a chance to engage them in the Western military style of linear tactics.

SIX

The End of a
Very Violent Year

Fall 1776

Fully two weeks before Rutherford began his expedition into the heart of the Middle and Valley Towns, Colonel William Christian received a letter from the Virginia Council of State placing him in command of Virginia's punitive expedition against the Overhill Towns. Before the sun set that day, Christian sent letters that ordered men and supplies to converge at his location in Botetourt County, Virginia. He estimated that the expedition would number some 1,450 men and require fifty days' worth of provisions. It would be two weeks before all had been assembled, and another two weeks to reach the "Big Island" (Long Island).[1]

Christian and most of his force arrived at Long Island on the Holston River on September 21. Evidently, Christian had a difficult time recruiting for his expedition. Even the commander of the fort on the island, dubbed Fort Patrick Henry, became discouraged from the lack of volunteers. Perhaps the constant ambushes by small groups of Cherokee warriors that occurred since Christian arrived at Long Island dampened recruiting efforts. To make matters worse, Christian observed that all the settlers from Botetourt County to Long Island had fled to the nearest fort. As a result, the stations had become quite crowded, and the people suffered from a lack of provisions because most of the crops in the area had been destroyed by Cherokee raids over the previous months. Something had to be done.[2]

First, Colonel Christian issued a notice "to all persons who have been in the country service in the forts or elsewhere . . . that all such must join some company and go on the expedition against the Cherokees. . . . [T]hose who refuse need not expect any pay for past or future service but will be called upon [to] pay for the provisions used and are to draw no more." Those who did not volunteer would be drafted and thereby receive nothing other than rations issued. Then Christian ordered his commissary to provide two wagonloads of flour for the families of those volunteers in the expedition. Estimates range as high as two thousand one hundred for the size of Christian's force after the issuance of his notice and the arrival of Colonel Joseph Williams's militia regiment and a contingent from Boonesborough. At that point he took the field, marching about six miles from Long Island to Double Spring, where they encamped for two days.[3]

To gather intelligence, Christian sent forward two scouting parties—one to lay on the main path from the Overhill Towns to warn him of any approaching force, the other to take a prisoner for interrogation. Christian did not know whether the Overhill Cherokees meant to oppose him or seek peace. He figured the French Broad River was where the question would be decided, as it offered the best position for the Cherokees to oppose him. If not, that was where they would attempt to negotiate peace.[4]

Christian resumed the march south on October 8 and reached the French Broad five days later. Just before they reached the river, on the evening of October 12, Christian's assumption about the French Broad being the point of decision proved correct, as a trader named Harlin appeared under a flag of truce. He advised Christian that the Raven had sent him in the hopes of negotiating reasonable terms, but that seven hundred to eight hundred warriors had gathered on the opposite bank with more en route. Before nightfall, the entire military force of the Overhill Cherokees would block his route; they meant to fight. By noon the next day, Christian's entire army had reached the river, making camp while he wrote a response to the Raven. Undeterred by the thought that hundreds of Cherokee warriors would be in position to inflict serious casualties and possibly halt his advance, Christian gave a bold speech to the Cherokees assembled before him.[5]

He scoffed at the idea of peace without the return of white captives and while the Cherokees continued to harbor Alexander Cameron, believing there would be nothing to stop the Cherokees from continuing their attacks if they rejected his terms for peace. Christian said he would distinguish between those towns that had attacked the frontier settlements and those that had not supported the attacks by not destroying the latter. Christian held his provisions nonnegotiable in order to preclude the possibility of a treaty conference. He feared the hostile towns intended to strike while the headmen of the three towns actually desirous of peace engaged Christian in a conference. Christian had a stratagem of his own.[6]

Realizing that either he or the Cherokees must end the stalemate, Christian sent scouts up and down the river to locate crossing points. The downstream reconnaissance located an unused ford, and at 10:00 p.m., October 13, Christian began marching toward it with about 1,100 men, including two hundred mounted militiamen. The river at the crossing proved deep, with a swift current. Fortunately for Christian, he had two hundred horses available, and he used them to ferry the entire force across, the river being impassable to men on foot. Since it was the night following a new moon, the total darkness forced Christian to have torches lighted frequently. It took about three hours for the entire force to cross the river and begin the march back up to where the Cherokees were encamped. An hour before daybreak, the column was within a mile of the Cherokees, and it took that hour to march the remaining mile. Upon arriving on the south bank at a point across from their previous camp, the militiamen surrounded the supposed Cherokee campground, only to discover the Cherokees had withdrawn. October 14 was spent crossing the remaining militia from their camp, as well as the supplies and baggage train.[7]

At about noon, the scouts Christian had sent out on the fifth to obtain a Cherokee prisoner came into the camp on the south side of the river. They had not captured a warrior but did convey intelligence that the Overhill Cherokee force remained in the area and had determined to engage Christian in sustained skirmishing and ambushes from there to the Overhill Towns. They intended to concentrate on the cattle and horses and seemed determined to heed John Stuart's advice "never to make peace but to fight and retreat on." From what information the scouts could gather, all of the towns except three did not condone the flag of truce on the 12th. The leaders of the militant faction—the Raven, his brother, and Captain Gist—commanded the warriors gathered on the south side of the river until their withdrawal. Upon the return of the trader, the militants sent him back to the Overhill Towns with the flag.[8]

At about the same time, Captain James McCall, who was captured by the Lower Cherokees in South Carolina back on June 26, entered Christian's encampment. The Cherokees had held McCall captive the intervening months, and he was forced to watch his fellow prisoners tortured to death. As word of the Whig expeditions spread, McCall warned his captors about the consequences of their torturing a peace emissary, fearing they might kill him before the Whigs could arrive. He even attempted to meet with Cameron, but the latter refused him an audience. Early in October, McCall managed to escape with one pint of parched corn, a few green ears of corn, and a bareback horse. On October 14, after nine days and about three hundred miles of rugged mountainous terrain, McCall entered Christian's camp on the French Broad River.[9]

Just after dark the same day, Captain Gist entered Christian's camp with another flag of truce. From Gist, Christian heard quite a different story from what his scouts had learned. When the trader Harlin returned and recounted Christian's intention to destroy the warlike towns, fear gripped their residents, fueled, no doubt, by accounts from Lower, Middle, and Valley Town refugees. Some hesitated only to gather what corn they could carry and fled down the Tennessee River in canoes, while others went down the Hiwassee River as they headed to Creek territory.[10]

Because only a few of the towns advocated war against the whites, Gist doubted that all the warriors of the Overhill Towns had gathered to stop the militia. After Harlin returned with Christian's overtures for peace, the Raven evidently harbored hopes that some of the Overhill Towns would be spared by Christian, and he persuaded many other Cherokees to also seek peace. His words must have had a great impact with the towns in favor of peace because they sent Gist out with yet another flag of truce. Gist said the Raven had sent him to persuade Christian to spare the Cherokee sacred town of Chota. The towns that did not support the war wanted to make peace with Christian.[11]

Cameron and Dragging Canoe, however, had no intentions of making a peace with Christian. The British agent so opposed a peace with the rebels that he offered a reward to anyone who would kill Harlin and Gist. Cameron implored the Overhill Cherokees to burn everything in the face of Christian's advancing army and depend on the British for provisions and goods. He intended to gather them around the Hiwassee River and continue the fight. But with most of Dragging Canoe's followers having fled and Christian crossing the French Broad, Cameron thought it prudent to flee to the Creek town of Little Tallassee.[12]

At first, Christian thought to arrest Gist and "put him in irons." But upon further reflection, he thought the flag of truce had been a ruse for Gist to join the Americans. If true, he could not justify arresting Gist, even though he had been counted among the British deputies. Christian noted that his entire camp had divided feelings toward Gist, "but most want to kill him." The militia commander did not know whether Gist wanted to return to the Cherokees, but he thought the manner in which he came to the Americans would preclude his arrest.[13]

Christian wanted to resume the march to the Overhill Towns on the fifteenth and believed it would require some four or five days to reach them. The distance being only about twenty-five miles, he knew the column of two thousand men plus packhorses would move slowly. Also, Christian realized the best defense would be a column in tight formation, not scattered about and subject to being cut off. He therefore ordered a drum to beat the march every day; he realized the Cherokees knew their location at all times anyway.[14]

Christian did not march his army the next morning; instead, he gathered intelligence and attempted to sift through conflicting information for three days. If he did nothing else, Christian fully intended to destroy Dragging Canoe's Great Island Town on the Tellico River. He finally led his army across the Tennessee River on October 18 and passed through Toquo before encamping at Tornattee. The next day he passed through Tuskegee and another town along the Tellico River before reaching Great Island Town, and Uivle across the river, where the army encamped. The Overhill Cherokees abandoned their towns on Christian's approach, probably evacuating in canoes down the river. They left their livestock, their crops, and some of their possessions. As a result, many militiamen feasted on fresh meat and acres of vegetables once Christian spread his army throughout a few towns within supporting distance of each other.[15]

After a couple of days, Christian sent out scouting parties toward the Hiwassee and up the Tellico River. He sent them with a message that since the Cherokees had offered no resistance, he would hear what the Raven and the other headmen had to say. His message said he had not come to make war on their women and children. Clearly, he desired a clash with Dragging Canoe and the militant young warriors who followed him. But he also sent them a warning that if, after meeting with him, they did not comply with his terms, they would be safely escorted from his encampment—and then treated like enemies.[16]

The Cherokee nation lay prostrate in a truly pitiable and disarrayed condition. About ten miles from Christian's camp, the scouting party to the south encountered an elderly woman and two children. They had been six days and nights without fire or food, except what they could scavenge from the countryside. Farther toward the Hiwassee, they found a young warrior who had lost his wife. It was difficult to distinguish where the scattered Cherokees originally lived in the wake of the Whig expeditions. Many of the Lower, Middle, and Valley residents fled west over the Appalachian divide, while some of the Overhill Cherokees fled south toward the Creeks. Many would eventually reach Pensacola.[17]

By October 23, Christian reached Chota and halted his advance. He gave Oconostota, the Raven, and Little Carpenter three days to appear and make a treaty of peace with him. If they did not, he would continue his drive toward the Creeks in Georgia. He had no intention to kill noncombatants or destroy any towns except those whose leaders actively participated in raising warriors to follow Dragging Canoe. While at Chota, he sent some of his troops to destroy the Great Island town (Dragging Canoe's town). He also destroyed the town where the Cherokees had burned young Samuel Moore, captured outside Fort Caswell in July.[18]

In Chota, Christian met with the Overhill headmen who desired peace and laid out his terms: (1) captives taken from the Virginia settlements, regardless of race, were to be returned by February of next year; (2) captives taken from South Carolina and Georgia at Keowee were to be returned as soon as possible; (3) property and livestock that had been taken was to be returned; and (4) no white was to reside among the Cherokees except designated officials of the states. All other matters pertaining to lands, agents, boundaries, armies marching through their territory, forts, etc., would be settled by commissioners from the states and no more than five headmen. War would cease and a state of friendship and brotherhood prevail between the Cherokees and the whites.

Oconostota and his fellow headmen agreed to the terms, and as an act of good faith, they returned fifteen captives to Christian, among them a Mrs. Lydia Bean, who had been captured near Fort Caswell just before the Cherokee attack the previous July.[19]

After concluding the peace, Christian invited Oconostota and the other headmen to meet with Virginia governor Patrick Henry in Williamsburg. Christian himself would conduct them there and back to ensure their safety. Christian left letters containing a speech to Dragging Canoe and the other militant Cherokee headmen.[20]

After the proceedings, Christian sent out detachments to destroy Uivle, across the Tellico River from the Great Island Town, for allying itself with Dragging Canoe's faction. Finally, Christian had Chilhowey destroyed because its representatives had met with him and promised hostages but had not produced any. Then Christian returned to Fort Patrick Henry with his army.[21]

Christian's expedition should have occurred simultaneously with those of Rutherford and Williamson, but it did not. To still provide a diversion for Christian, Rutherford ordered his brother-in-law, Captain William Moore, to lead his company of militia back into the Cherokee towns. Rutherford could not lead another expedition himself because he had been elected to the Fifth Provincial Congress of North Carolina and had to leave for the capital, Halifax. Moore's expedition would not be a mere expedient, for Rutherford had learned of Cherokee towns he had not known about during his expedition and therefore had not destroyed. Rutherford also ordered two other militia captains to muster their companies of light horse militia and outfit them for an expedition into the Cherokee towns. The ills of eighteenth-century communications, however, plagued the coordination yet again.[22]

Not until October 29 did Captain Moore and his troop set out for Cathey's Fort, where Captain Joseph Hardin and his company joined them, the two continuing on to Swannanoa. The next day the column encountered fresh signs of four or five Cherokees before it crossed the French Broad River, which compelled it to quicken its pace. Upon reaching the ford of Harney Creek, the column encamped to wait for more militia to join them.[23]

After seeing the signs of the war party, the men became so eager to pursue them that once the moon rose, Captain Hardin and a detachment of thirteen men set out. After some eight miles, the detachment could discover no sign of the Cherokees and halted for daylight. Once day broke, they could discern in the frost that one of the warriors had continued along the trail, and they set out after him. After moving rapidly some five miles, they caught up with the Cherokee, whom they killed and scalped. Hardin determined that the others had gone into the countryside to hunt, so the detachment returned to the camp at Harney Creek.[24]

The Tryon militia did not arrive at Harney Creek until around noon, at which time Captain Moore decided to remain in camp that day and get everything in readiness. On November 1, the column got under way after being delayed gathering some horses that had gone astray. The men marched as far as Richland Creek, where they made camp for the night. Despite the presence of pickets, and guards for the horses, the Cherokees managed to take three of the mounts during the night.[25]

The next day Moore began tracking the Cherokees, who appeared to be numerous and moving quickly. This indicated to the militia that these Cherokees had learned of their presence and beat a hasty retreat to the nearest town, Toocowee (Stecoah). The objects of the militia expedition were the Cherokee towns untouched by the previous expeditions. In order to close the gap, Moore and his column took a treacherous blind path through the mountains to the Tuckasegee River. They hurried along, intending to reach the town before dark, but they miscalculated the distance and had to make camp before crossing the river. The next morning they located a ford and crossed the river, only to encounter a "Very large Mountain." At last they struck the main path from the Middle Towns to Toocowee, and after a couple of miles came into view of the town, spread over a small valley.[26]

After a council of war, Moore and Hardin concluded that they could not surround the town with their ninety-seven men and decided to rush into the center of the town and hopefully surprise the inhabitants. Upon entering the town at a gallop, the militiamen found it to be deserted except for two Cherokees, whom they shot down. The town consisted of twenty-five dwellings, some of them newly constructed, and "one Curious Town house framed & Ready for Covering." The Cherokees had taken their possessions with them upon abandoning the town, except large stores of corn, pumpkins, beans, and peas. The militiamen took what they wanted, then set the town ablaze.

Scouting the perimeter, the militiamen found the trail of the residents heading in a northerly direction and began to follow them. After only a mile, the militiamen saw a great column of smoke rising above the mountains—a fire set by the retreating Cherokees to cover their trail. After deploying their men on good defensive ground, Captains James McFadden and William Moore went forward with a squad of men to scout. Crossing a river unknown to them and a large mountain, they encountered abandoned Cherokee campsites. Farther on they encountered more abandoned camps with fires that had been started. With the sun setting around five thirty and no moon until some eight hours later, the scouting party prudently decided to return to the main body.[27]

The next morning the militiamen readied and advanced to where the scouting party had stopped the evening before. There, an advance guard encountered two females and a young boy, whom they captured. But in the process they discharged their firearms, giving notice to the Cherokee camp nearby. Upon reaching the camp they found it abandoned, but they captured many horses and baggage. With supplies beginning to run low, the column began the return trek homeward. That night, the men encamped "upon a prodigious Mountain" and experienced an earthquake tremor, providing the only excitement during the trip home.[28]

Neither Christian's nor Moore's expedition seemed to deter Dragging Canoe. Almost immediately after Christian left the Overhill area with his army, Dragging Canoe arrived there. Cameron had sent a letter to Dragging Canoe and his followers, but Dragging Canoe did not widely distribute its contents and withheld them from those Cherokees who sought peace with Christian. He did not want the Virginians finding out about the Cherokees' determination to continue the war and reenter the Overhill Towns before they had prepared to meet them in combat. After being told that Christian had left messages for him and the other headmen, Dragging Canoe refused them. One of his lieutenants, Lying Fish, had a black belt from Toquo and Uilve, and Dragging Canoe was intent upon sending them to Cameron to show they intended to continue the war. A couple of days later, another letter arrived from Cameron reassuring Dragging Canoe that the British would supply all the provisions and supplies the militant Cherokees required. After receiving Cameron's letter, the followers of Dragging Canoe bragged about the British having sufficient troops to defeat the Wataugans, and that the headmen who met with Christian did so only to save their corn. Cameron made good on his promise, as a British trader arrived in the Overhill Towns with a large supply of goods and ammunition.[29]

While Christian was invading the Overhill Towns, John Stuart was busy in Pensacola brokering an end to the Choctaw-Creek War. Stuart assured the British secretary of state, Lord Germain, that as soon as the Upper Creeks returned to their towns, they would assist the Cherokees. Little did he know their assistance would not be needed: the damage already wrought by the Whig expeditions had eliminated the Cherokees as a viable threat, at least for the time being. Stuart then cautioned the Upper Creeks that only after they attacked the frontiers could they enjoy Britain's "powerful protection and trade."[30]

Word of the destruction of Cherokee towns soon reached Creek towns, as did Cherokee refugees recounting the horrors they had experienced. Because the Creeks now feared Whig expeditions coming to their towns and destroying them, the British had a hard time creating reliable alliances with them. Because the British had no intention of mounting an offensive in the south, Lord Germain stressed to Stuart the importance of American Indian alliances so they could keep up the offensive pressure on the Whigs. Not yet knowing of the devastating Whig expeditions, Lord Germain further expressed his hope that the Creeks would "soon join the Cherokees against the rebels." From Little Tallassee, Emistiseguo and other Upper Creek headmen sent a letter to Stuart indicating their willingness to attack the frontier if British troops from Pensacola supported them. After the Cherokee travesty, they stated in no uncertain terms, "We do not wish to begin and then to be abandoned."[31]

With their summer offensive, the Cherokees had driven most of the white settlers off the lands west of the 1771 boundary, but the punitive Whig expeditions left practically all their towns and crops in ashes. They could rebuild their towns in the same locations, but they would obviously be susceptible to destruction again. Crops could not be planted until spring 1777. Those militant Cherokees not deterred by the Whig expeditions had to select a different location to rebuild their towns, preferably near a means of supply. These Cherokees called themselves the "Real People" or "Principle People" and intended to continue waging "the good war" against white encroachment. Many of the refugees from the Lower, Middle, and Valley Towns migrated west to the Chickamauga region (near present-day Chattanooga) in the wake of the Carolina expeditions. The new towns would not only serve as their homes but also as their new base of operations. In essence, these Cherokees seceded from what had been known as the Cherokee nation and came to be known as Chickamaugas.

Dragging Canoe was among those who decided to relocate his militant followers to the Chickamauga towns. Conveniently, a British trader, John McDonald, also resided there, and they could procure supplies and sustenance from him. Militarily, the location had the advantage of being on or near the main trails passing from the southeast to the north. Also, their towns would be far from the reach of any Whig expeditions. Though the Whig militias paid a heavy price for implementing their scorched-earth policy, they remained a potent military force. Dragging Canoe obviously could not discount them.[32]

The settlers who had fled Carter's Valley and Powell's Valley (in present-day northeast Tennessee and southwest Virginia) because of the summer attacks by the Cherokees began to return in the fall. Some even encountered Christian's column returning to Virginia from the Overhill Towns. The militiamen with Christian knew the area would be susceptible to attack by the still-warring Chickamaugas and did not believe the returning settlers would be as safe as they believed themselves.[33]

Farther south, George Galphin had been vigorously courting the Lower Creeks during the summer and early fall, trying to persuade them to remain neutral. Even as early as late

August, he began to warn them about attacking the frontiers, knowing it would provoke a counterattack from the Whigs. As an example he used the Cherokees and the Whig expeditions ranging through Cherokee territory at the time. As a result, only two parties of Cussitas, seeking revenge for a murder in the spring, attacked the Georgia frontier. Because Georgia could not afford to mount an offensive at the time, officials noted that the Cussitas had acted in accordance with Creek law and made no effort to respond.[34]

SEVEN

An Uneasy Peace

January–July 1777

In mid-January 1777, the Raven ventured to Fort Patrick Henry to meet with Colonel Christian to ensure peace still existed between them even though Dragging Canoe's warriors still raided frontier settlements. Although the Raven was unexpected and unannounced, Christian received him as a diplomatic guest. Christian reassured the Raven that the Virginia headmen desired nothing but peace, as evidenced by his latest expedition into Cherokee country in which he only burned the towns of those warriors still attacking frontier settlements. He spared all the towns that had met with him to seek peace and "took pity" on their "families and helpless ones." The Virginians did not intend to war against women and children.[1]

The Raven told Christian that he would not be able to accompany him and Oconostota to Williamsburg for the meeting with Governor Patrick Henry. Christian expressed his disappointment but reassured the Raven that as soon as the delegation returned from Williamsburg, he was authorized to deliver all the goods and supplies the Cherokees selected on the trip. He would also provide the Cherokees with whatever provisions they required during their journey. Christian emphasized that the Americans felt the Cherokees had been influenced by Cameron and the British in starting the war. The Americans wanted the Cherokees to remain neutral, and if the British urged them to war again, it would merely be a sign of their weakness to finish the job themselves. As long as the Cherokees did not participate, the Americans would provide them with all the goods and supplies they required. If any towns did continue to war against the Americans, they would be targeted for destruction; peaceful towns would be left alone. Then Christian wrote a letter to Oconostota, to be delivered by the Raven and read to him by a trader, in which he reiterated much of their discussion.[2]

Christian made it a point to distinguish between those towns that wanted peace and those that did not for a reason. He knew that Dragging Canoe had many followers and that he did not intend to make any kind of peace. In fact, as the Raven met with Christian at Fort Patrick Henry, a Chickamauga war party made its way past Carter's Valley and into Poor's Valley, where settlers who had been driven out by the earlier Indian attacks felt safe enough with Christian's army in the area to return. The Chickamaugas attacked with unbridled ferocity as before, and again survivors spread the warning. Settlers fled from Carter's and Poor's Valleys as quickly as they could, while a few remained and gathered in forts to await the expected onslaught.[3]

While the Chickamaugas conducted their military operations, the Creeks seemed to be walking a thin line between words and deeds. The Cussita King, a headman of the Lower Town of Cussita, sent a message to John Stuart affirming his town's loyalty to the British, in case Stuart had any doubts. Stuart had provided them with supplies and goods as he had promised. The Cussita King then warned Stuart that the trade must be maintained. Georgians constantly encroached on their lands, and they desperately needed more supplies and weapons to drive off the settlers. Long before the new year, the Creeks had heard about the devastation wrought upon the Cherokee towns in retribution for their attacks. At that time, a few hundred Cherokee refugees had traveled as far as Pensacola to seek assistance from Stuart, who informed Lord Germain of their utter dependence upon "His Majesty's bounty" for their survival. Lord Germain conveyed to Stuart his belief that the Creeks would militarily assist the

Cherokees, who should "keep South Carolina busy." The minister evidently could not grasp what Stuart had been trying to convey through his letters—that the Cherokees had been devastated by the Whig attacks and that made the Creeks much more cautious in contemplating any aggression toward the Whigs. Their letters would cross each other in a few weeks, but in the interim several Lower Creek headmen wrote Stuart, saying they were "resolved to hold you fast. . . . We need goods." As both Stuart and his Whig counterpart Galphin knew, their loyalty seemed based upon whoever could supply them.[4]

Dragging Canoe and his followers had no such conflicts. On February 1, Colonel John Carter wrote to North Carolina governor Richard Caswell from the Washington District about the killing of settlers not two miles from Fort Patrick Henry. Other such reports reached the governor, and he authorized the raising of one hundred militiamen to reinforce the Washington District, as well as 150 more to range the frontier on the east side of the mountains to protect the frontier of Rowan, Surry, and Tryon counties.[5]

While the Chickamaugas struck the frontier, a delegation of Cherokee headmen representing the Lower Towns, led by the Bird and the Mankiller, traveled to Charleston accompanied by Colonel Andrew Williamson. On February 3, 1777, they addressed South Carolina president Rutledge and the Privy Council. The Bird began by stating the Lower Towns had "seen their folly" and hoped South Carolina would extend a peace. He spoke for his town of Neowee, Tomatley, and several others, even for those that "had been walking through the Long Grass [a euphemism for being at war], but wanted now to stay at home." Importantly, a beloved woman from the Valley Towns expressed her hope that peace would be secured. They had made the path between the Lower Towns and Charleston white (for peace) by their talks and agreement to make peace. The Bird carried tokens of peace from the Prince of Chota and also sent a message of peace to Virginia. Last, but certainly not least, they desired to now have Carolina traders in their towns again.[6]

Mankiller spoke next and told his audience that he did not stand before them as a messenger, like the others. He had come of his own volition and endured the hardships and dangers of the way through the settlements to speak his mind. He admitted his participation in the recent war by saying he "had met the Warrior Beloved Man (Colonel Williamson) in the Long Grass," but that he had come "with good Talks" of peace. The young warriors he represented had not heeded the advice of the Whigs the previous summer not to make war, but he "was now come into the light, when he entered the Council Room." The Mankiller also spoke for the Beloved Woman of Little Chota, who sent a token of peace and asked the Carolinians to make peace, saying, "The young men are great rogues, and are out in the woods—which, she does not like: and she hopes you will make it up with them [make peace]." The Mankiller had been one of the headmen at the 1773 treaty cession between the Cherokees, the Creeks, and the state of Georgia called the New Purchase. In front of the council he now explained "he was ready to make further gifts, for the peace and safety of the nation."[7]

What Rutledge and the Privy Council said in response to the Cherokee headmen was not recorded, but it was noted to be a "friendly" talk. The Cherokees received goods from the state as part of customary diplomatic relations. The headmen and the Carolinians agreed to meet at DeWitt's Corner in May to conclude the peace with a treaty. With that, all returned home to prepare for the coming meeting.[8]

In southwestern Virginia, the initial panic that had swept through the frontier settlements had dissipated. Not all the settlers had left the region, and Virginia militia officers sought support for those who remained. Toward the end of February, militia officers went throughout the Watauga settlements "to placate the people" so they would not abandon the region. By March 1, 1777, another officer traveled to far-off Williamsburg to impress upon Governor Patrick Henry the dangerous state of the frontier. He intended to return with support for the frontier and implored Captain Joseph Martin to make every effort to prevent settlers from fleeing.[9]

On March 14, Governor Henry wrote to North Carolina governor Caswell to share information and try to arrange for

the two states to work in concert. By that time, the establishment of Dragging Canoe's followers apart from the rest of the
Cherokees had become common knowledge, as Henry conveyed to Caswell. More importantly, Henry said that
Dragging Canoe's followers "are determined for war" and that
another war with the Cherokees appeared likely that spring.
On a more positive note, Henry said the older chiefs and warriors seemed to be in favor of peaceful relations with the
Whigs, and he planned to have a peace conference with them
that spring at the Long Island of the Holston. Henry then
invited Caswell to have North Carolina commissioners participate in the peace conference.[10]

Though Henry had ordered Colonel Isaac Shelby to raise
four hundred militiamen and station them on the frontier, he
stressed to Shelby that he should take defensive positions and
not go on the offensive. Several reasons prompted Henry's
orders, and they all had to do with the planned peace conference with the majority of Cherokee headmen in a few
months. He feared that offensive operations by the Whigs
would only facilitate British designs. Besides, the state could
not supply any force at that time, it being the end of winter
and no provisions or crops available. Henry hoped that the
peace conference would "neutralize" that part of the Cherokee
nation and might, perhaps, "render the disaffected part inef-
fective."[11]

At that opportune moment, Henry received some valuable
aid from an unexpected quarter. Nathaniel Gist, who had
joined the Whigs when Christian invaded the Overhill
Towns, had gone north to join General George Washington.
In March 1777, Washington sent Gist south to recruit
rangers and as many Cherokees as he could for the
Continental Army. But before he recruited them, they had to
make peace with the Americans, and he agreed to assist
Virginia state officials in securing that peace. Gist wrote a letter to the Overhill Cherokee headmen, rebuking them for listening to those of the Delaware and Shawnee who advocated
war against the whites. He told them he had traveled to the
north and met a great many Americans who wanted peace
with the Cherokees. He told them that France and Spain had
allied with the United States, a statement that was a bit pre-

mature. As a result, the United States had an overabundance of supplies and goods for the Cherokees, something they desperately needed at that time. Gist ended his letter with a warning that Dragging Canoe and some others had not listened to him the year before and paid the price with the destruction of their towns and the impoverishment of their people. Another war would be even more devastating.[12]

While an uneasy peace settled over the Overmountain settlements, violence erupted in Kentucky. In the wake of previous warfare, Virginia organized a militia for the region, and commissions were issued for officers. The commissions arrived on March 1, and four days later the officers organized militias at Boonesborough, Harrodsburg, and Logan's Station. The next day, Shawnee warriors struck near Harrodsburg. Outlying settlers took refuge within the fort at Harrodsburg and readied it for defense. After the Shawnees lured a mounted party from the fort to weaken the garrison, the remaining militiamen prepared for a siege by bringing in corn stored in outlying cabins. At the same time, another Shawnee war party attacked settlers in the neighborhood of Boonesborough. Some Shawnee war parties remained in the area throughout the year.[13]

As the Shawnees fell on the far western frontier of Virginia with uncontrolled fury, Governor Henry wrote to Oconostota, seeking peace with the Cherokees. Henry said the political leaders of his state desired peace with the Cherokees. As a bribe, Virginia offered the destitute Cherokees salt (necessary for preserving meat), food, and goods. Further, the Virginians offered the Cherokees protection from their enemies. The Cherokees had several enemies at the time. Unfortunately for the Cherokees, one of them was Virginia. Cleverly, Virginia even offered to "adopt" the Cherokees and house them in homes throughout the state, which would have diminished the Cherokees' military strength. Knowing full well that neither Cherokees nor Virginians would agree to such an arrangement, Henry then offered to build forts in the Cherokee country for their protection. This was a seemingly magnanimous gesture on the part of Virginia politicians, no doubt, and an equally appalling one to the Cherokees, no doubt. To complete the veil of sincerity, Henry pledged all the resources of Virginia in the pursuit of Cherokee enemies.[14]

Up to this point in Cherokee-Virginia relations, it would seem that either Virginia entirely underestimated the intellectual capacity of the Cherokees or it was extremely naïve in diplomacy with them. Though Virginia offered protection to the Cherokees, the underlying intent of the letter was a veiled threat. Lastly, Henry extended an offer to make peace with Dragging Canoe and his warriors. Knowing that they represented the primary warring faction of the Cherokees, it is unknown whether the Whigs would have honored their offer or not. Dragging Canoe ignored it.[15]

While Henry attempted to thwart any future Cherokee aggression, a party of Creek warriors left their homes to join the Chickamaugas under Dragging Canoe. Still others patrolled the Georgia frontier, while the remaining pro-British Creeks hunted or otherwise remained close to their towns in case of an attack by Georgia. Stuart still had a difficult time influencing the Creeks, especially many Lower Creeks, because of the ability of Galphin to supply them with goods, ammunition, and plenty of rum. Since the failed British attack on Charleston the previous summer, the Whigs had enjoyed a relatively uninterrupted commercial trade with the French West Indies.[16]

Though the Whigs had asked the Cherokee headmen to meet the Council of the State of Virginia in Williamsburg, upon further consideration the Virginians decided that Long Island would make a better meeting place for several reasons. The trip to Williamsburg would be a long one for the Cherokee headmen and at a time of year, planting season, when they would be needed in their towns. Additionally, the council thought Dragging Canoe's party might take the opportunity to exert their influence in the absence of the headmen. Williamsburg had not heard about the recent murder of a family near Fort Patrick Henry, but Colonels Christian, Preston, and Shelby had. The colonels sent a messenger, Samuel Newell, to inquire about the murder, but some Chickamaugas attacked and killed him. Appalled at the killing of their messenger, even in wartime, the colonels still referred a letter of invitiation to a peace conference from Williamsburg to the Cherokee headmen.[17]

Newell wasn't the last victim of American Indian aggression that spring. Indians shot and scalped one Frederick Calavatt and stole some horses in the Watauga settlements. Captain James Robertson quickly gathered some volunteers and chased them. They caught up to the war party and recovered ten horses. The Chickamaugas fell on them the next night, suffering two casualties. About the same time, Indians attacked some settlers in South Carolina next to the Creek Nation. Everyone in that quarter expected a major conflict to erupt every day afterward. The Shawnee attacks continued unabated in Kentucky, with Blackfish simultaneously attacking Boonesborough, Harrodsburg, and Logan's Station. With only three centers of settlement left, and their futures precarious at best, Richard Henderson, who began the Kentucky settlements, sent a written plea back to Virginia for reinforcements.[18]

In the midst of all the attacks on the frontiers, the advance of the Overhill Cherokee peace party reached Fort Patrick Henry and requested that the recently promoted Colonel Gist bring provisions for a large group of Cherokees approaching the fort. The next day, April 18, Gist and a group of militiamen left the fort with ample food supplies. They returned on the nineteenth with over one hundred Cherokee men and women of all ages. The commissioners from North Carolina and Virginia met them on the Long Island and asked them to form an encampment, opposite the fort and across the Holston River. After introducing themselves, they invited the Cherokees to rest from their journey that day and enjoy the provisions.[19]

Old Tassel, father of Dragging Canoe, spoke for the Cherokees and told the commissioners that they looked forward to the talks. They had not planted all their corn because they did not know what the future held, but they knew there would be peace. Their stay at the fort could not be long because they needed to return and finish planting. He warned the commissioners that Dragging Canoe remained on the warpath even as they spoke. The Old Tassel also said that they had made contact with some Creeks who had attacked the frontier. He concluded by explaining that Cameron tried to dissuade them from making peace with the Americans and told them that if they did they would have to return the medals the British had given them. Cameron also warned them that they would be taken prisoner if they went to Fort Patrick Henry. Old Tassel said they desired to return soon and prove Cameron wrong. With that, both sides retired for the day.[20]

The following day, April 20, the commissioners began by reading letters sent to the Cherokees from Governor Henry and General Washington. The commissioners did not know if the letters had been deliberately misinterpreted by a Loyalist trader when read to the Cherokees, and the commissioners wanted the Cherokees to know exactly what the letters contained. After the commissioners read the letters, Oconostota said he needed time to consider their contents, which implored the Cherokees to make a lasting peace with the Americans and take no further part in the Revolution. He said some Cherokees remained on the warpath, but he would try to persuade them to make peace when they returned. The Cherokees wanted peace, and that is why they came to Fort Patrick Henry, "although whites now live here on Cherokee land," he said. Then the Cherokee headmen and the commissioners smoked tobacco together and talked of such "indifferent matters" as a pending conference among South Carolina, Cameron, and Loyalist traders.[21]

The official beginning of the talks started on April 21. The commissioners spoke first, greeting the Cherokees as neighbors and ancient allies. They nostalgically remembered that the headmen of the Cherokees and Virginia used to meet and "workout any difficulties and that should still be the case." Then they turned to the late war and how the Cherokees initiated it "without just provocation." Because they believed the Cherokees had been influenced by the British, Colonel Christian did not wreak widespread destruction as he could have, but spared their peaceful towns. Oconostota agreed to a peace, and the Raven came to Fort Patrick Henry to confirm that peace. However, the recent killing of the messenger Newell had to be rectified by the apprehension and execution of his murderer.[22]

The commissioners then turned to the topic that still concerned them most: the warlike faction among the Cherokees. Dragging Canoe continued to be their foremost concern, and in a desperate effort to stop his operations, the commissioners told the headmen that they would forgive Dragging Canoe for initiating the war and that he would be well treated if he made peace. If their machinations did not have the desired effect of persuading Dragging Canoe to stop his attacks, the commissioners warned the headmen that making the Americans their enemies forever would have dire consequences, because "the white people are like the trees of the woods for number and therefore cannot be all destroyed."[23]

Although Dragging Canoe led the militant faction, the Americans blamed the British agents, traders, and Loyalists residing among the Cherokees for being the catalyst in urging the Cherokees to attack the frontier. Previous efforts to enter the Cherokee towns and capture these individuals precipitated violent reaction. To preclude any such incidents in the future, the commissioners said that the Cherokees must deliver these individuals to the Americans, who only desired to prevent any other Loyalists from entering their towns.[24]

They implored the headmen to use every means possible to persuade Dragging Canoe to attend a peace commission that would begin on June 26. At that time, they would conclude the peace, settle all unresolved issues, and mediate any complaints the Cherokees might have. Before then, a group of headmen could journey to Williamsburg and be presented with clothes and other goods. They would meet with the governor and select all the goods and supplies they desired, have them loaded onto wagons, and return to Fort Patrick Henry in time for the treaty. The commissioners ended with yet another request that Dragging Canoe's operations be curbed so "that there be no more blood lost" until the meeting in June "least it might destroy the peace we are now making."[25]

Old Tassel rose to speak on behalf of the headmen present. He suggested they all smoke the white pipe of peace to symbolically clear the negotiators' minds so they all could speak openly and honestly. They passed around a pipe until everyone had smoked from it. Then Old Tassel proceeded to the business at hand.[26]

He recounted the dark times during the war, but after they made peace, everything became light. Even on their journey to Fort Patrick Henry, they encountered those who had been attacking on the frontier, but they persevered onward. The commissioners stated their belief that the war began at the behest of British agents, but Old Tassel reminded them, "Brothers, do you not remember that the difference is about *our* land?" He then extolled the virtues of peace between the Cherokees and Virginians. Then, turning to the obvious source of apprehension, Old Tassel told the commissioners that he and one of Dragging Canoe's brothers, the Young Tassel, would speak with Dragging Canoe when they returned. Surely, a father and brother could persuade Dragging Canoe to make peace with the Americans.[27]

April 22 dawned overcast and dreary as rain settled upon the Holston River valley. The place where the headmen and commissioners usually met had no roof, and the conference was postponed as a result. In the evening, a militiaman's musket discharged accidentally, wounding a warrior in the shoulder just below the collarbone. The warrior retreated to the Cherokee encampment, and the commissioners arrested the militiaman. Then they went to the Cherokee encampment to try to ameliorate the situation. Fortunately for the Americans, the Cherokee headmen acted "with great prudence and candor" in calming the alarm the incident had caused among the Cherokees.[28]

The conference resumed the following day with Old Tassel speaking first. As expected, he mentioned the accidental wounding of the Cherokee and declared his surprise "that while we were talking the good talks they should be made bloody by your people." But he said he would not allow the incident to disrupt the peace talks. Rather, he focused on the belt of beads he held as he spoke and on similar symbols of peace their predecessors used to create "a long peace." Similarly, he said, he hoped that the peace created with the belt he then held would also be a lasting one between the Americans and the Cherokees. And when they who had met there to create the peace had long ago died, their successors could uphold the peace symbolized by the belt.[29]

The commissioners said they would draft a letter to Dragging Canoe and read it to the headmen the following day. Then the commissioners said they would speak "on some other matters," and the meetings ended for the day.[30]

As promised, the commissioners began the talks on April 24 by reading the lengthy letter they had drafted for Dragging Canoe. Again, the Americans ascribed the cause of the war initiated by the Cherokee leader to British influence. As a result, the commissioners could forgive Dragging Canoe and his followers, inviting them to attend the planned formal treaty in two months. Invoking biblical teachings, the commissioners avowed that they would receive even their enemies as brothers in friendship and peace. In other words, if Dragging Canoe and his warriors came in to Fort Patrick Henry and made peace, the Americans would not hold his previous actions against him. They even offered to send Colonel Gist, personally well known to Dragging Canoe, to meet and guide them to the fort under his protection. Besides all the provisions and supplies they may need, Virginia would come to their assistance against any of their enemies. The commissioners suggested assistance be provided to the Cherokees against the Creeks, probably because they were traditional enemies of the Cherokees—and maybe because the Creeks represented the other potential Indian enemy near the southern frontiers. In conclusion, the commissioners appealed to Lying Fish, brother of Dragging Canoe, in hopes he could persuade his brother to stop attacking the frontier. With that, the commissioners ended the conference so that the Cherokees could return to the Overhill Towns and "prove Cameron a liar."[31]

No doubt the commissioners did not expect that Dragging Canoe would attend the peace treaty conference, even if they did appeal to his brother. War parties under his authority conducted raids throughout the time the conference was taking place. Even as the headmen left the conference to return to their towns, Dragging Canoe raided white settlements. On April 25, a rider arrived at Fort Patrick Henry with the intelligence that two settlers had been killed on the Clinch River. From the time the Cherokee delegates left Fort Patrick Henry to April 27, a dozen settlers were killed in the region.[32]

As the conference at Fort Patrick Henry ended and the Cherokees prepared to return to the Overhill Towns, warfare reignited in Kentucky. Boonesborough resident Simon Kenton and two others stood just outside the town's stockade on April 24, preparing to go hunting. Suddenly, they saw two men who had been sent out to drive in some stock running as fast as they could toward the fort. Kenton saw a party of about five Shawnees chasing the men, and when they came within one hundred yards of the fort, a warrior tackled and toma-hawked one of them. Kenton and his fellow hunters then shot the warrior and began pursuing the small war party. Hearing the attack from within the fort, Daniel Boone gathered about ten armed men and immediately followed Kenton's group. Once the pursuers were sufficiently far from the stockade, a party of about fifty warriors sprang from their hidden posi-tion. Kenton, Boone, and the others halted their pursuit when they noticed a group of warriors moving to encircle them and cut them off from the fort. Boone, a militia captain, gave orders to head for the fort, firing at the warriors attempting to cut them off. The race back to the fort began, and the settlers fired on the warriors. The Shawnees returned fire, and before anyone could reload, the two groups mingled in a hand-to-hand struggle that involved knives, tomahawks, and the butt ends of rifles. Kenton, after shooting one warrior and club-bing another, carried Boone with his shattered left ankle into the fort. All the settlers entered the fort, and others immedi-ately closed the gate. The Shawnees remained in the area, just outside of rifle range (about four hundred to five hundred yards away), for several more days before withdrawing.[33]

A few days later, on April 29, Harrodsburg residents James Ray and Francis McConnell stood outside the town's stock-ade engaged in some target practice when suddenly, McConnell fell from a gunshot. About the time Ray turned and began to sprint toward the fort gate, a large party of Shawnee warriors attacked. Aware of the war party's presence, the garrison of Harrodsburg closed the fort gate before Ray reached safety. The occupants feared the war party would dash into the fort if they opened the gate, so Ray threw him-self flat on the ground between a stump and the stockade. The gunfire from the fort prevented the Shawnees from approaching Ray. McConnell signaled those in the fort that he was alive but could not move. Finally, those inside the fort dug under the stockade, which allowed Ray to enter the fort. Those inside the Harrodsburg stockade knew they had to retrieve McConnell before dark, but the guns of the Shawnee war party were trained where McConnell had fallen. A detachment of the garrison took position on the cabin roofs and laid down covering fire while another detachment, including Ray, sprinted out of the fort toward McConnell. While some of the rescue party fired and dispersed the warriors in the immediate area, the others grabbed McConnell, and all raced back to the fort. Unfortunately, McConnell died of his wound later that day. As at Boonesborough, the war party lingered in the area before withdrawing.[34]

In light of the incessant Shawnee attacks on the settlements in the Kentucky lands in 1777, the Virginia legislature authorized a militia in the beginning of May.[35] This meant that a regular body of troops would be available to defend the forts and stations in the region. It also meant that a supply of ammunition would be allocated for their use to alleviate shortages. The only problem with the legislation was that the region did not contain a population that could support itself militarily.

Fortunately for southern Whigs, they still only faced a one-front conflict. Stuart's hope of Indian operations supported by regular British troops was not a part of British strategy as conceived by the British commander in North America, General Sir William Howe. In the beginning of May, Howe wrote to Stuart to advise him that no British troops would be sent to the southern theater. The only support he could count on would be from Loyalists. To assist in that area, Howe sent Moses Kirkland, a well-known Loyalist figure on the South Carolina frontier, to recruit His Majesty's supporters. Then Howe drafted a letter to the southern Indians in which he promised them friendship and supplies. Unfortunately for Stuart and the American Indians of his department, that would be the extent of British assistance. The Cherokees and Creeks had to make their own war—or peace.[36]

As agreed upon, the headmen and warriors of the Lower and Valley Towns met with South Carolina and Georgia commissioners to conclude a treaty at DeWitt's Corner, South Carolina. The first article required the Cherokees to cede all their lands east of the Unicoi Mountains (near the present-day northeast border with Georgia), but they could harvest whatever crops of corn they had already planted. A regular trade would be established by licensed Whig traders, and the Cherokees would apprehend all other traders, along with all their livestock and property. The commissioners provided for a reward to be paid if the Cherokees brought in any British agents or commissaries, such as Cameron. The treaty also required the return of all prisoners and livestock taken in the recent war. Curiously, the treaty bound not only Georgia and South Carolina to be at peace with the Cherokees, but also their ancient enemy the Catawba, though none of the latter attended the treaty conference.[37]

While the Lower Town headmen negotiated with the Georgia and South Carolina commissioners at DeWitt's Corner, a delegation of Overhill headmen traveled from Fort Patrick Henry to Williamsburg. Oconostota, Little Carpenter, the Pidgeon, and an entourage of some thirty other headmen and warriors arrived in Williamsburg before the end of May. Between meetings with the governor and the Virginia Executive Council, the administering body of elected officials in the state, the Cherokees on at least one occasion performed some dances on the green in front of the Governor's Palace. Within a few days, the council received intelligence that some Virginians intended to assassinate the Cherokees on their return to Fort Patrick Henry. The council issued orders that all county lieutenants (the chief militia officer of a county in Virginia) provide "well armed Men of the Militia of their respective Counties for the Protection of the said Indians."[38]

While the Cherokees made peace, during the spring the Creeks remained inactive. But in May 1777, Sempoyaffe of Coweta requested that the Upper Creeks come to their assistance by attacking the Georgia frontier. Some Chickamaugas had urged a small group of Cowetas to attack the frontier. The group targeted the head of the Little River, near the Buffalo

Lick, where the settlers had constructed three forts. The war party selected one, Fort Roger, but when the Cowetas asked if they should attack it, the Chickamaugas advised against it. Undoubtedly their experience against the Watauga forts taught them the folly of attacking settlers protected by a stockade. But some of the younger warriors could not resist and initiated a general attack.[39]

The settlers drove off the war party, but Sempoyaffe's cousin was killed in the exchange. Sempoyaffe then requested the Upper Creeks come to their assistance and take the field against the Georgians. Fortunately for Sempoyaffe, the Upper Creeks had just ended a council in which they agreed to attack the Georgia frontier following the Green Corn Ceremony either in July or August. Upper Creek headmen Alexander McGillivray and Mad Dog then persuaded the Tuckabatchies, the Savannahs, the Coosadas, the Okchai Towns, the Alibamas, and the Tuskegees—all a part of the Creek confederation—to join in the attack.[40]

During the council of Upper Creeks, a subject arose that reveals the true nature of American Indian alliances. When the delegations of northern and western Indians held their conference in the Cherokee Overhill Towns back in 1776, the Cherokees sent the wampum belts the delegates gave them to the Creeks. In essence, the Cherokees were asking the Creeks to join them and the northern and western Indians in the war against the Americans. At the time, the Creeks would not accept them and join forces with the Cherokees in their newly formed alliance. That created a diplomatic rift between the Creeks and their neighbors to the north that had to be resolved before any future alliance could occur.[41]

In the May 1777 meeting, the Upper Creek headmen decided to resolve the issue. Apparently, some young Okfuskee girls and boys had been captured on the north side of the Cherokee (Tennessee) River. The Creeks suspected the Twitawees, who had been represented in the delegation that visited the Cherokees the summer before. If so, the Upper Creeks intended to arrange the exchange of a Twitawee woman they had captured some four years earlier. The Upper Creek headmen asked John Stuart for the wampum belts the delegation had brought the Cherokees so that Shawnee

Warrior could carry them on the diplomatic mission. While in the north, he could also determine the northern tribes' involvement in the Revolution.[42]

While the Cherokees sought peace, except for the Chickamaugas, and the Creeks vacillated between supporting whomever could provide them goods, the Shawnees had no such qualms about continuing the war against the Americans. A Shawnee war party attacked Boonesborough on May 23, firing on the stockade until the evening. Continuing the next day, it attempted to set the fort ablaze, but to no avail, and it left the area that night with both sides having suffered casualties.[43]

Perhaps the same war party that attacked Boonesborough began operations on May 30 against Logan's Fort, whose garrison had strengthened the stockade earlier that month. The attack began with the war party firing on the garrison detachment guarding the women assigned to milk the cows outside the stockade that morning. Of the four guards, one was killed and two wounded, but the women and the fourth militiaman retreated inside the stockade. One of the wounded men apparently died shortly thereafter, but one remained visibly alive to the garrison. At length, two of the remaining twelve militiamen volunteered to retrieve their wounded comrade and dashed out the fort gate. Although one turned back, the other retrieved him, with only a sack of wool for protection. After killing all the livestock they could find in the area, the Shawnees withdrew that night.[44]

Neither John Stuart nor his deputies seemed to be aware of the Shawnee activity in the Kentucky lands. One of his deputies, Henry Taitt, mentioned that some Creeks had attacked the Georgia frontier but lamented that "many Cherokees are making peace with the rebels." Shortly thereafter, Taitt added that the Upper Creeks planned to attack Georgia after the Green Corn Ceremony, but only if they had enough provisions and supplies. Echoing his deputy's despondency, Stuart advised Lord Germain that even he did not have enough provisions and supplies for the Cherokee refugees who had arrived in Pensacola, much less all the others scattered throughout the Creek towns. Stuart also lamented the fact that many Cherokees (actually a vast majority) had agreed to a peaceful neutrality with the Americans—at least for now.[45]

Relations between the Creeks and southern Whigs had become so precarious by 1777 that the matter came before the Continental Congress. In response, it authorized George Galphin to hold a conference with the Creeks. As one of the two federal superintendents of Indian affairs of the Southern Department, he planned to attend the upcoming treaty conference with the Cherokees at DeWitt's Corner. But after he was directed to meet with the Creeks, he sent word to their towns and began planning to hold a treaty conference with them at his place in Georgia on the Ogeechee River at Old Town. Galphin knew that many Creeks would attend and avail themselves of Whig hospitality. He also knew that such a large number of Creeks moving through the settlements would precipitate violence. With the meeting at Old Town, the situation seemed precarious enough to Georgia governor John Treutlen that he issued a proclamation explaining to Georgians the importance of the congress and pleading that the Creeks not be molested in any way.[46]

Tensions between Creeks and frontier settlers stemmed partially from both sides stealing each other's horses. If one settler stole another's horse, the crime could be punishable by hanging. However, if a settler stole a Creek's horse, it was not even considered a crime. Georgia officials, therefore, found it extremely difficult to deter such activity and preclude a full-scale war with the Creek Nation. On more than one occasion, George Galphin complained bitterly about the frontier settlers' stealing horses, murdering Creeks, and surveying Creek lands. He did not mince his words when he wrote "if it was not for these Damed villians upon the frontier I Should tacke a plasure in Serving my Contrey."[47]

Handsome Fellow, from the Upper Town of Okfuskee, and the Cussita King gathered about four hundred to five hundred Creeks from Okfuskee, Cussita, Apalachicola, Tallassee, and Yutchi for the journey to meet with the continental and state commissioners at Old Town. The vehemently pro-British Emistiseguo did not attend, nor did anyone from the Lower Town of Coweta. Handsome Fellow and the large party of Lower and Upper Creeks arrived at Old Town during the first part of June.[48]

All the Creeks had arrived by June 17, and Galphin began the talks by congratulating those Creeks who had not attacked "your old friends," the white settlers in the Ceded Lands. But he expressed regret about those who had attacked the Georgia frontier. True, some Cowetas had been killed, but they had been warned about the penalty for horse theft.[49] The Cowetas sought satisfaction in retribution, and he hoped the killings would stop. For good measure, Galphin mentioned the Cherokees as an example of what would happen to the Creeks if they continued attacking the frontier. To emphasize the threat, he also noted that Georgians outnumbered Creeks.[50]

Galphin had noticed that the headmen did not bring two prisoners who had recently been captured in the Ceded Lands. As an enticement for them to bring in the two prisoners, he noted that he had plenty of goods to send them and desired to send some traders back with them so they would be protected. Before he did that, however, they had to drive off the British traders David Taitt and William McIntosh from the Upper and Lower Towns, respectively. In conclusion, Galphin alluded to the current tension between their people and lamented that they could not all coexist peacefully. At that point, he extended the invitation of the Continental Congress for a group of them to visit Philadelphia.[51]

Old Tallassee King's son and Handsome Fellow responded to the Americans the following day. Old Tallassee King's son represented the three towns of Cussita, Utchies, and Pallachuitas, and he brought tokens of peace and friendship from them, including a white pouch with tobacco, a string of white beads, and an eagle's feather. He then stated the crux of the dilemma facing the Creeks: the tokens represented the desire of the towns to be at peace with the Americans, but they also did not want to make "ourselves poor," and wanted Galphin to at least send a few packhorses of goods into their towns with their return. Stuart and his deputies had told them not to go to the congress, because the Americans were poor, but as Galphin had shown with all the goods, the British proved to be "great liars." [52]

Handsome Fellow spoke next, recounting in flattering terms the history of the Creeks and Anglo-Americans since the founding of Georgia in 1733, diplomatically overlooking the violent episodes. He had received messages of peace sent from Philadelphia, Charleston, and Savannah, and likewise wanted to be at peace with the Americans. Taitt, Big Fellow, and Tallassee Second Man had all told him not to accept the invitation to Philadelphia, because Galphin would only lie to him in order to persuade him not to make war against the Americans. If Galphin supplied them with goods and they brought them back to their towns, that would negate anything the pro-British Creeks could say. Instead of a few pack-horse loads, Handsome Fellow advised Galphin that his town alone would require fifteen to twenty loads of goods and four loads of ammunition. Handsome Fellow declined the trip to Philadelphia but said they would go to Charleston instead. With that, the conference ended and preparations were made for the trip to Charleston.[53]

On July 9, Galphin arrived in Charleston with Handsome Fellow, Head Tallassee Warrior, Handsome Fellow's son (name unknown), Handsome Fellow's nephew (name unknown), Oakchee Warrior, Cussita Second Man, Hallowing King, Singee, Singee's son (name unknown), and Palachacola Second Man. Charleston received the Creek headmen with great fanfare, including a military parade. The headmen toured Fort Moultrie, heard the story of its successful defense the year before, and viewed the large quantity of arms and ammunition obtained from the French. Then the tour moved to some vessels in the harbor, including one from France, emphasizing the new alliance with that country. Handsome Fellow and his entourage seemed quite impressed with all that they saw. He said Cameron had told them many things in the past that "they now found to be Lies, that they would never believe 'em again." No doubt, Galphin's gathering enough goods to require twenty to thirty horses impressed them enough to rebuff Cameron's disparaging remarks concerning the poverty of the Whigs.[54]

On Saturday, July 12, South Carolina president Rutledge called a special session of the General Assembly in its chambers to receive the headmen. Rutledge addressed the Creeks by speaking of an American victory in the war and reiterating Galphin's demand that Taitt, McIntosh, and the other British traders be driven out of their towns. This would be for their own benefit, Rutledge stressed, because the British only wanted to embroil them in a war with the United States that would result in their own destruction. Besides, the French and Spanish (expected to ally themselves with the Americans) would begin a naval blockade of the gulf ports of Mobile and Pensacola, which would seriously diminish their trade.[55]

The visit to Charleston proved quite a revelation for Handsome Fellow and the headmen accompanying him. Contrasting what Stuart and his deputies had said about the poverty and weakness of the Americans with the realities of what they saw, the delegation determined to make a legitimate and lasting peace. Handsome Fellow produced the commissions he had received from past British colonial governors, saying, "he was now done with them." Instead, he urgently asked a commission of President Rutledge, who obliged him most willingly. The incident so impressed Rutledge that he mentioned it in detail to Henry Laurens, Continental Congress delegate from South Carolina and future president of the Congress.[56]

At that point, Handsome Fellow genuinely regretted not being able to visit Philadelphia. He cited the great distance and the heat of the season as the primary reasons for him and his entourage not being able to make the trip. To convey the sincerity of their regret, Handsome Fellow gave an eagle tail and a rattletrap to Rutledge, to be forwarded to the Continental Congress. The eagle tail signified perpetual peace; the rattle was used for certain dances and ceremonies. Neither of these tokens would be presented to someone the Creeks did not consider a true friend. Handsome Fellow asked that the Congress "shew them to the Northward Indians that they may see them & be thereby convinced, that the Creeks are at Peace" with the Whigs. In other words, it would serve no purpose for the northern Indians to send emissaries down seeking allies against the Americans. [57]

At least a significant number of Lower and Upper Creeks sympathized with the Whigs enough not to attack the southern frontier. Handsome Fellow and his fellow Creek leaders who agreed with his perspective would ally themselves with the Whigs for the remainder of the war. As long as the Whigs maintained that relationship, they would have a segment of the Creek warrior population that could dissuade pro-British warriors from taking to the warpath against the southern frontier. The Whigs had not demanded more Creek land, a crucial factor, probably, in the sentiment of those pro-American Creeks. More importantly, Galphin promised to supply them with goods and provisions necessary for their survival.

EIGHT

Peace & War

July–October 1777

By summer 1777, the political leaders of the Overhill Cherokees and the Whigs of Virginia wanted to establish peaceful relations. Not all Cherokees or whites desired peace: Dragging Canoe and his followers attacked frontier settlers even as the conference at the Long Island of the Holston River convened. And though settlers did not directly attack Cherokee towns, they encroached on Cherokee lands and killed some warriors out hunting.

In mid-June, Colonel Isaac Shelby had been informed that except for Dragging Canoe, the Overhill Cherokee intended to make a peace with the Whigs. Colonel Nathaniel Gist left the Overhill Towns about June 20 with a large body of headmen, warriors, women, and children because of their destitute condition. Shelby and others at Fort Patrick Henry had to procure additional provisions in order to feed the group that would soon arrive. A few Cherokees had just left the fort after Shelby provisioned them well. It must have struck Shelby as odd when he received news of the violent attacks on settlements in Kentucky at the same time a peace conference was about to convene.[1]

On June 28, 1777, Colonel Gist arrived at Fort Patrick Henry with some headmen and a large group of the Overhill Cherokees. Two days later, Oconostota and his entourage of headmen arrived with Colonel Christian from Williamsburg.

Immediately behind them came the North Carolina commissioners. While everyone rested from their long travels, a Cherokee named Big Bullet was shot and killed. The Cherokees had encamped on the Long Island, and the shot came from across the river near the fort. That day, July 2, Oconostota addressed the commissioners, saying the headmen would not let the incident derail the peace conference. He understood the incident to be perpetrated by "a bad man" beyond the control of the commissioners. He knew this because of the many supplies they had already given the distressed Cherokees.[2]

The commissioners expressed their gratitude for his wisdom concerning "this horrid Action . . . done by some Devlish evil minded person who wants to destroy the good talks that are now between your brother and you." They pledged their "utmost endeavors" in finding the culprit and punishing him in accordance with the law. That afternoon, the commissioners posted a reward of $600 for whoever identified the culprit. The headmen and commissioners then retired for the day.

The Fourth of July occasioned a great celebration among the Whigs. The commissioners explained the significance of the day to the Cherokee headmen in a speech and presented them with copious quantities of rum. The Cherokees responded with a dance performed by several of the warriors. No negotiations occurred for several days. But that did not translate into a delay in beginning the treaty, because neither all the Cherokee headmen nor all the Whig commissioners had arrived.

In the days after the headmen arrived, the Whig commissioners met with them informally to discuss the nature of the upcoming formal treaty talks. During those meetings, the Whigs emphasized to the Cherokee headmen that they should keep nothing from each other—that everyone should say whatever was on their minds that would have a bearing on the talks. Old Tassel took those words to heart, for on July 10, he met with the commissioners and recounted an incident on his way to the treaty conference late the previous month. Old Tassel had met with a small party of Mingos in Chota. Remembering the talks of the delegation from the "Norward Indians" the previous summer urging the Cherokees to war against the settlers, the venerable headman admonished them for those talks and the devastation that had befallen the Cherokees. He told the Mingos that peace talks had already commenced between the Cherokees and the Whigs, and nothing they could say would interrupt the negotiations. Old Tassel ended his talk to the Mingos with the advice that he hoped they, too, would meet with the Whigs and form a lasting peace with them.

Whether the Mingos intended to again ask the Cherokees to war against the Whigs will never be known. If they did, the Mingos changed their speech in the light of Old Tassel's admonishment, for they claimed to merely want to find out if the Cherokees had been cut off by their recent war with the Whigs. Considering the fact that Cherokee territory lay far to the south of the Ohio River, it is doubtful that the Mingos journeyed forty days just to discern whether they had been cut off. In response, the commissioners advised Old Tassel that he should initiate the talks to begin the peace treaty.

Once again, violence threatened to derail the planned peace treaty. Though Old Tassel told the Mingos a particular path to take and return to the north, when he passed the location where the path crossed the Tennessee River, he did not see any sign of them. That is because they had gone another way and attacked a farmstead about thirty miles from Fort Patrick Henry. The next day, the Whig commissioners received a courier who informed them that some settlers on the Nonachuckie and Watauga rivers might be organizing to attack the Cherokees assembled on the Long Island across from the fort. Immediately, North Carolina commissioners Waightstill Avery and Joseph Winston rode out to intercept the settlers and persuade them to return to their settlements. After their departure, the Overhill Cherokee chiefs Raven and Willanawaw arrived at the Long Island. All the Overhill Cherokee headmen who would attend the conference and the commissioners from Virginia and North Carolina having all finally arrived, Old Tassel addressed the commissioners and deferred beginning the conference to them, since he considered them his "elder brothers."

Though the Overhill Cherokees wished to return quickly to their towns so crops could be tended, the conference had to be postponed for two days until Avery and Winston returned from their successful mission to avert an attack on the Cherokees. When the meetings began on July 13, the commissioners addressed the murder of Big Bullet to settle that matter before proceeding with a peace treaty. They observed the proper rituals for the death of a Cherokee warrior and offered three large coats and three shirts (it was customary to offer goods in the place of a deceased warrior who hunted deer to provide skins used in trading for goods). The assembled headmen returned to their encampment on the Long Island to discuss the matter. Later, about a dozen returned, and Potclay and Mankiller of Great Hiwassee spoke on behalf of the Overhill headmen. They essentially agreed that the incident stemmed from the evil of an individual and should not interfere with the peace treaty. Then, all retired to begin the true peace conference the next day.

Finally, the day to begin the peace conference arrived. On July 14, Colonel Christian, representing Virginia, and Avery, representing North Carolina, opened the talks as the Overhill Cherokee headmen had requested. The two Whig leaders greeted the Overhill Cherokees and expressed their hope of a lasting peace and boundary. No doubt, the Cherokees also hoped the boundary would be a lasting one. In regards to the boundary, it is significant that representatives of both North Carolina and Virginia attended the conference because the boundaries would not separate the Cherokees and the United States, but the Cherokees and Virginia on one hand and the Cherokees and North Carolina on the other. The meeting, in essence, was a dual treaty. That arrangement must have seemed quite confusing for the Cherokees, especially after the great celebration made on the Fourth of July, which emphasized the unity of the thirteen states.

In their greetings, Christian and Avery mentioned the primary points that concerned them most and addressed the issue of trade that they knew weighed heavily on the minds of the Cherokees. Christian advised the headmen that better trade would be established as soon as the war (the cause of the trade's interruption) ended. Then he lamented the fact that Dragging Canoe, Judge's Friend, Lying Fish, and Young Tassel continued to attack the frontier, even during the conference.

The next day, the commissioners had the articles of the Treaty of DeWitt's Corner between the Lower Cherokees and South Carolina along with Georgia read to and interpreted for the Cherokee headmen, setting the tone for the conference. With that, the Raven addressed the commissioners as the Cherokee spokesman and expressed his great pleasure at the meeting where Cherokee, Virginia, and Carolina could come together and make a lasting peace. He went on to explain that he had made professions of wanting to be at peace before, but he had made them to John Stuart, and now the Raven believed that Stuart did not send the Cherokee warriors to Virginia and Carolina. Rather, he conveyed how Stuart had told him that it would be all right if the Cherokee took all the possessions of any white settler encroaching on Cherokee land, and even killed them—an obvious reference to the attacks the preceding year. He then advised the commissioners that other American Indians had recently been in his town and attempted to persuade his people to make war again against the settlers, but he spurned them and came to the conference. Most importantly, the Raven told the commissioners that he needed to return to tend to his crops; that the "peace and safety of both parties" had been achieved before the conference, and that the Cherokees had merely come to indicate their goodwill toward the agreement and to see the commissioners again.

Old Tassel then reminded the commissioners that the conference they had three months earlier established the peace then existing between them. In reference to the treaty, Old Tassel explained his difficulty in understanding how South Carolina could justify taking so much land because they had driven the Cherokees from it. The Cherokees returned, he continued, just as the settlers returned to the areas the Cherokees drove them from the previous year. By such logic, could not the Cherokees claim the lands they drove the settlers from? Further, the Cherokees in attendance at DeWitt's Corner returned to their destroyed towns "as naked as my hand and crying with hunger." In other words, the DeWitt's Corner commissioners provided the destitute Cherokees with nothing, yet touted peace while insisting on obtaining land. But, Old Tassel continued, he felt assured that the commissioners of Carolina and Virginia would "do us justice" in terms of providing the Cherokees with provisions and "give us a little room, because your people have encroached upon us verry close and scarcely given us room to turn round."

Having had enough of the Cherokee position, Colonel Christian cut to the chase in plain language, saying that the commissioners had come "to settle a peace and fix a boundary line." He explained the boundary to the Cherokees as "this important part of the peace now making between us." Conceptually, the commissioners considered the boundary to be inextricably tied to any peace, in direct contradiction to the Cherokee notion that the peace had already been established during the talks of April. He then questioned the Raven's claim that they been encroached upon by demanding to know which settlers had encroached on what land claimed by the Cherokees. Then his claim would be addressed when they proposed the boundary lines the next day.

The Raven began the talks on July 16 by responding to Christian's question regarding encroachment, saying their land had been trespassed on by many groups of settlers. Then he reminded Christian that Colonel Evan Shelby lived near the boundary line (in present-day Bristol, Virginia) "to see that each party kept on their own side of the line." Even though Shelby had obviously not enforced the boundary, the Raven told the commissioners that if they intended to establish another boundary and have it marked, the settlers outside the line who had crops growing on Cherokee land could first harvest them and then move. He then suggested that Virginia extend the boundary line west to the North Fork of the Holston River and then north to Cumberland Gap. To North Carolina, he suggested extending the boundary west to the Holston River near present-day Bristol, then south to the Nolichucky River.

As delineated by the Raven, the boundaries would require the removal of many hundreds of settlers already established along the Watauga and Nolichucky rivers. North Carolina commissioner Avery flew into a rage. He became belligerent and began to hammer away at the Raven with rapid-fire questions. Avery asked if the Cherokees objected to all the Watauga and Nolichucky settlers or just some of them; the

Raven said only the settlers south of the boundary he had earlier delineated. After trying to get the Raven to say the Cherokees had given their consent to the settlement of the lands in question to no avail, Avery questioned his intent by asking, "Did you not afterwards agree to sell those lands and receive pay for them?"

At this point, Oconostota stood to take the floor. He told Avery that he had already explained to the Watauga and Nolichucky settlers that he would seek the consent of the British king for the land cession. Before that consent could be obtained, however, the settlers planted crops and started raising livestock, which "destroyed our hunting." The outbreak of the Revolution precluded any consent of the king—why would the king consent to anything "rebels" wanted? Therefore, Oconostota explained, he could only take "rent" from the settlers and not "payment." Oconostota's lucid and cogent explanation ended Avery's harangue.

With a break in the diplomatic action, someone presented the commissioners with a petition on behalf of Richard Henderson and his partners. The petition had been drafted specifically for the peace conference. It stated that the Cherokees had sold the land in Kentucky and along the Watauga and Nolichucky rivers to Henderson and his partners several years earlier. Since a boundary would be determined with the Cherokees, the petition implored the commissioners not to exclude any of the lands that had been purchased. If the commissioners recognized the validity of the transaction stated in the petition, then the states would realize no income from the sale of those lands. The commissioners concluded that they did not have the authority to decide matters of a private nature (which, in fact, they legally did not possess), and that the petition had no place in any of their conferences with the Cherokees. With that decision, the conference adjourned for the day.

The next day, July 17, Colonel Christian attempted to strengthen the commissioners' position when he opened the meetings with a speech to the Cherokees. In an effort to legitimize the encroachment on Cherokee lands, he explained how King George had actually consented for the settlers to locate themselves on the Holston River and its tributaries. Then Christian attempted to place the Cherokee war effort in a negative context by explaining that once the Revolution began, the king had his servants Stewart and Cameron lie to the Cherokees in order to persuade them to attack the settlers by advising the Cherokees that the king had never given his consent. Christian even offered to produce evidence of the king's consent and authorization for the settlement of present-day southwest Virginia, though it is unclear what that evidence would have been. Christian then turned to the primary goal of the commissioners: establishing a boundary that "will stand firm and unshaken through many generations." To avoid another complication like the Henderson episode, he told the headmen not to make any other private deals to sell or rent any of their lands.

Christian had crafted an interesting combination of truth and propaganda, one that the Cherokee headmen had not heard before. They retired for a short time to consider what he said. Upon their return, the Raven declared surprise at what Christian said, no doubt referring to the consent of King George. Regardless, the Raven spoke for all Cherokees when he said "if the land ever belonged to him [King George] it's more than I know of." He could not consent to where the commissioners wanted to establish the boundary. It would be only a few miles from some of the Overhill Towns, and the Cherokee had already seen the whites' idea of a boundary that would "stand firm and unshaken through many generations." But the Raven did not want to thwart the peace conference and suggested that all parties consider their proposals further. He would not have to wait long to see if his diplomatic ploy would work.

Avery took another tack from his previous diplomatic efforts with the headmen. In response to their complaints of settler encroachment, he reminded them that they had asked the governor of North Carolina for a boundary some years earlier. After one had been agreed on, the Cherokee then made bargains with private individuals against the advice of the governor. The settlers from those deals are the ones who encroached on the Cherokees, but rather than turn to North Carolina for redress, the Cherokees turned to the British, who urged them to attack the frontier. Because of their attacks, the settlers asked North Carolina to include them in the state, which they did, and protected them (with Rutherford's and Moore's expeditions). Avery explained that the boundary the state sought would include all those settlers. To make the boundary more palatable to the Cherokees, he insisted that laws would be made to punish any and all encroachers for whatever reason.

With the commissioners not retreating from their desired boundary, Old Tassel rose to address the conference. He said that the Nolichucky settlers lived too close to the Overhill Towns and that, therefore, the boundary to include them would be too close—something to which he could not agree. Old Tassel even suggested that the commissioners did not realize just how close to the Cherokee towns they had drawn the boundary. He expressed surprise at the proposed line, but he would not let that interfere with the peace between the Cherokees and the two states. At that point he had nothing more to say on the matter, and he expressed a desire to write a letter to General Washington. The conference then ended for the evening.

The next day, July 18, Old Tassel began the talks and spoke plainly to the North Carolina commissioners. He expressed pleasure at the peace Governor Henry and Oconostota made and at the present conference. He reiterated the headmen's surprise at the talk of a boundary, especially one encompassing so much Cherokee land. They thought the conference would only address peace, not a boundary. In fact, Old Tassel wondered whether Governor Henry knew that the commissioners asked for so much territory. Even if a great amount of goods had been brought to pay for the land, Old Tassel told the commissioners it would not be enough. Again, he said, "It seems misterious to me why you should ask so much land so near me." He then revealed the purpose of his having a letter written to General Washington when he said, "But I will leave the difference between us to the great Warrior of all America." He then addressed the Virginia commissioners, assuring them that the Cherokees would keep the peace.

Having been flatly rejected on the boundary, and with Old Tassel redirecting the talks to the matter of peace, Colonel

Christian then extended the invitation of General Washington for some of the Cherokee headmen and warriors to accompany Colonel Gist to observe the northern army. Those who made the journey would be well treated and see that other American Indians fought alongside the Continentals. The Old Tassel responded that the Pidgeon would accompany Colonel Gist but that he could not speak for any others.

He continued by indicating the Cherokees' desire to return to their towns and tend to their crops, adding his personal hope that the conference would end soon so he could leave in three days. By stating his intention to leave within a few days, Old Tassel conveyed to the commissioners they had but a short time to reconsider and compromise on the boundary, if they wanted one. He and the other Cherokee headmen had come to make peace, not a boundary. Because the commissioners predicated a peace upon a boundary, there was an impass. Peace or no peace, boundary or no, the last of the Cherokees would depart in three days.

Perhaps the incentive provided by the Old Tassel prompted the commissioners to reconsider their hard-line approach to the boundary issue—their position as victors of the 1776 war against the Cherokees notwithstanding. After the talks ended on July 18, the Virginia commissioners drafted a formal letter to the North Carolina commissioners, urging them to reconsider their boundary demands and perhaps even consider compensating the Cherokees for the land they demanded as in previous land negotiations. The Virginia commissioners labored under the assumption that when something is obtained, it is usually purchased. The North Carolina commissioners, however, calculated that the cost of Rutherford's and Moore's expeditions constituted a large enough expenditure. Because the Cherokees had attacked the frontier, which prompted the punitive expeditions, they forfeited any amount due them, and the North Carolinians refused to offer any recompense for the territory they demanded. Nor would they take any less territory than they came to acquire.

The next day of talks proved enlightening to the Cherokees. Christian began by finally overtly stating the

Whig position: only through the Cherokees' ceding territory and agreeing to a boundary would there be peace. He then proposed the Virginia boundary to include the Carter's Valley settlers (southwest of present-day Rogersville, Tennessee). In return, Virginia allied itself with the Cherokees there at the conference and also offered two hundred cows and one hundred sheep. As Christian then said, "In short, on your agreeing to this boundary, our peace will be confirmed."

After a short break, the Raven stated the Cherokee position about another boundary in no uncertain terms. He said the commissioners should make the boundary impassable, "As if it was a wall that reached up to the skies." The Cherokees were agreeing to yet another boundary, but this would be the final one. He then countered Virginia's proposed boundary with one that ran from Robinson's Fort (just west of present-day Kingsport) to Cumberland Gap. Given the continued plight of the Cherokees, his request for some livestock—which Christian had already offered—seems sincerely earnest. In an effort to end matters on a positive note for the Cherokees, the Raven said he understood that the Virginians had some ammunition for them and that they would like to receive it later that evening so they could return to their towns.

It is important to note that the boundary proposed by the Raven placed the Long Island within Cherokee territory. The Long Island had always been a place to hold peace conferences such as the current one. The headmen wanted to ensure that it would be preserved for such meetings, especially with the Whigs wanting to make the boundary farther to the south of the island.

Christian apologized for having to again propose a boundary, but he agreed it should be "like a wall, high and strong that none can pass over or break down." The line, however, should include all the settlers, and if it ran as the Raven proposed, there would be some twenty settlers already outside the wall. He therefore reiterated his proposed boundary so as to include all the current settlers. The Raven consented. Christian advised that Virginia would send someone to facilitate communication between Chota and Williamsburg, and that the Cherokees would receive a true copy of the treaty, which would contain all that had been said and agreed upon. He then implored them to reach an agreement with the commissioners from North Carolina, and the conference adjourned for the day.

When the conference met again the next day, July 20, 1777, Avery rose to address the headmen. Although he began by admonishing the Cherokees for rejecting the peace overtures from North Carolina the previous year, he proposed sending an agent to reside among them, as Virginia had proposed. Avery, as Christian had done, also linked the boundary with peace by saying, "If you will not settle a boundary line with us the peace cannot be lasting." Perhaps in an effort to make the land cession more palatable, Avery also indicated that much of the Cherokee homeland had been invaded and conquered so that the Whigs could actually claim all of it by right of conquest.

Astonishingly, the North Carolina commissioners had actually reconsidered their proposed boundary, and they offered another that did not include the settlers' receiving so much Cherokee territory. Their new boundary proposal included the Carter's Valley settlements and came east to Chimney Top (about ten miles southwest of Kingsport) to the mouth of Camp Creek, or McNamies Creek, on the south bank of the Nolichucky River (south of Greeneville, Tennessee), then southeast back over the Eastern Divide. This new proposal would include all the settlers then in the Watauga and Nolichucky regions, as well as those along the Holston River below Kingsport. Still, the Long Island would be north of the proposed boundaries. There seemed no escaping that fact for the Cherokees. The conference adjourned so the headmen could discuss the matters among themselves.

Upon resumption of the conference, the Raven rose and began by designating Colonel Gist the caretaker of the Long Island. The Long Island must be kept neutral for both sides to meet in peace as they had been doing, the Raven said. The headmen probably thought the Whigs would be more amenable to the island's being kept neutral if a Whig had charge of it. The Cherokees knew Gist well, and he had even married a Cherokee woman. Further, the Raven insisted that a copy of the proceedings be sent to General Washington, as the head warrior of the United States, as the final arbiter in the matter. Notwithstanding the fact that the Whigs had claimed their right to the land via conquest, the Raven reminded the headmen that some form of payment usually accompanied a land cession. He hinted that a good time to bring "some acknowledgement" would be when they came to mark the boundary, or "run the line." Finally, he agreed to the commissioners' insistence on the territory cessions and concluded, "Now I am done; I give up the land you asked; I shall say no more. If you ask for more, I will not give it." Fittingly, about the time the Raven had finished, it began to rain, and the conference ended.

On July 21, 1777, the headmen heard the articles of the Virginia treaty and then the North Carolina treaty interpreted to them. The treaties mirrored each other in substance and the order of articles, except for the different boundaries each delineated and the fact that the seventh article in the Virginia document ordered the delivery of goods by Virginia to the Cherokees. Despite the urgings of the Raven, North Carolina made no such promise of goods to the Cherokees. Both treaties allowed the Cherokees to drive off trespassers and squatters and confiscate their property. They also provided that all settlers and slaves who had been taken prisoner, as well as all livestock that had been taken, would be returned. And the treaties included a special provision regarding the surrendering of murderers.

Curiously, neither treaty stipulated that the Long Island remained Cherokee territory, essentially under the stewardship of Colonel Gist. After the fifth article, delineating boundaries, was read, Old Tassel and the Raven objected because of the lack of that caveat. The Old Tassel said, "I told you yesterday so plain that no one could misunderstand. We will not dispose of this Island but we reserve it to hold our Great Talks on. . . . [P]eople may settle around it but not on it." Only Gist could settle on the island, because the headmen considered him "our friend and Brother."

When it came time for the headmen to commit their signatures, or marks, to the treaties, Old Tassel said, "Ever since I signed a paper for Colonel Henderson I am afraid of signing papers. He told me many lies and deceived us." Only after being reassured that the treaties would be between the Cherokee people and the states of North Carolina and Virginia, and that the Cherokees would receive a copy of each treaty, did Old Tassel sign them, "verry readily."

After the signing of each treaty, Christian and Avery spoke to the headmen, expressing their pleasure with the agreement and the peace that they made. After the second treaty (North Carolina's) had been signed and Avery made his speech, Old Tassel spoke. He expressed his surprise at the commissioners' insisting on a Whig agent residing among them. Evidently he had given the matter much thought, because he then insisted on having not just one agent, but one from each state—which was logical, because he had entered into a separate treaty with each state. He justified his position by concluding, "They can do the business better than one." The North Carolina commissioners immediately appointed Captain James Robertson as their agent to reside in Chota with Old Tassel and the Raven. After formally drafting instructions to Robertson, the conference adjourned for the day.

The next day opened with a joint message from the commissioners to the headmen, commending what had transpired over the past several days. Then a chief from Cowee and a messenger from the Valley Towns spoke of their approbation of the proceedings and the peace that had been made. In a complete turnabout, the North Carolina commissioners wrote instructions to the state commissary to have six hundred pounds of flour delivered to Fort Patrick Henry for the Cherokees.

Immediately after this humanitarian gesture, the North Carolina commissioners invited some of the headmen and warriors to visit Halifax and meet with the governor. Five Cherokees offered to go to visit three friends who had been taken prisoner during the previous year's military operations. The five Cherokees would be escorted to the home of Commissioner William Sharpe, some 150 miles away in North Carolina, where they would meet their three friends. This would be quite a convenient arrangement for the states, having visitors stay with friends who were prisoners. Actually, after the course of the treaty negotiations, the commissioners realized they could not secure hostages, but this invitation to the five Cherokees to stay with their friends would suffice. They would, in essence, become de facto hostages without even realizing it. With this last subterfuge, the treaty conference ended, and all departed the Long Island in the Holston River.

While Virginia made peace with the Cherokees, it took steps to place the Kentucky region on a more stable military footing. In light of the incessant Shawnee attacks on the settlements in the Kentucky lands in 1777, the Virginia legislature authorized a militia in that region toward the end June. [3] This meant that a regular body of troops would be available to defend the forts and stations in the region. It also meant that a supply of ammunition would be allocated for their use to alleviate the chronic shortage they had experienced since their arrival. The only problem with the legislation was that the region did not contain a population that could support itself militarily.

In July, British superintendent Stuart became aware that the Overhill Cherokees had left their towns to make a peace treaty with the Americans. He harbored a dim view of them as military allies and expressed his displeasure with their actions to Cameron. Stuart stressed to Cameron that the goods sent him were not for general distribution, "But to Reward such as go upon service and have merit of which you are to be the Judge." Stuart charged Cameron with reminding the Cherokees that they had gone to war to recover their lands and in defense of themselves, not on account of the British. Stuart did promise support to those Cherokees who "behave properly," that is, who followed Loyalist leaders against the rebels at his discretion. Many of the refugee Cherokees had already left the Lower Creeks to return to their homes. The Cowetas told them that if they joined the rebels, they would be treated as enemies, something Stuart clearly endorsed. Obviously, Stuart intended to support the Chickamaugas and those Creeks who would openly attack the southern frontier. [4]

Although Stuart received instructions to send the Creeks against the frontiers, he and his deputies knew that they would not begin large-scale military operations unless supported by British regulars. By mid-July, David Taitt advised Stuart that the water levels of the rivers through Creek territory would "not allow boat transport of goods and supplies." The Creeks had overcome their apprehension of British troops moving through their country, but the logistics could not be managed. Taitt cautioned Stuart that not even enough horses could be obtained to transport all the materiel that would be required. Taitt further warned that he must receive advance notice of any British operation in the southern states if the Creeks were to be of any assistance, so they could gather supplies and prepare to attack the Georgia frontier.

Evidently, Stuart had not informed his deputy that the British high command entertained no such thoughts as an operation conducted by British regulars. Taitt reaffirmed what Stuart believed, that Handsome Fellow and the Cussita King were "influenced by [George] Galphin." Conversely, the Cussitas, Ussichies, Broken Arrow, and some Hitchities supported the British. To preclude any retribution against Handsome Fellow by Taitt and Stuart, White Lieutenant, an Upper Creek headman from Okfuskee, told them that Handsome Fellow merely participated in Galphin's conference at Old Town so he could obtain goods from him, something the British could hardly fault him for in such difficult times.[5]

While Oconostota and other Overhill Cherokee headmen met with the American commissioners at Fort Patrick Henry, Cameron assessed the situation of the militant Cherokees for Stuart. The Loyalist traders and the militant Cherokee headman Judd's Friend all lived at the newly established Chickamauga towns. Rumor had it that the Shawnee offensive succeeded so well that the Kentucky settlers sought assistance from the Holston River settlements, but the latter had to contend with attacks from Dragging Canoe and his followers. Rumors circulated that the Americans would take the Cherokee headmen hostage at the peace talks if Dragging Canoe continued his attacks, but that did not deter the Chickamauga leader. The only reason for the Chickamaugas to halt their attacks would be lack of supplies. Cameron warned Stuart that some shirts, blankets, knives, a paltry few other goods, and a ridiculously small amount of ammunition was all he could give the Chickamaugas. If Stuart wanted them to continue attacking the frontier, a large shipment of ammunition would be required.[6]

At about the same time, but farther south, small parties of Cowetas attacked stockade forts on the Ogeechee frontier with some success. With their initial attack failing to force the capitulation of a fort, the Cowetas withdrew. Once confident the garrison was pursuing them, the Cowetas picked a location and established an ambush. As the pursuing militiamen entered the ambush, the Cowetas attacked, inflicting serious losses. Upon reaching Coweta, the warriors assured Taitt that even more Creeks would attack the Georgia frontier as soon as they secured enough corn to support them in the field. However, only parties from Coweta among the Lower Creeks attacked the Georgia frontier, despite Taitt's reassurances to Stuart that the Lower Creeks did not pay attention to what the Americans told them. It is no coincidence that Galphin sent a message to the Lower Creeks in response to the Coweta attacks, warning them against any future such operations. He emphasized his warning by alluding to what had happened to the Cherokees, something quite familiar to the Creeks through Cherokee refugees.[7]

Stuart admonished his deputies to designate Loyalists to lead the Creek war parties. General Howe and Lord Germain envisioned waves of American Indians attacking the rebel frontier, led by intuitive Loyalist officers, rather than red-coated battalions. After Taitt and Stuart's other deputies among the Creeks attempted to carry out these instructions, their headmen finally explained to Taitt that the scenario envisioned by the British high command would never come to fruition. Taitt informed Stuart that "they would give us any Assistance in their power by Excursions in Small parties upon the Settlements." Stuart managed to supply them with a large quantity of goods and ammunition but revised his expectations to conform with the Creek manner of war.[8]

Only a few weeks later, Taitt wrote to Stuart what the superintendent had already realized: that the American Indians in his department would not openly assist the British without the support of regular troops. The British had not been able to supply the Creeks with any consistency, nor had a regular British force been deployed in the southern theater to support the Creeks. With no hint of British troops to be deployed in the southern theater, Taitt attempted to persuade the Lower Creeks to confiscate the supplies of Galphin's traders. Taitt knew that the Whigs would then refuse to send any goods or traders into the region. But the Lower Creeks also knew this, and they would not do as Taitt suggested, because of the scarcity of supplies.[9]

Taitt then tried to sway those Upper Creek headmen who sympathized with the rebel cause, particularly the White Lieutenant and Will's Friend of the Okfuskees. He did not fare well, and a war party from Little Tallassee heading to attack the Georgia frontier turned back after the Okfuskees threatened to send out their own war parties against Pensacola while Handsome Fellow remained among the Georgians. Taitt failed in his attempt and later discovered that Galphin had promised all Creeks a regular trade and amnesty for all previous attacks if they remained neutral henceforth.[10]

Throughout the fall of 1777, Stuart made every effort to convince Whitehall, the administrative center of the British government in London, that for the British to rely on the American Indians of the southeast, regular troops would have to be deployed. Stuart explained that the Creeks had thus far only "harassed" the frontier of Georgia, and that the "Cherokees are distressed" because the Whig expeditions of 1776 destroyed their crops and livestock. But in an effort to secure British troops, he told Germain that the "whole Creek nation is now unanimous for war." A planned offensive against the Georgia frontier had been thwarted by the return of some Lower Creek headmen from Galphin's conference at Old Town, the neutralist faction of the Creek Nation. In other words, Stuart maintained that unless the British government committed troops to the southern theater, the Creeks would soon suffer the same fate as the Cherokees did in 1776 and be unable to assist the British.[11]

The ink had hardly dried on the 1777 Treaty of Long Island before settlers began moving in as far down as the headwaters of the Watauga, Nolichucky, and New rivers. On August 7, Commissioner Avery implored the governor to have the boundary line surveyed and marked immediately. His primary concern lay in acquiring a large tract of land between the Blue Ridge and Iron mountains that was claimed by the Cherokee Middle Towns. Then the Overmountain settlements could be linked with roads to those east of the mountains. Therefore, Avery concluded that the treaty with the Middle Town headmen should be vigorously pursued. Avery seemed bent on acquiring as much Cherokee territory as possible.[12]

While Avery tempted future conflict with the Cherokees by endeavoring to secure more of their land, Colonel John Carter, one of the original Overmountain pioneers feared that other rapidly developing events might precipitate more attacks. He learned that the Nolichucky settlers had obtained authorization from General Rutherford to raise a troop of twenty-five horsemen to patrol their frontier. Carter could not understand the necessity for the patrol, as there had not been a single instance of a clash between Cherokees and settlers since the peace treaty. He did, however, foresee clashes arising from the rangers themselves, especially with the hunting season approaching. It was true that four settlers had been killed on the Clinch River about sixty miles northeast of the Carter's Valley settlements, and that fear of a widespread attack by the Cherokees had created a general alarm. But Carter believed that the attacks were isolated incidents and that "Norwards" (including Shawnees, Wyandots, Miamis, and Delawares) were responsible for them. The alarm prompted Colonel Shelby to raise a force and pursue the marauders. His efforts confirmed Carter's belief about who was responsible for the attacks, which calmed settlers' fears and cleared the Cherokees of guilt. As additional evidence of the Cherokees' peaceful nature toward the Americans, Carter informed the Virginia governor that Little Carpenter had gone to the Long Island with twenty-five to thirty warriors and offered the service of five hundred warriors for the American cause against the English or any American Indians. Carter could not discover any attacks that had been made by Cherokees. He therefore realized the authorization for the militia had been obtained on a pretext so that a war could be

initiated against the Cherokees, which would more than likely result in another Cherokee land cession. Any mobilization
of militia seemed a sham and an outrage to Carter, who
became so disgusted at the thought of the impending catastrophe for the Cherokees that he stated plainly to the governor, "if my dignity is to be sported with, under these circumstances; I have no need of your Commission as Commanding
officer for the Washington District."[13]

Over a month later, in October, the North Carolina agent
to the Cherokees, James Robertson, wrote to his governor of
the Cherokees' continued peacefulness. Oconostota had
approached him about being supplied by the states rather
than Cameron and the British. Stuart's policy of not supplying Cherokees who made peace with the Revolutionary
Whigs remained in effect. Cameron even chided them,
Robertson said: "The Indians say he makes much diversion of
their having Bark Trade with the Americans," a reference to
the poverty and paucity of goods that the states could supply
to the Cherokees. Robertson speculated that if the Cherokees
could be supplied, the states would no longer have cause to
fear attacks from them.[14]

Most historians agree that the 1777 Treaty of Long Island
represented yet another agreement in which the Cherokees
ceded more land to the ever-encroaching white settlers moving west. Certainly Dragging Canoe and his followers shared
that sentiment. A few dissenters claim that the land had
already been ceded by the Cherokees in the meetings with
Richard Henderson in 1775, the so-called Henderson
Purchase. Because the land the Cherokees ceded in the Treaty
of Long Island was a part of the Henderson transaction, some
tout the 1777 treaty as the only one in which the Cherokees
ceded no land.

The reality lies somewhere in between. Given Oconostota's
comment on Avery's questioning of the Raven, and Old
Tassel's remark at the signing of the treaty about Henderson's
duplicity, it is doubtful that the Cherokees actually thought
they had sold the territory. Since the Henderson Purchase in
1775 and the Treaty of Long Island in 1777, however, settlers

had poured into present-day northeast Tennessee and middle Kentucky. The Cherokees, therefore, had in fact lost the territory. In a strictly technical, or legal, sense, the Cherokees did not concede possession of the land until the treaty of 1777.

But that is not why the treaty was important, especially for understanding subsequent events. The Whigs made it clear that any peace would be predicated on this new boundary—that is, on the Cherokees' ceding more land. That came as quite a shock to the Cherokee headmen, who thought that a lasting peace had already been achieved. To them, the treaty conference would merely confirm the lasting peace. They were told it was to be a peace conference; no one had said anything before it took place about their ceding additional territory.

Of even more importance is what seems to have been lost on the Whigs: the full gravity of the meaning the Cherokees placed on the boundary. Because the commissioners had been so insistent on establishing a new boundary and had predicated achieving peace on doing so, it must have represented something very important to them. The Cherokees, therefore, made it equally important to themselves. They made it clear that the peace would be predicated on the inviolability of the boundary. Any breach of the boundary would be tantamount to a declaration of war by the whites on the Cherokees. Without foresight, the commissioners had empowered the Cherokees to violate the basic premise of every previous treaty—that the Cherokees would become and remain peaceful—by including the article allowing them to drive off settlers located in the Indians' territory.

The combination of new boundaries and allowing the Cherokees to drive off trespassers created a recipe for disaster. Whether either side realized it or not, it would only be a matter of time before violence resumed.

NINE

The Calm before
the Storm

1778

The Shawnees conducted the only major American Indian offensive during 1778. Throughout the year, their war parties traversed the Kentucky Territory, attacking and besieging settlements. Eventually, those settlers who did not flee Kentucky gathered at Boonesborough, Logan's Station, and Harrodsburg. There they erected stockades around their cabins and constructed bastions in the corners to protect the garrison within and repel attacks. Probably because of the fame of Daniel Boone, the most complete account of a siege by Indians (in this case, the Shawnees) is that of Boonesborough. It is atypical for others along the frontiers, and it is also noteworthy for being the longest of any American Indian siege.

In February, Boone and a party of over twenty settlers drawn from all over Kentucky traveled to the Great Salt Lick, north of Boonesborough, so salt could be distilled there and distributed to the stations in the territory. While they were engaged in that occupation, a large war party of Shawnees captured Boone, who was out hunting, and intended to march on Boonesborough and reduce that settlement. The war party had undoubtedly kept the men at the Great Salt Lick under surveillance for several days, and Boone persuaded the Shawnees to accept their surrender rather than attack them. Knowing the weakened condition of Boonesborough at that time, he then implied he would help arrange the surrender of the forted settlement in the summer, when the weather would not create further hardships for the women and children. Boone went with the war party to the Great Salt Lick and persuaded the men to surrender without resistance. The Shawnees took Boone and the others back to their town of Little Chillicothe on the Little Miami River in present-day Ohio.[1]

The Shawnees adopted most of the salt makers they captured at the Great Salt Lick. The great Shawnee headman Blackfish adopted Boone himself as his son. Boone accompanied Blackfish when the latter took those settlers not adopted to Detroit as prisoners, where the British would buy them. Upon Blackfish's return to Little Chillicothe, the Shawnees exercised less and less vigilance in guarding Boone until, on June 16, he escaped after seeing the largest Indian force sent against Kentucky preparing to make the journey to Boonesborough to attack the settlement. The attack would be no ordinary two- or three-day siege. With a great sense of urgency, Boone traveled the 160 miles from Little Chillicothe to Boonesborough in four days.[2]

Upon arrival, he found Boonesborough in worse condition than he had imagined. The palisade had all but completely deteriorated, and the gate and both blockhouses were in serious need of repair. After he warned the settlers of the impending attack by Blackfish, the people immediately began to get the stockade on a proper defensive footing. They repaired and strengthened the palisade that served as a common back wall for all the cabins. Next they added two additional bastions on the southern side so that the fort had one in each corner, though neither of the additions was given a roof, due to time constraints of the pending attack. They also strengthened the existing two blockhouses. In the center of the enclosed compound, an American flag fluttered in the breeze atop a fifty-foot pole.[3]

With all the preparations done that they could accomplish quickly, the Boonesborough settlers awaited the attack. Days passed and there was no sign of any Indian force. Then on July 17, William Hancock, a fellow captive of Boone's, arrived with the news that the attack had been postponed for three weeks. He also conveyed a dreadful rumor he had heard: Blackfish would be armed with four swivel guns. Artillery is the only thing the garrison of a frontier fort feared, even that of a small caliber. It had already been nine days since Hancock left Little Chillicothe, but Boone, who expected the attack in about twelve days, wrote to Colonel Arthur Campbell, commander of the Washington County (Virginia) militia, requesting reinforcements to arrive in "five or six weeks."[4]

Two weeks passed with no attack. It was now the beginning of August, and six weeks since Boone had escaped. Many of the settlers thought the attack may have been canceled because of that escape. Blackfish may have surmised that the attack would meet with a reinforced and prepared Boonesborough. Boone decided to take the fight to the enemy rather than stand and wait. A great many of the settlers did not agree with the strategy, including Boonesborough's commander, Colonel Richard Calloway, who doubted Boone's loyalty to them after his stay with the Shawnees. In spite of the opposition, thirty men volunteered to accompany Boone on his scouting raid.[5]

After passing the Blue Licks, about a third decided to return to Boonesborough. The rest pushed on. Once across the Ohio River, Boone and his party headed for the Scioto Valley, home of the Shawnees where Boone had been a captive. They ambushed several small groups of Indians and a war party that seemed to be gathering. Making their way to the outskirts of Paint Creek Town, they found no warriors. Boone surmised that many tribes other than the Shawnees had begun gathering for the intended offensive against Boonesborough. Boone and his party began their return trip to Boonesborough, slipping around Blackfish's force, and reached the stockade just ahead of them on September 6, 1778.[6]

The two forces prepared for the pending struggle. Boone brought back detailed information on the enemy and its proximity—just across the Kentucky River. The garrison of Boonesborough readied weapons, made bullets, harvested as much of the corn in the fields around the fort as possible, and gathered up as many cattle as they could and herded them into the fort. About ten to fifteen men had arrived from Logan's Station and Harrodsburg.[7]

Blackfish's force crossed the river on the morning of September 7, about a half mile west of Boonesborough. The force then came down Hackberry Ridge to the south of the fort and appeared in a meadow several hundred yards away, out of effective rifle range. Blackfish had an arbor constructed of poles, boughs, and tent material for use as a headquarters. Boone counted 444 Shawnees, Mingos, Wyandots, Delawares, and Cherokees,[8] as well as about a dozen French Canadian militiamen led by Lieutenant Daginaux De Quindre of the Indian Department in Detroit. They came with a large supply train of packhorses.[9]

Blackfish called for Boone to meet with him outside the fort, and they did, within one hundred yards of the gate. After a personal conversation with Boone through Pompey, an ex-slave acting as interpreter, Blackfish insisted that Boone fulfill his promise to surrender Boonesborough and all would be well treated and taken to Little Chillicothe. If they did not surrender, he would kill all but the young women, whom he would make his wives. Blackfish then presented Boone with letters from Henry Hamilton, British superintendent of Indian affairs at Detroit, in which he posed two options: either surrender and all would be treated leniently, or resist and he could not be held responsible for the bloodshed that surely would occur. Blackfish then gave Boone a belt of wampum—the Shawnee version of Hamilton's letter. The belt consisted of rows of red, white, and black beads, with Detroit being one end and Boonesborough the other. Red represented the warpath the Shawnees and their allies had taken there, white stood for the path for all of them to take back to Detroit, and black meant death in the massacre that would follow their failed defense.[10]

Boone replied that during his captivity, others had been placed in command in Boonesborough. It no longer fell to him to decide what to do. Understanding the vicissitudes of leadership, Blackfish allowed Boone to return to the fort and present the options to the current commanders. Boone offered the livestock roaming outside the stockade and the corn left in the fields for Blackfish's warriors. Blackfish, in return, presented Boone with seven smoked buffalo tongues, considered a great delicacy. All seemed civil and courteous. The Indians butchered only a few cattle and gathered just enough corn to meet their needs, unlike their traditional practice of destroying all livestock and crops.[11]

Boone returned to the fort and explained the situation. Those inside had seen enough of Blackfish's force to realize it was immense compared to their numbers. They faced a stark reality: either surrender and be taken back to Detroit, or make a successful defense—an unsuccessful one would spell doom for all. Reinforcements were expected from Virginia, but no one knew when they would arrive. Also, Blackfish's force supposedly had four swivel guns, which eventually would create a breech in the stockade wall. Initially, about half the men supported a surrender, while the other half wanted to fight. Colonel Calloway threatened to kill the first man who attempted to surrender. At that point, they needed to stall in order to give the Virginian reinforcements time to arrive, and to determine whether Blackfish did have swivel guns.[12]

Boone met again with Blackfish, this time accompanied by Major William Bailey Smith, who looked every inch the commander, bedecked in his crimson tunic and tricorn hat replete with plume. Smith informed Blackfish that the women and children could not endure the long trek to Detroit. In turn, Blackfish informed Boone and Smith that he had brought forty horses for the women and children in anticipation of alleviating the hardship of such a long journey. Somewhat surprised, Boone and Smith asked Blackfish to allow them to consult on the matter with the other militia officers for the rest of that day and the next. Blackfish consented, and he agreed that his warriors would not approach the fort, as long as the settlers would not leave the fort with weapons.[13]

This parley with Blackfish revealed two important facts to the Boonesborough garrison: Blackfish and De Quindre believed the garrison's strength to be far greater than it was, and they had not brought any artillery with them to reduce the stockade. Both of these factors would greatly aid in their resistance. The exaggerated strength of the garrison stemmed from supposed intelligence Hamilton had given to Blackfish before his departure. To strengthen Blackfish's mistaken belief that the garrison numbered close to his forces, all the women donned men's coats and hats. They even made scarecrows and placed them strategically around the palisade and blockhouses. The gate remained open to the fort so Blackfish's force could see the size of the "garrison."[14]

On the evening of September 8, Blackfish and the accompanying headmen appeared before the fort bearing a white flag. Boone met with Blackfish and conveyed the garrison's desire to defend the fort to the last man. This seems to have taken Blackfish aback, especially because De Quindre had explained that they had come on a peaceful mission, not a destructive one. In fact, Hamilton had ordered them to avoid bloodshed. Because the residents did not wish to return to Detroit with them, and all the British really wanted was to neutralize the outpost as a possible source of future military operations against them, De Quindre suggested a peace treaty. If nine of the Boonesborough leaders would sign it, the entire force arrayed against them would leave. To avoid a desperate and prolonged engagement, in which failure would mean a massacre, Boone and Smith agreed. The two sides agreed to meet the next day and sign a peace treaty. Blackfish insisted that a representative of each Indian town be present, which would amount to about eighteen. Boone and Smith objected because the Boonesborough leaders would be greatly outnumbered outside the fort and therefore susceptible to capture, but Blackfish explained that the other headmen would not consider the treaty binding on them unless they attended. Boone and Smith had no choice but to agree if they wanted to stall for more time.[15]

On September 9, the settlers brought tables, complete with tablecloths, out to the meadow in front of the fort and spread a feast of venison, buffalo, vegetables, even bread and milk. Warriors spread skins for Blackfish and the other headmen to sit on, and all fully enjoyed the repast. Afterward, all repaired to the hollow of Lick Spring, about sixty or eighty yards from the fort—a position clearly visible and easily swept with rifle fire from the stockade. Blackfish had wanted to meet inside the fort, but that would have exposed the numerical weakness of the garrison. Boone had instructed the riflemen manning the loopholes facing the spring to fire into the group if anything happened, for their odds of hitting a warrior would be two-to-one.[16]

After everyone seated themselves, a warrior took position behind every white man, his face painted black and red (for war). Blackfish initially offered to withdraw his army if the settlers left Kentucky in six weeks. When the Boonesborough leaders rejected this outright, Blackfish demanded to know, "By what right did you come and settle here?" Boone responded that the land had been purchased some three years earlier at the Sycamore Shoals, and a Cherokee with Blackfish confirmed that. In light of the response, Blackfish conceded that the settlers could stay and continue in peace. He suggested that the Ohio River be the temporary boundary for both sides and said he would withdraw his army after both sides took an oath of allegiance to the king. Surprisingly, all the Boonesborough leaders, including Colonel Calloway, agreed.[17]

Blackfish announced that he would have to explain the agreement to his assembled warriors and proceeded to deliver a speech supposedly to that affect. He then told the Boonesborough delegates that to consummate the treaty, they all must shake the "long hand," Indian-style, with their hearts next to each other. At that moment, each delegate was grabbed by two warriors, one on each arm to give the "long hand" shake, while Blackfish embraced Boone. Then the warriors attempted to pull the delegates away from the treaty site down the bank of the river, out of sight from the fort. A melee ensued in which the delegates struggled with the warriors to break free and race back to the fort. The riflemen from the fort began to fire as instructed, and some warriors Blackfish had placed in defilade also opened fire on the group. Boone threw Blackfish to the ground and made his way toward the fort. Miraculously, the other eight delegates managed to free themselves also. It is difficult to exactly reconstruct the ensuing events, but Boone credited the fort's riflemen for hitting enough of the warriors to allow the delegates to dash back to the fort. Squire Boone, Daniel's younger brother, received a debilitating wound, and Daniel Boone suffered a minor wound, but all made it back inside the fort. The garrison barred the gate, and the siege began in earnest.[18]

Both sides began firing until it became general and created much confusion among the noncombatants and livestock. Between the screams and shouts from inside and outside the fort, powder smoke from the rifle fire, and dust from the livestock running around inside the compound, the scene was sheer pandemonium. That afternoon, the warriors attempted to storm the stockade, but heavy rifle fire made them withdraw. The firing continued sporadically that night and all the next day. On the night of September 10, a group of warriors gathered some flax growing in a field outside the stockade and piled it up against a fence that ran to a corner of the stockade. The next day they lit the flax on fire, hoping it would reach the stockade and light it as well, but some of the garrison crawled out under the stockade wall and separated the fence from the palisade. Clearly, Blackfish had not brought swivel guns, or he would have used them. The use of fire took its place.[19]

On Friday, September 11, some of the garrison noticed something unusual—muddy water in the Kentucky River. Upon further investigation, they could hear the muffled sounds of digging coming from the river, and a cedar pole was seen shaking periodically. De Quindre had persuaded the warriors to dig a tunnel from the bank of the river to the fort. The stratagem seemed to be either to enter the fort under the palisade wall or blow up a section of it and attack through the breach. To thwart the effort, the garrison began digging a countermine: a trench that would be perpendicular to the attacker's tunnel and expose them when they reached the countermine. Also, the garrison constructed a six-foot observation tower of sorts and placed it on top of Richard Henderson's kitchen to try to observe the progress of the besiegers' tunneling.[20]

That night, the warriors "shot arrows, with powder in a little rag, and a little punk. They set only one house on fire, the only shingled roof house that was there, Col. Henderson's."[21] A seemingly endless line of warriors ran up to the palisade and threw over torches they had fashioned out of oily inner hickory bark and flax. Some landed on the ground, but others landed on cabin roofs. Squire Boone, known for his inventive ingenuity, fashioned old rifle barrels with a mechanism that shot water up onto the roofs. Those fires that could not be so extinguished were doused by going through the roof from inside the cabin itself. The burning arrows that stuck into the roofs could be swept off with poles.[22]

As preparation for the expected siege, Squire Boone had also made two swivel guns by drilling a bore in gum tree logs and wrapping them with iron wagon-wheel bands. One of the improvised swivels burst upon testing; the garrison did not use the other swivel gun after its first fire because it cracked, but the shot scattered a group of warriors in the meadow. Afterward, the warriors did not cluster together again in the open. The besiegers noticed the absence of the swivels after their bursting and tauntingly inquired why the militiamen no longer used them. But the rifle fire of the garrison proved effective enough, even at distances considered long-range— three hundred yards or more.[23]

After days of sporadic gunfire and night attacks, the warriors made a determined effort on the night of September 17. Time and again, waves of attackers came at the stockade and threw their torches over the palisade. By now, the warriors had learned to mask the fire of their torches with a blanket, but still the accurate rifle fire proved deadly for many. Blackfish designated a segment of his force to use fire arrows, and they came in a seemingly incessant stream. The battle raged with such intensity that Moses Boone, Squire's son, noticed that the sky was so bright from all the fires and firing that "any article could be plainly seen to be picked up, even to a pin." After some time a heavy rain began to fall, and it finished putting out the fires. With the onset of the stormy weather, calm settled over Boonesborough.[24]

Friday, September 18 dawned with only sporadic gunfire, which continued through the morning and then curiously ceased. Late in the afternoon, some of the garrison ventured outside the fort gate and scouted the area. Blackfish and his force had withdrawn suddenly. The tunnel his warriors began had collapsed, probably from the torrential rain the night before. Some thirty warriors, probably the Cherokees, had gone south; other bands had headed toward Logan's Station and Harrodsburg. They withdrew with all their casualties, so their losses are unknown, but Boone estimated thirty-seven. The Boonesborough garrison suffered only two killed.[25]

William Patton, a resident of Boonesborough who had been away hunting since before the siege began, returned the night of September 17 and observed the major assault on the fort. Fearing the worst, he made his way to the nearest settlement, Logan's Station, and conveyed the sad news that Boonesborough had fallen.[26]

Captain Benjamin Logan, the ranking militia officer at Logan's Station, realized that if what Patton said was true, then his stockade would be Blackfish's next target. He ordered a deep trench to be dug from the fort to the spring located about fifty yards to the east and then had it covered, probably with felled trees, to provide protection from gunfire during the expected attack. Then all the residents took to the fields to harvest corn, pumpkins, and other vegetables. Also, Logan ordered every container that could hold water to be filled. After going to a nearby salt lick to round up cattle, he returned severely wounded: the war party had already arrived. A few days later, some of the garrison noticed an approaching force, which turned out to be a group of horsemen from Boonesborough. The horsemen refuted Patton's claim that Boonesborough had been captured, but they understood the reason for his assumption, given the utter chaos and terror of that night. No Indian force attacked Logan's Station or Harrodsburg. Kentucky passed the rest of 1778 in relative peace.[27]

The same could not be said for Georgia. Not content with waiting for a British army, if one would ever come, pro-British Creeks intensified their attacks in August. Led by the Cowetas, they killed some two dozen settlers in the Ceded Lands that month. At least seven Creek towns participated in the attacks, according to Galphin. On August 25, a party of Chickamaugas joined the general offensive and attacked Fort Nail, taking the horses and killing the cattle. To counter the attacks, South Carolina authorized Colonel Williamson to

advance into Georgia. He gathered over five hundred militiamen and took up a position in the Ceded Lands, forcing the
Creek warriors to retreat.[28]

After the August attacks, the Fat King, a Lower Creek
headman, sent a message to Galphin warning him of a possible full-scale Creek invasion of Georgia. Galphin immediately notified the Continentals. Colonel Samuel Elbert put the
Continental establishment in Georgia on a full defensive
footing by canceling all military leaves and calling a complete
muster of all personnel. He then ordered the 1st Battalion
Georgia Continental Infantry to the Ceded Lands immediately, and the Savannah detachment of Continentals to
Augusta as a reserve. Those troops guarding against incursions from Florida would replace those in Savannah, while he
authorized the arming of prisoners of war for the defense of
the western frontier. A full-scale Creek war was something no
one wanted—Loyalist or Whig.[29]

One way to keep the neutral Creeks from changing allegiance was through supplies. Galphin believed that if he had
a regular supply of goods and provisions for them, not only
would neutral Creeks remain so, but many of the Creeks making the attacks would support the Whig cause. Galphin
already believed that a majority of Creeks did, or at least were
willing to, remain neutral. He even thought that the neutral
Creeks would retaliate against Loyalist settlers for the pro-
British Creeks' attacking the settlers on the Ceded Lands.
Galphin's belief proved accurate, as the Old Tallassee King's
son actually led a war party against West Florida, known as a
haven for Loyalists.[30]

The pro-British Creeks, sensing the growing division in
the Creek Nation, sought allies who could provide a martial
presence. They sent appeals to the Cherokees, asking them to
join in attacks on the western frontier, but the Cherokees did
not hesitate to refuse. The Cherokees of the Valley and Lower
Towns would not even let Creek war parties pass through on
their way to attack the South Carolina frontier. In September,
the peaceful faction of the Valley, Middle, and Lower
Cherokee towns sent a lengthy message to Colonel LeRoy
Hammond and Indian agent Edward Wilkinson at Fort

Rutledge to inform them of their stance and actions. At least the Whigs would not have to be concerned with all the Cherokees.[31]

Before the end of September, Galphin sent a message to one of his staunchest supporters in the Creek Nation, the Tallassee King, asking that he kill Big Fellow, one of the most active pro-British Creek headmen organizing attacks on the Ceded Lands. The Tallassee King advised Galphin that he could not kill Big Fellow, because he "was very much on his guard." Around the first of October, about two hundred warriors had left to attack the Ceded Lands. Also at that time, a party of Cussitas had just returned from an excursion against Loyalists toward Pensacola. The Fat King had received a message Galphin had sent and immediately took some of his warriors to Pensacola. On their way there, they killed three Loyalists, cut them up, and hung them in the trees, sending a clear message. A British trader demanded the Fat King return his horses, but the latter told him they would not get the horses back until the pro-British Creeks stopped attacking the frontier. They then went to the Okmulgee River and laid ambushes for returning pro-British Creek warriors.[32]

In mid-October, the pro-British Creeks resumed their attacks on the Ceded Land settlements. Shortly thereafter, Galphin sent two of his men into the Creek Nation. Galphin's agents went to Cussita and spoke with those sympathizing with the Americans. They told the Cussitas that the French and Spanish had allied themselves with the Americans, and it would merely be a matter of time before they captured Pensacola and Saint Augustine. Many Creeks from Parachuckla, the Halfway House, and Tallassee went to meet Galphin at Old Town, led by the Smoke King and the Tallassee King. In light of the news about France and Spain and the closing of the gulf ports, a Lower Creek named Alligator decided to go to Havana, Cuba, and meet with the Spanish. He sought confirmation that they would return to the Gulf of Mexico (which they left after giving Florida to the British under the 1763 Treaty of Paris), and, if so, he also sought an alliance between them and the Creek Nation. While Alligator was in Havana, a group of Tuckabatchees and fifteen Cowetas attacked the frontier. After other groups of

pro-British Creeks attacked the frontier, the Whigs constructed Fort Oconee on the Upper Path.[33]

Despite the attacks on Loyalists, pro-British Creeks and
their Chickamauga allies continued to attack the Georgia
frontier on the Ceded Lands. In early November, some
Chickamaugas attacked Fort Nail again, inflicting a casualty
and capturing a small boy. In the Creek Nation, one of
Galphin's traders, Patrick Carr, heard rumors that the pro-
British Creeks might even attack Old Town, and he warned
Galphin. About one hundred neutral Creeks had gone there
to receive goods and supplies. If the pro-British Creeks did
attack, civil war would certainly erupt among the Creeks.[34]

Such a war would be a welcome turn of events for the
Whigs, especially with a British army bearing down on the
south. Southern Whig leadership had received intelligence of
a British army numbering some two thousand five hundred
that would sail from New York City for Georgia. If the
Creeks mobilized on a grand scale and a British army landed,
the southern states could not defend themselves against both.
They had to prevent a "general Creek Indian war" in any way
they could. If that meant facilitating civil war among the
Creeks, so be it.[35]

Patrick Carr told Galphin, "I believe if they are supplied
with goods till we are ready to come against them with an
army, that we will find a large body of them to back us." If the
Whigs could send goods, the neutralists would stand fast with
the Americans, even to a civil war; if an American army went
into Creek territory (as it had done to the Cherokees in
1776), many Creeks would join it against the pro-British
Creeks. Lower Creek headman Patuey Mico even asked
Galphin to send a Whig army into the Creek Nation—at
least then they would have peace, he thought. To prove Creek
sincerity, Patuey Mico reminded Galphin that he had been
among the delegation that went to Charleston on a peace
mission the previous year. Also, Stuart had sent a British flag
for them to fly over their town, but he threw it away.[36]

Surely the actions of the neutral Creeks proved their wor-
thiness of being supplied by Galphin. The Fat King appealed
to Galphin's sense of responsibility, pointing out that because
they had taken such an overt stance in favor of the Americans,

they would not have the ammunition to defend themselves if the Americans did not supply them. When Galphin inquired about their visit to Pensacola, they replied that they had been to see Stuart in Pensacola, but only reluctantly and only after they had repeatedly refused to go. Their sole reason for going to Pensacola was to obtain ammunition, which Galphin could not supply. Now, however, they needed more supplies, so about a dozen went to Old Town. They did not ask for much, the Fat King reassured Galphin, even if all they received was "an old blanket to cover ourselves now it is cold." But they again needed ammunition, and other goods, if he had them. Fortunately for them, a Spanish merchant ship made port in Savannah toward the end of November, and Galphin could meet their needs.[37]

Only one month later, Lieutenant Colonel Archibald Campbell and over three thousand British troops arrived off the coast of Savannah. On January 3, 1779, the British captured the lightly defended capital city in a flanking maneuver. Brigadier General Augustine Prévost marched north from Saint Augustine with two thousand troops and arrived in Savannah a couple of weeks later. By mid-January, over five thousand British troops occupied Savannah. The southern theater became the focus of the American Revolution in North America, and the worst fears of Whigs throughout Georgia and South Carolina had been realized. From that moment, they would be forced to wage a two-front war.[38]

TEN

The Two-Front War

1779

By the beginning of January 1779, numerous attacks by the Chickamaugas prompted Virginia governor Patrick Henry to authorize an expedition against the Chickamauga towns. He ordered Colonel Evan Shelby to raise a militia force of three hundred for the expedition. As Shelby organized the militia, he had it construct boats to float the entire force down the Tennessee River to the Chickamauga towns in the spring. Henry then wrote North Carolina governor Caswell, asking for that state to augment the expedition with two hundred militiamen. In early spring, the expedition would float down the Holston River from Fort Patrick Henry to the Chickamauga towns and destroy them. Henry reasoned that with a British army recently landed in Savannah, the frontiers would only become more of a battleground. Perhaps an attack on the Chickamauga towns would stem the wave of violence.

According to the plan, after the destruction of the Chickamauga towns, part of the Virginia militia, under Lieutenant Colonel John Montgomery, would join Colonel George Rogers Clark in the Illinois country as a reinforcement, while the remainder returned to the Overmountain settlements. Clark had previously suggested such a twofold operation. For the next couple of months, militia from North

Carolina and Virginia gathered at the Long Island in the Holston, engaged in constructing canoes and pirogues.[1]

While those preparations were being made, James Robertson and a handful of other Holston frontier settlers ventured overland to an area on the Cumberland River in middle Tennessee near present-day Nashville. Rather than encroach upon the Overhill Cherokees (for whom he had been the Virginia agent) like so many others, he decided to escape the increasingly crowded conditions of the Holston settlements by going west. Besides, the Cumberland lands had supposedly already been bought from the Cherokees as part of the Henderson Purchase in 1775. Further, to anyone's knowledge at the time, the region contained no American Indian towns. Robertson and his party of intrepid settlers intended to plant a crop of corn so that other settlers could be brought to the area during the fall harvest season. The abundant hunting would provide meat for all the settlers the first year.[2]

About the end of January, British superintendent John Stuart and his deputies finally received news of Lieutenant Colonel Archibald Campbell's presence in Georgia and Lord Germain's orders to raise Cherokee and Creek warriors to join the British army. David Taitt had been in Pensacola, and Stuart issued him his written instructions. Two days later, Taitt set out for the Creek Nation, sending out calls to all headmen and warriors to return to their towns. On February 9, the few headmen who had returned set February 24 as the day for all to assemble, and March 7 as the day the war parties would leave to join Campbell. Too ill to make the journey and go on an active campaign, Stuart sent a message to the headmen with Taitt. Stuart told them that the time they had all been waiting for had finally arrived: a British army was in the southern theater. However, Stuart still did not know the precise time of the anticipated British invasion of the interior, so his directions regarding when to mobilize remained vague. He did not know that Campbell had already advanced as far as Augusta, arriving there on February 1, and there awaited the war parties.[3]

While Campbell advanced toward Augusta, he intercepted a letter from Galphin to the Creeks that the British commander interpreted as a call to attack the British. No doubt Galphin asked the neutral Creeks who had already attacked Loyalists in West Florida to become active against Campbell. Another letter from Galphin got through to the pro-American Creek towns, however. To counter Galphin's letter, Campbell sent a message to the pro-British Creeks, notifying them of his arrival in Augusta and telling them he greatly anticipated their arrival.[4]

On February 3, Campbell received a letter from the inhabitants of Wilkes County, Georgia, offering to surrender several of the forts they had constructed, either because they felt secure with the presence of regular British troops or they did not want any confrontations. He immediately ordered out eighty mounted Loyalists under two captains named Hamilton and Campbell to take possession of the forts. He also sent a response to the Wilkes County settlers, offering them the king's protection and saying he desired nothing but for them to continue their daily pursuits rather than joining Whig militias and opposing him. Those who could not pledge their allegiance to the king had twenty-four hours to depart the country. This led to a precipitate flight of Whig-leaning settlers across the Savannah River into South Carolina.[5]

A few days later, Andrew Pickens, now a colonel, arrived at the Savannah River with part of his South Carolina militia regiment, amounting to about three hundred men, and met Colonels John Dooley and Elijah Clarke, who had about one hundred Georgia militiamen. The next morning, Captain Hamilton arrived at the river opposite the Whig militia on the west bank and started looking for an unguarded crossing point. After two days of searching, he withdrew from the riverbank. Realizing that Hamilton had withdrawn entirely from the area, Pickens crossed the river throughout the night of February 10 and pursued the small British force.[6]

Hamilton had withdrawn to Heard's Fort, but upon arriving there, Pickens discovered that Hamilton had just withdrawn to Carr's Fort, some twelve miles away. Pickens ordered two men on horseback to Carr's Fort so they could arrive before Hamilton and have the settlers there close and bar the fort gate. The two men did not arrive first, and

Hamilton arrived to secure Carr's Fort. But Pickens caught up with the rear of his column, and the action became general. The Whigs managed to position a few men in a structure near the fort whose marksmanship proved "annoying" to the British. Pickens issued a summons for surrender, which Hamilton refused. He further declined to release the women and children in the fort. Lacking artillery, Pickens prepared to set fire to the fort after dark. In the evening dusk, the Whigs received intelligence that Colonel James Boyd and seven hundred Loyalists were approaching the Savannah River. "There was no time then to be lost" for the Whigs to prevent Boyd from joining Campbell, according to Pickens. He ordered the wounded to be removed, and after a council of war, had a line of fires started just on the top of a ridge directly opposite the fort to make it appear as if the besiegers had encamped for the night. They then mounted and made for the Savannah River. But they were not in time to prevent Boyd from crossing. It took two days for them to catch up to the Loyalists, whom they dispersed near Kettle Creek in a sharp engagement.[7]

British military commanders and administration officials did not understand that all Indian warriors would be out hunting during the winter and would not be available to fight. Campbell did understand that he had advanced too far from Savannah without support from Boyd's Loyalist militia or the warriors. Campbell was also too far away for Brigadier General Augustine Prévost, who had come up to Savannah from Saint Augustine, to support him. Facing a gathering host of Whig militia across the Savannah River, and with Boyd's forces having been defeated, Campbell began withdrawing back to Savannah on Valentine's Day. Although disgusted by the failure of Creeks to support him, he did send them a message. He told them he had to retreat but would send another army to meet them when they got to Augusta. No doubt Campbell felt as Governor Peter Chester of West Florida articulated to Germain some months earlier, "after the great expenses which it has cost this Government in supporting these Savages, . . . they cannot be depended upon."[8]

After regrouping and refitting on the South Carolina side of the river, Pickens recrossed to attack a small party of Loyalists reported to be about thirty-five miles from Augusta.

Near Wrightsborough, Pickens learned of a large Creek war party, some seven hundred or eight hundred strong, on the Ogeechee River about twenty-five miles to the north. Though the Creek warriors did not number quite so many, they still outnumbered Pickens's force. Besides, Pickens knew the Cherokees and Chickamaugas might mobilize and could soon be in the field.[9]

Matters grew worse for the Whigs as Pickens's apprehensions came true. Some of the Cherokees agreed to participate in the all-out offensive and join the British army in Georgia. They met British agents Walter Scott and John McDonald at Selacoa in mid-March. Then word arrived of a Whig expedition making preparations at the Long Island, and the Cherokees' enthusiasm began to wane out of fear that their towns would be destroyed in their absence. Scott impressed on McDonald the need to bring all the warriors he could muster to join the British army in Georgia. McDonald could not leave the towns defenseless, nor could he disobey orders, so in early April he left seventy-five warriors in the towns under the direction of Judd's Friend and led seventy-five more warriors with a few Loyalists south to the Creek town of the Standing Peachtree. In the meantime, word of casualties stemming from a Whig attack on a war party near Seneca reached Selacoa, convincing its warriors to revenge them before joining the British army. Left with no other alternative, Scott sent runners to meet McDonald at the Standing Peachtree, on the path from Selacoa to Augusta, while he continued with his group of warriors to the Seneca area.[10]

As Scott gathered warriors to head south, Taitt had already gathered some four hundred to five hundred Creeks and led them to join Campbell in Augusta. This is the Creek force Pickens had heard about as he neared Wrightsborough. The Creeks arrived at Fulsom's Fort in the Ceded Lands and prepared to attack the stockade but found it deserted. Learning of Taitt's large band, Andrew Williamson, who had recently been promoted to brigadier general in the South Carolina militia, ordered colonels LeRoy Hammond, Pickens, and Dooley to attack the Creeks and prevent them from joining Campbell. He also sent Lieutenant Colonel Joseph Kershaw and Colonel John Twiggs with about two hundred men to either make a show of force against or attack Hammond's flank and hopefully meet Taitt in a decisive action.[11]

Taitt and his force reached Fulsom's Fort but found it deserted. They proceeded to Roger's Fort but found it deserted as well. After burning the stockade on March 24, the large group decided to break up into smaller war parties. Some set off toward Seneca to seek their revenge, while many returned to their towns, and a party of seventy or eighty went on with Taitt to Savannah. Hammond and Pickens caught up with Taitt and attacked at 10:00 a.m. the next day, killing several warriors and taking some Loyalists prisoners.[12]

When Hammond and his command returned to Williamson's camp on March 30, British trader Wilson Scott, along with the Raven and a headman named Calegishu, left Citico with fifteen warriors. A few Loyalists and a half dozen Cohutta warriors joined Scott soon thereafter, followed by Young Turkey of Turropine, Oconostota's son Terrapin, and seventy-five warriors. Within a few days, Tukewee and Little Bird led Cherokee warriors from Ustanaula, Toqua, and Cusawahlahie south. Some Loyalists and a large number of Chickamauga warriors joined them on their march to connect with Scott and then the British.[13]

Tukewee spoke for all those warriors who followed him south, for the fourth time they had been called upon to assist the British, when he said, "I am glad the King puts it in my People's power to revenge the injuries done us by the Rebels. I have but a few with me and the Rebels are many but I am resolved to give them battle where I shall find them." He had been waiting a long time for British troops to actually be in the southern theater so they could have direct military support. Many of his followers, like himself, worried about the Whigs attacking their towns in their absence as they had done many times before, but they now could look to British troops keeping them "busy at home."[14]

Simultaneously, a large group of warriors from Great Hiwassee and Chistowee went to join McDonald at the Standing Peachtree on the Ocmulge River. There they would be supplied before moving on to attack the Georgia frontier. Though previously peaceful, both the Raven and Old Tassel had been to see McDonald. Oconostota gave his son,

Terrapin, the medal given him by the British years ago. Wearing it meant Terrapin supported the British and would wage war against the Americans. Once returned from their expeditions against the Georgia frontier, the Cherokees would all go to meet with Cameron, from whom they could obtain more supplies and goods for future attacks.[15]

By the time the British agents mobilized the Cherokees, Chickamaugas, and Creeks, Colonel Evan Shelby's men had completed construction of all the boats needed to transport them down the Tennessee River. After securing the necessary provisions, they set off on April 10 for the Chickamauga towns. The flotilla slipped down the river all the way to the Chickamauga River on the spring flood waters. At the mouth of the Chickamauga, the flotilla secured a prisoner and forced him to be their guide. The Chickamaugas lived in several towns along the river, with the main town stretching along the banks for about a mile. When Shelby's force attacked Chickamauga, Judd's Friend and the seventy-five warriors left in the town by McDonald offered a stiff resistance to the surprise attack, buying enough time for the evacuation of the women, children, and elderly. Shelby's force burned all the buildings in Chickamauga and surrounding towns, destroyed twenty thousand bushels of corn, and confiscated a large amount of hides, pelts, horses, cattle, gunpowder, and lead— the military quartermaster's supplies for the Chickamaugas. Even though Shelby did not inflict severe casualties on the Chickamaugas because of their absence, he rendered them militarily impotent until they could resupply.[16]

Shelby's expedition did not deter the pro-British Creeks from attacking the frontier. By the first of May, war parties from Tuckasegee and Cussada went to seek revenge for the deaths near Seneca in South Carolina. A few days later, warriors from Little Tallassee, the Hillabies, and the Alabamons also went. Jacob Moneac, a British agent in Little Tallassee, distributed shirts, knives, and paint to the warriors heading to Seneca. Meanwhile, neutral Creek headmen Opaya Hadjo and Phiamingo led a party of warriors against Loyalists along the road to Pensacola. Moneac tried to prevent them from going by telling them smallpox had broken out in that area, but they went anyway; they were not to be dissuaded.[17]

Evidently, Shelby prevailed on Oconostota to send a message to the Chickamaugas after his devastating raid on their towns, saying the Whigs wanted the outlying Cherokees to relocate into the established Cherokee towns they had left. This, no doubt, was to make them more susceptible to attack. In May the Chickamaugas replied, explaining why they could not immediately relocate: some of their headmen had not returned from hunting, and they had planted some corn. When the headmen had returned, and they had harvested their corn and made bread, they would move back to their old towns. They made it a point to ask that Governor Henry also read their message; the Chickamaugas did not want to be the targets of another expedition.[18]

The Raven and Hanging Maw went to Fort Patrick Henry and met with Colonel Shelby and Major Joseph Martin. They asked for goods of "ammunition, paint, and other necessaries" as a reward for their not having joined the Chickamaugas. Knowing that Virginia did not have many trade goods, they hoped Governor Henry would give them special attention, because the goods they had thus far received from the state were "not half sufficient." Besides, they had no other means of supply except the British, who continually tempted them with goods, but Hanging Maw said the Cherokees refused to trade with the British. As further evidence of the Cherokees' good faith, the Raven said he would go to the "Norward Indians" on a peace mission.[19]

Shelby passed along to Henry their professions of peace and their pleas for goods. Shelby believed that his expedition against the Chickamaugas had awed the old Cherokee towns and that his attack had forced the British traders among the Cherokee towns to leave. It now seemed that the Cherokees could become truly dependent on Virginia for supplies, and Shelby recognized the opportunity to establish their dependency on the Whigs. Shelby asked Henry to procure whatever goods he could for the Cherokees. He did not include the Chickamaugas. Throughout the ensuing months, Henry gave directions to various state entities to provide them with goods.[20]

The Chickamaugas sent yet another message to Shelby on May 22, reiterating that as soon as they had harvested their corn and made bread, they would relocate to the old towns. They explained that they would not have seceded in the first place had not the British agents insidiously persuaded them to leave their traditional towns. Now they could not stress strongly enough their urgent need for salt and ammunition, and they vowed to return within the fold of the Cherokee Nation. But their emphatic and seemingly genuine pleas only echoed empty promises: the Chickamaugas did not relocate to the old towns. Because the Americans did not keep their promises to prevent encroachment, the Chickamaugas no doubt felt justified being duplicitous in their diplomacy.[21]

The settlers of the Kentucky lands also decided to exercise an offensive strategy. Their having been on the defensive for the past few years had not convinced militant Indians to relent in their attacks. In May 1779, Colonel John Bowman assembled a force to invade the Shawnee territory. Bowman targeted their main town, Chillicothe, in his surprise attack, and the Shawnee abandoned the town. In the attack, the primary chief, Blackfish, received a mortal wound. The Kentuckians tarried too long, however, and the Shawnees rallied to counterattack, forcing Bowman to retreat. Casualties were slight on both sides, but the action did persuade the Shawnees to relocate farther up the Mad River. [22]

Shortly after Bowman's ill-fated expedition to Chillicothe, a delegation of Cherokee headmen made the arduous trek north to the Ohio country and the home of the Delawares. The Raven led a delegation of fourteen Cherokee warriors to Lichtenau, ostensibly to pay their respects to their leader, Coquehagechton, or White Eyes, in the wake of his untimely death. A "councellor" met the Cherokees a mile outside the town to perform cleansing and healing ceremonies after their long journey. After resting, they continued the next day. When they reached the town, they discharged their firearms to announce their arrival. The warriors of Lichtenau discharged a volley in return, then began singing and escorted the visitors to the longhouse, which had been built especially for their reception. The Cherokee and Delaware warriors, as well as an envoy of the Wabash and other northern tribes, spent the balance of the day in the longhouse, observing periods of silent remembrance punctuated by speeches by the Raven and Gelelemend.[23]

In his speech, the Raven noted the visit by a delegation of northern and western tribes to the Cherokees in early 1776. He remembered how the Cherokees attacked the southern frontiers during the summer that year as the delegation had requested even though they were outnumbered by the white settlers. The Cherokees bore the retaliation of the punitive expeditions and lost not only their towns but their crops as well. Still, despite all that tragedy, he stood before them "to convince you that we have not thrown away your talk" and to prove his point, he produced four strands of wampum that the delegation had given to the Cherokees in 1776.[24]

The Cherokees and northern Indians evidently engaged in some duplicity of their own against the whites. A white observer did not know of the meeting where the Raven reaffirmed the Cherokee alliance with the northern tribes. Instead, the white observer recorded that the Cherokees met with the Delaware headmen on "business relating to national concerns," resulting in an agreement that the two would not participate in the war. Evidently, the observer attended an altogether separate meeting. Then the Cherokee delegation, including two women, exchanged various articles that each had made indicative of their respective cultures, including tobacco pipe bowls and baskets. The Cherokee delegation then proceeded to Fort Pitt.[25]

At Fort Pitt, the Cherokees met with the commandant of the post, Colonel Daniel Brodhead, whom they called Maghingwekeeshuch. On the first day of talks, the Raven told Brodhead that the Cherokees were friends with the Whigs to the south and there was an open line of communication that maintained the peace between Virginia and the Overhill Towns. The agent who issued their passports also attested in writing to the "Amity subsisting between the Cherokee nation and the Americans." The next day, the Raven stated that the Cherokees had at one time been on a similar footing with the British, but he sounded like a true rebel when he added, "thank God now that I have freedom of Speech with my American Brethren." Astonishingly, the Raven then told

Brodhead that he spoke for the entire nation—Oconostota would no longer act as the spokesman for the Cherokees.[26]

Brodhead congratulated the Cherokees for rejecting the British in favor of the Americans. Those Indians who had chosen to fight against the Americans, like the Cherokees years earlier, felt the retribution. The Delawares resisted attacking the Americans, and because the Raven declared a similar intention of the Cherokees, he desired they enter into a formal peace accord as their "grandfathers" had done. The Raven and the other headmen and leading warriors of the Cherokees then agreed to a formal peace treaty with the Americans at Fort Pitt.[27]

Meanwhile, far to the south, Cameron advised General Prévost that he would mobilize as many warriors as he could and lead them against the frontiers. He only had to wait for the corn to be harvested and made into bread. Unfortunately for Cameron, Colonel Williamson and the Whigs received intelligence regarding Cameron's plans and activities. Williamson decided to preempt the British agent's offensive and mobilized upward of seven hundred militiamen at Fort Rutledge in early August. By mid-August, he had marched his force to Beaver Dam Creek in the Ceded Lands. On August 25, the Mankiller came into Williamson's camp and informed him that the Terrapin and nine others had arrived at Chota the day before and knew of Williamson's approach. They had pushed on for Estanore, a town on the Tugaloo River, to advise Cameron of the Whig force.[28]

In response, Williamson dispatched about forty horsemen to try to run down Cameron; they returned about noon with the Terrapin and his nephew as prisoners. The next day, Williamson marched his force to Soquee, which he burned along with all the cornfields. He ordered Colonel Pickens to lead 160 men to capture a couple of British traders known to supply the Chickamaugas, but they had fled into the mountains. Williamson then marched his column to Estanore in an effort to capture Cameron, but he, too, had fled into the surrounding countryside. The Whigs laid the torch to Estanore and five other towns, along with all the cornfields and stores they could find.[29]

On August 28, two Chickamauga headmen, the Wolf and Good Warrior, entered Williamson's camp to negotiate an end to the expedition. Williamson said that for him to end the destruction of their towns, they would have to move back to their old Cherokee towns. Eventually the two headmen consented and agreed to meet with him at Seneca upon his return. With that, Williamson slowly returned to Seneca in mid-September.[30]

Not to be deterred, Cameron sent runners out to have all the Chickamaugas gather. The board of Indian commissioners directed Cameron to mobilize as many of the Indians as he could. The sting of Williamson's expedition and attempt to capture him also surely prompted Cameron to act. With hundreds of warriors on their way, Cameron purchased about three hundred bushels of corn and instructed the traders to mill it into flour. He then made other preparations to be completed by September 25, when they would all march to Savannah. Then Cameron left the Cherokees and went to the Hillabies. Arriving on September 9, he found the Creeks had grown weary of the war, preferring to hunt bear. In addition, smallpox had hit several towns, and many Creeks had fled. Those pro-British warriors who did not flee would be ready to leave by the first of November. Some Creeks had gone to attack Fulsom's Fort in the Ceded Lands even before Williamson had returned to Seneca.[31]

On the coast of Georgia, French and American forces converged outside Savannah in an effort to recapture the capital city. Though the French forces under Jean Baptiste Charles Henri Hector, the Comte d'Estaing, could not tarry in Georgia for more than six weeks, the allies began to lay siege lines outside the city. But not having enough time for a formal siege, after a brief bombardment, the allies launched an assault. The motley British force behind the defensive works of Savannah repelled the attackers. By mid-October, the allied forces had quit the siege of Savannah, opening the way for further British conquest of the south.

By this time, James Robertson had arrived back at the Holston settlements and aided in the preparations for the journey back to the new settlements along the Cumberland River. Some of the emigrants prepared to go overland, guided by Robertson, while others had been constructing boats to float down the Tennessee River to the Muscle Shoals. There they would meet Robertson and a party from the Cumberland. Surveyor and settler John Donelson would lead the flotilla of emigrants down the river.

The overland route was a circuitous, winding way over the Wilderness Road through the Cumberland Gap, up to stations in Kentucky (some ventured as far north as Lexington), then southwest until passing Kilgore's Station on the Red River northwest of the French Lick, or the Bluffs on the Cumberland River. The expedition began in early November and included some two hundred emigrants. Captain John Rains brought along his herd of cattle. By then "the hard winter" of 1779–1780 had set in, making the trek extremely arduous. Fortunately for the settlers, they did not experience any attacks by Indians, but the "extraordinary severity" of the inclement weather created great hardship. By mid-December, all the emigrants with Robertson had reached the north bank of the Cumberland River. The emigrants crossed over the frozen river—an indication of the intensity of the weather—and tradition has it that Captain Rains drove his cattle across on Christmas Day 1779. On New Year's Day, the last of the caravan crossed the river safely at Fort Nashborough (present-day Nashville, Tennessee). Donelson's flotilla had been detained by a frozen Tennessee River and would not arrive until the next spring.[32]

ELEVEN

The Changing Tides of War

1780

A s 1780 began, the Whigs' new allies, France and Spain, began operations in the southern theater. These operations had the salutary effect of drawing some American Indian forces away from the frontiers. Unfortunately for the Whigs, the distraction did not last long and did not affect all the frontiers. In January 1780, France and Spain sent a combined force against the British at Mobile, West Florida. By mid-March, the British defenders had surrendered the Gulf Coast port. The most logical next step for the Spanish would have been Pensacola, the only other port of any consequence on the Gulf Coast, but British reinforcements there deterred the Spanish invasion force then being prepared in Mobile. Additionally, over one thousand pro-British Creek warriors went to the aid of Pensacola by May, stalling the Spanish attack for several months.[1]

Colonel Williamson and his South Carolina militia occupied Augusta in the wake of Lieutenant Colonel Archibald Campbell's withdrawal from the town, and with the British-aligned Creek warriors down in West Florida, they passed a relatively undisturbed spring on the Georgia frontier. With no

Spanish attack in the offing, and the Creek warriors becoming unmanageable due to the lack of action, the British commander of Pensacola, Major General John Campbell dismissed them to avoid problems and minimize his expenses.[2]

Other pro-British American Indian allies, most likely Chickamaugas and Chickasaws, focused their attention on the settlements in the newly established Cumberland region of present-day Middle Tennessee. They had discovered the settlements by the spring, probably because of the passage of the Donelson party down the Tennessee River once it had thawed. In response, the Indian raiding and hunting parties began regular attacks on the scattered settlements throughout the spring. When settlers tended their fields, they always placed a rifleman in an elevated, strategic location to give sufficient warning. Though constantly vigilant, individuals still were killed during the course of their daily chores. At the beginning of the season there were about 250 settlers along the Cumberland, but that number dwindled as casualties mounted.[3]

As a result of the Indian attacks, the Cumberland settlers constructed forts, or stockades, during the spring since they had completed their individual dwellings. In a general meeting, they decided that the primary fort should be constructed at the Bluffs, or the French Lick, and other, smaller posts at the settlements known as Freeland's, Eaton's, Kasper's, Asher's, Bledsoe's, Donelson's, and Fort Union. The main fort at the Bluffs, named Fort Nashborough, consisted of the traditional frontier fort palisade that encompassed about two acres and twenty cabins. It had blockhouses in each corner and two gates.[4]

As the Chickasaws and Chickamaugas attacked the Cumberland settlements, on the other side of this two-front war, the British had landed an invasion force in South Carolina and laid siege to the largest city in the south, Charleston. When the revolutionaries surrendered that city on May 12, 1780, the entire nature of the struggle changed radically. The outlook for the war along the southern frontier looked bleak for revolutionaries as it did throughout the south.

After the capture of Charleston, the British commander of North America, General Sir Henry Clinton, offered lenient terms to those Whig militiamen who surrendered to British authorities, gave up their weapons, and returned to their homes. With the surrender of the largest city in the south, many Whig militiamen throughout the region came in to take the oath of allegiance to the British Crown. That left the entire region open to occupation by British troops, and posts at Ninety-Six, South Carolina, and Augusta, Georgia, were quickly established. The newly appointed British superintendant for Indian affairs for the southern colonies, Colonel Thomas Brown, occupied Augusta with several hundred troops the first week of June.[5]

Brown lost no time in establishing communications with the Cherokees and Creeks, his primary responsibility. He gave notice to all settlers on the southern frontier below the lines established by treaties before the Revolution to remove themselves by the end of June or face the vengeance of Indian warriors. He then asked the British commander of the southern theater, General Lord Cornwallis, for authorization to order the Cherokees and Creeks to drive off the settlers in force. Brown's predecessor, John Stuart, had always been too timid about checking settler encroachment because he realized colonial officials would not act against British subjects in favor of American Indians. Brown knew he would ingratiate the Indians solidly to the British war effort with official directives for them to reclaim their lands from settlers and British support of their actions. Further, "from the distressed miserable condition of near 700 families" he expected some one thousand two hundred warriors, women, and children to arrive in Augusta in three to four weeks hoping for Brown to sustain them, since they still had no crops. In addition, some one thousand four hundred Creek warriors had recently returned from Pensacola.[6]

Brown realized that Augusta served as the gateway to the backcountry because it had served as the main supply point for the Cherokees and Creeks. The primary trading paths led from Augusta to the Lower and Upper Creek towns, as well as into Cherokee territory. The British occupation of Augusta now meant that trading could be done much closer to the Cherokees and Creeks than Pensacola. Brown wanted to gain friendship and alliance with them to show that it would be in their best interests to ally themselves with the British and to show a clear difference from when the Whigs controlled the backcountry.[7]

Cornwallis, however, did not share Brown's views on the southern American Indians. In fact, he could see no use for them at all for the present and ordered Brown to placate them without mobilizing them. Cornwallis expressed to Brown his belief that perhaps the boundary issue could be better dealt with when the British had completely consolidated the province. As if to confirm his views, Cornwallis had received a report from General Campbell in Pensacola about the great expense of providing for the Creek warriors until their departure just before an expected attack by the Spanish. Worse, Cornwallis had received reports that some of the Creeks had visited the Spanish commander, Brigadier General Don Bernardo de Galvez.[8]

Cornwallis did order the destruction of Fort Rutledge. Built by General Williamson at the Seneca town site, it had secured that part of the frontier in northwestern South Carolina. In the intervening years, it had served as a base of operations for the Whigs against the Lower Cherokees, now scattered throughout northeastern Georgia and the northwestern corner of South Carolina. Evidently, its Whig garrison abandoned the post without even removing the military stores there. A company of King's Rangers that Brown sent to occupy the post took possession of ammunition and artillery. No doubt the British destruction of Fort Rutledge met with the approbation of the Cherokees, as it represented "a standing insult" to them, according to one historian. In August, Whig hegemony over the region was broken with the demolition of the fort and the occupation of Ninety-Six.[9]

Meanwhile, uncertainty and apprehension prevailed among the Cumberland settlements. With the combined Chickasaw-Chickamauga attacks continuing through the summer, residents in the scattered settlements began to gather and consolidate themselves. The outlying settlers along the Red River, some forty-five miles northwest of Fort Nashborough, decided to abandon their homesteads for the safety of friends and family at Freeland's or Eaton's stations. They gathered after loading what they could and headed south, but after making camp the first night several decided to return and retrieve some of their belongings they had hastily left behind. The next night an Indian war party attacked those who had gone back, killing all but one, a Mrs. Jones, who miraculously escaped and made her way on foot to Eaton's Station. By the end of the summer, only Eaton's Station and Fort Nashborough had any sizable population, though there may have been a few inhabitants still at Freeland's and Mansker's.[10]

Chickamauga attacks had become so frequent by June that Virginia governor Thomas Jefferson issued orders that began the preparations for a punitive expedition against the Indian towns. He authorized Colonel Arthur Campbell to raise 150 militiamen from Washington County and 100 from Montgomery County. Jefferson also ordered enough gunpowder and lead for the intended strike. The governor then notified North Carolina of his intentions and invited that state to send a militia force in conjunction with Virginia's. He made it clear to Campbell, however, to take "great care that no injury be done to the friendly part of the [Cherokee] nation." He stressed that the Cherokees had the pledge of Virginia for their protection and that Campbell, therefore, should not cooperate with the Carolinians against them. A week later, Jefferson again stressed the point to Campbell, saying, "Take great care to distinguish the friendly from the hostile part of the Cherokee nation, and to protect the former while you severely punish the latter."[11]

The need for concern about attacking friendly Cherokees stemmed from Colonel Campbell's having communicated with North Carolina militia commanders about the expedition. Their response conveyed a distinct desire to attack the friendly Cherokees to secure more land instead of punishing those responsible for attacks on the frontiers. Jefferson, informed of the North Carolina militia's intent by Campbell, wrote to the newly elected North Carolina governor, Abner Nash, to caution against such action, which would only make matters worse and was, he said, unjust. Then Jefferson stated bluntly that Virginia would not participate in such action.[12]

After the fall of Charleston, the Continental Congress sent General Horatio Gates to form another Southern

Continental Army. In mid-August 1780, Gates led his force south and ran into the main British field army, led by Cornwallis. The British defeated the Continentals at the Battle of Camden, in South Carolina, driving the Whig militia from the field. In the wake of such a stupendous victory, Cornwallis readied British forces to begin the reconquest of the southern provinces.

The surrender of most of the Whig militias made Cornwallis's planned offensive possible because there would be no threat to his rear. With the British solidly in control of the Georgia and South Carolina backcountry, the new British superintendent of Indian affairs, Thomas Brown, called a conference of Cherokees and Creeks. He intended to mobilize them to occupy the attention of those few Whigs who had not capitulated and keep them from attacking Cornwallis.[13]

Georgia militia Colonel Elijah Clarke was one Whig who had not surrendered, and he began rallying others who had not taken the oath of allegiance to the Crown. He spent the next several months moving between the Ceded Lands and the South Carolina backcountry, attacking British troops whenever the opportunity presented itself. Then, after a couple of skirmishes in South Carolina, he gathered several hundred Whig militiamen and headed for Augusta. Clarke learned of the conference Brown called with Cherokee and Creek headmen and knew that hundreds of Cherokees and Creeks would gather there. He also knew that a large supply of goods had been sent to Augusta for Brown to distribute among them. Only one thing could come from such a meeting: Cherokees and Creeks would be supplied by the British and then attack the Georgia frontier. If Clarke could break up the conference and capture the goods, perhaps he could prevent the impending attacks.[14]

Sometime during the second week of September, Clarke crossed the Savannah River into the Ceded Lands of Georgia. In South Carolina, Lieutenant Colonel James McCall recruited for Clarke's attack on Augusta. In the Ceded Lands, Clarke recruited more with threats than anything else. Those able-bodied men who did not join him would be put to the sword. The British paroled the Whig militiamen who had surrendered, which meant they had sworn an oath to not bear arms against the Crown again. As a result, McCall could only raise about eighty men; when added to Clarke's force, there were around five hundred troops.[15]

Early on the morning of September 14, Clarke attacked the Creek encampment some three miles west of Augusta. By 9:00 a.m. Brown received information of Clarke's attack, gathered his force, consisting of about three hundred troops with two field pieces, and marched to the Creek encampment. Upon his arrival, he received intelligence that Clarke had marched around his force and entered Augusta on the Savannah road at his rear. Brown then immediately counter-marched back to Augusta, joined by about three hundred Creek warriors.[16]

By the time Brown arrived back in Augusta, Clarke had already attacked the guard at the former site of Mackay's Trading Post by the Savannah River. Brown formed his men in an old field to the left of the road on Garden Hill, west of the trading post site, anchoring the line on each end with a field piece. Clarke immediately attacked Garden Hill, but the British line held, with the Creeks on the left performing like European soldiers, maintaining their position on the left of the British line. Although the Whigs captured one of the field pieces, Brown had the other brought up to Garden Hill when the action became intense. Eventually, the Whigs retreated. Brown then thought it advisable to take up a position at the houses. Just as he positioned his forces, the Whigs opened fire; the ensuing firefight lasted two hours. At about 1:00 p.m., the Whigs broke off the engagement and went into Augusta to secure all the plunder. The scene remained quiet for the rest of the night.[17]

The next day, the British began digging entrenchments, and around noon they learned that the Whigs had made their headquarters at Grierson's fort, about a mile and a half east of Mackay's former trading post, where they busily mounted cannon. At 1:00 p.m., about fifty Cherokees appeared on the north bank of the river and crossed over safely, joining Brown at the houses. As soon as they deployed among the defenders, the Whigs advanced. The Whigs brought into action two artillery pieces, and the engagement became general.[18]

During the day, Clarke had earthworks dug so that no more than one hundred yards separated the Whigs and British. Clarke had the British and Creeks surrounded to the point that they could not even procure water. Occasionally, some of the warriors would sally out from the British position, attack the Whig militia, and return with scalps. Both sides continually fired at each other as the operation settled into a veritable siege, and throughout the next couple of days, a stalemate ruled.[19]

On the evening of September 17, Clarke sent a summons to surrender under a flag of truce; Brown replied that he would defend his position to the last man. He also warned Clarke of the destruction his actions would bring on the Ceded Lands. When communications between the two commanders ended, firing commenced; it continued for about an hour and became sporadic throughout the night.[20]

Before daybreak of the eighteenth, the Whigs initiated the engagement again, and the firing became general until the fog cleared. The arrival of Lieutenant Colonel John Harris Cruger from Ninety-Six with British reinforcements to relieve Brown forced Clarke to lift his siege and withdraw his men north into the Ceded Lands.[21]

At first, Cruger received information that Clarke had crossed the Savannah River with only one hundred of his men. Then, on September 20, Cruger learned that Clarke had actually gone into the Ceded Lands to gather the many Whigs residing there. Cruger began to pursue Clarke while he dispatched one hundred Loyalist militia to march north up the Wrightsborough road to cover his left flank. That day, Clarke crossed the Broad River, which put him out of Cruger's immediate reach. Cruger arrived at Colonel Dooley's house, forty-five miles north of Augusta, on September 23 and crossed the Broad River two days later. Afterwards, he learned that Clarke and the Whig refugees had crossed the Savannah River at Cherokee Ford two days before.[22]

Though Cruger did not overtake Clarke, he used the opportunity to "settle all the Ceded Lands business." This he did with ruthless efficiency. Not everyone in the Ceded Lands had Whig tendencies, and those who did not he formed into Loyalist militia units. During his pursuit, Cruger sent forward the Cherokees and Creeks who had helped defend Augusta to perform a dual function. First, they sent back accurate information on Clarke's movements. Second, they attacked the rear of Clarke's group at every opportunity. In their wake, Cruger burned courthouse, forts, and the homes of Whig leaders. By the end of the month, Cruger had recruited over one hundred militiamen. With Loyalist militias to enforce British authority over the southern territory, regular British troops would be free to reconquer the southern provinces on their way north. The Whitehall strategy of conquering the south and organizing Loyalist militias seemed to be working.[23]

Before Colonel Campbell could mount his expedition against the Chickamaugas, a larger and more dangerous threat developed. Lord Cornwallis ordered Major Patrick Ferguson to raise Loyalist militias in the western part of the Carolinas to help guard the left flank of his main column as the British army advanced into central North Carolina. Ferguson learned that small units of Overmountain militia had participated in recent engagements against the British. He now issued them an ultimatum: desist from opposing the British; if not, he would march his army of about one thousand troops over the mountains, "hang their leaders, and lay their country waste with fire and sword." The Overmountain militias decided not to wait for Ferguson. They assembled, marched over the mountains, surrounded Ferguson, and annihilated his force at the Battle of Kings Mountain.

After that, Cornwallis directed the Cherokees to attack the frontier to weaken the Whigs arrayed against him. The British commander surmised such attacks would result in the Overmountain militias returning to defend the frontier. Evidently, Ferguson's defeat completely changed Cornwallis's mind about not employing southern American Indians.[24]

Superintendent Brown now instructed the Indians as he had wanted to back in the summer: to make a widespread offensive against all the settlers in order to reclaim the areas they had lost since 1775. He gave the Indians a speech designed to motivate them militarily and even designated "the

Raven as the principle chief of the Nation and received the customary medal and was received by the warriors in room of [in place of] Oconostota." They had been told to kill all the American traders and that they would be compensated for all prisoners and livestock.25

By December, the "Distress of the frontier Inhabitants" had become quite apparent to Virginia's Cherokee agent, Joseph Martin. Because they had not yet arrived, he was unable to deliver the letters and medals sent by Governor Jefferson to the Cherokee headmen signifying their recognition as men of leadership. Cherokee warriors had begun their offensive against the frontier settlements, some led by the Raven himself. Campbell could not advise Jefferson whether the attacks would continue through the winter, but "from every circumstance a war with them seems inevitable."26

Campbell's prediction stemmed from the news that Brown, in Augusta, had made a treaty with the Cherokees, giving them back their lands "if they would conquer" them. He also learned that the Raven vowed to reclaim the lands by force of arms and never be driven off again. The Cherokees already threatened the American traders in their towns, who later escaped with the assistance of Nancy Ward, the Beloved Woman of Chota, and others. Campbell received a letter from Clarke describing how he and the Whigs had been driven out of the Ceded Lands in Georgia. Brigadier General Edward Stevens in Charlottesville also believed a war with the Cherokees was inevitable. Campbell ordered his militia to muster at the Block House in Carter's Valley on the Kentucky Path.27

In early December, Colonel John Sevier called out the Washington County militia. About three hundred men gathered, armed with rifles and providing their own mounts. They assembled at Long Creek (in present-day Jefferson County, Tennessee) and began their expedition the next day before dawn. The advance scouts exchanged shots with a group of about seventy warriors on the south side of the French Broad River. After crossing that river at Buckingham's Island, Sevier encamped for the evening.28

Early the next morning, December 16, Sevier reached Boyd's Creek and located the camp of the Cherokee warriors they had encountered the previous day. The warriors had withdrawn before Sevier's advance, and he suspected an ambush, the favorite tactic of Cherokee warriors. Sevier decided to prepare his own and instructed his scouts to make contact with the warriors, then fall back to the abandoned Cherokee camp. Then Sevier divided his force into three divisions: a right wing under Major Jonathan Tipton; the center, which Sevier commanded; and a left wing under Major Jesse Walton. When the scouts fell back they would lure the warriors onto the center division, which would engage them at close range. Then the wings would fall on the center and trap the entire Cherokee force.[29]

As planned, the militia scouts encountered the warriors, exchanged some shots, and promptly fell back. The Cherokees gave chase, and when they came into point-blank range, Sevier's command rose up from hiding and delivered a withering fire. Walton's men immediately charged forward, closing off the left flank. But for some inexplicable reason, Tipton did not move with haste, and the stunned Cherokees were able to retreat through the gap in the lines. They fled into a swamp and then scattered. If the official report can be trusted, the Cherokees suffered thirteen killed while the militiamen incurred no casualties.[30] In their flight, the Cherokees dropped much of their personal baggage. Among the captured items the militiamen found a collection of letters, treaties, and commissions from previous years.

His force not being of sufficient strength to continue, Sevier returned to Buckingham's Island in the French Broad River and encamped there for the next week. While awaiting Colonel Arthur Campbell's force from Virginia, Sevier's supplies ran out and the troops resorted to living on hickory nuts, walnuts, and wild grapes. On December 22, Campbell crossed the French Broad River with his force and joined Sevier, where the Virginians shared their scant supply of provisions with Sevier's men. Sevier handed over the collection of papers they had retrieved from the Cherokees. Campbell believed Oconostota had carried the papers and dubbed them the "Archives of the [Cherokee] nation." Since many originated from British authors, it confirmed in Campbell's mind "the double game that People [the Cherokees] have been carrying on, during the present War." At that point, it seems, Campbell no longer made any effort to use restraint in his dealings with the Cherokees, whether in war or in peace.[31]

The next day the combined force made a quick march toward the Tennessee River. Having intelligence that the Cherokees had obstructed the usual fords of the river and positioned warriors at them to oppose the crossing, Campbell knew their immediate security lay in passing the entire command to the south bank.[32]

On Christmas Eve morning, Campbell made a feint toward the Great Island Town (Dragging Canoe's town), lowermost on the river, and with the main body crossed at Tomotley without resistance. The Cherokees detected the crossing and withdrew from their positions on the river. Campbell divided his force and sent one part to the towns farther south, while Campbell led the other part of the army toward Chota. As the militiamen passed a canyon above Toqua, they noticed the Cherokees in force along the hills below Chota. The Cherokees seemed about to attack the advance of the column, which had just come into their view, but the main body then appeared, and the Cherokees decided not to attack. Soon the column entered Chota and found much needed provisions.[33]

Campbell dispatched Major Joseph Martin on Christmas Day to discover the Cherokee route of withdrawal. Martin caught up with a small group and dispersed them; the remainder seemed to be heading toward Tellico and the Hiwassee River. Campbell detached about sixty Virginian militiamen to burn Chilhowee. The Virginians burned that part of the town on the south side of the river but came under attack by a larger force of warriors, compelling them to withdraw.[34]

The following day Campbell sent 150 mounted Carolina militiamen to cross the river and force the Cherokees to retreat, then to occupy and destroy Tallassee. Colonel Christian and 150 infantry crossed the river and burned the rest of Chilhowee and inflicted a few casualties, taking nine prisoners. The mounted militia failed to cross the river, and it took two days to accomplish the crossing, during which time

Nancy Ward, Beloved Woman of Chota, entered Campbell's camp. She informed him that the headmen desired peace, but Campbell said he intended to destroy the towns whose warriors had made the frontier attacks, primarily the towns of Hiwasee and Chistowee.[35]

The militiamen spent December 28 burning Chota, Citigo, and Little Tuskegee, after which the entire column moved to Kaiatee on the Tellico River. There Campbell intended to establish a post as a magazine for provisions and a rally point in case of a forced retreat. That evening skirmishes broke out around the town. The next day Campbell left Christian with 150 troops as a garrison and marched the rest toward Great Hiwassee, about forty miles away.[36]

Campbell found the town abandoned when he arrived there on December 30. In the vicinity, his men captured a young warrior who told them that a force of warriors, Loyalists, and the British trader John McDonald awaited them at Chistowee, about twelve miles away. Campbell knew the Cherokees were keeping them under surveillance, so he had the men encamp and kindle campfires. Sometime after 6:00 p.m., Campbell led about three hundred troops out of the camp and crossed the river by the light of a full moon. Marching toward Chistowee, they arrived early on the morning of December 31 and found yet another deserted town. The inhabitants had also taken with them most of their provisions, utensils, furniture, and even some of their livestock. The Whigs had previously found corn and other provisions in the towns, but now there had been enough time for residents to remove their stored harvests.[37]

Campbell realized all the towns they encountered from then on would be deserted and they would find no provisions. The scarcity of provisions and the fact that the North Carolinians refused to go any farther than Chistowee forced Campbell to end the expedition. He sent Major Martin with a part of the troops through Satogo and other towns along the Tellico River. They first entered the ruins of Chota the night of January 1. The next day about two hundred mounted militiamen entered Chilhowee and came under fire while burning the town. They then went down the river to Tellico, where a part went to destroy Chestoa.[38]

In the course of their route, Martin learned through prisoners taken that several headmen had met some days previously to discuss approaching Campbell for a peace conference. In Kaiatee, Campbell felt satisfied with the destruction
his expedition had carried out and wrote a letter to the headmen, essentially rebuking them for all the recent attacks—the
cause of his expedition. He invited them to a peace conference
at the Long Island within two months, and said any
Cherokees who did not support a war against the Whigs
could move to the vicinity of the island, where the Whigs
would sustain them. If they did not respond, it would be
understood that the Cherokees maintained their hostile
stance, and another expedition would enter their country—
this time to hold and occupy their lands. In fact, Campbell
suggested to Governor Jefferson that the peace he proposed
be made on the basis of acquiring land from the Cherokees
that would then be sold and the proceeds used to pay for the
expedition. Prior to finding the Cherokee archives, this would
have been quite uncharacteristic of Campbell.[39]

Although the combined militia force once again did not
bring the entire Cherokee force to battle, as it had desired, it
did destroy Chota, Citigo, Chilhowee, Toqua, Great Island
Town, Kaiatee, Satogo, Tellico, Great Hiwassee, and
Chistowee—with a total of around one thousand dwellings—
an estimated fifty thousand bushels of corn, "and large quantities of other kinds of Provisions" after the Whig force sustained itself from the confiscated foodstuffs.[40]

While Campbell led his militia force down into the
Cherokee Overhill Towns, warriors attacked settlers in
Powell's Valley and travelers on the Kentucky Path near the
Cumberland Gap. Evidently the militias of Botetourt and
Montgomery counties responded too slowly to repel the
attackers. On Campbell's return, his militia ran into one of
the marauding parties and recaptured a number of horses.[41]

Though the Whigs believed the Campbell-Sevier expedition would have a salutary effect on the Cherokees, its useful-
ness was dubious at best. During the entire expedition and
into the next year, raiding parties from Chilhowee continued
their attacks along the Holston River and into Powell's Valley.
As had frequently been the case recently, their objectives

included the capture of every horse within their reach. Even the previously amenable John Watts, nephew of Old Tassel, led a party of warriors from Toqua against the settlers. Watts would soon become a leader among the Chickamaugas.[42]

TWELVE

Winning Battles

1781

Soon after Colonels Arthur Campbell and John Sevier returned to the Overmountain settlements from their expedition, Captain James Robertson arrived back at the Bluffs with desperately needed ammunition. His return from Kentucky on January 15, 1781, proved fortuitous. After staying only briefly at Fort Nashborough, he continued on to join his family at Freeland's Station. The reunion lasted into the night, and Robertson issued the portion of ammunition he had brought. Around midnight, a distinct noise aroused Robertson. He looked out into the stockade compound to see intruders in the moonlight. Grabbing his rifle, Robertson yelled an alarm, and the firing began. At Robertson's alarm, a Major Lucas ran out of the blockhouse that he and Robertson occupied, only to be immediately shot down. The firing became general, and the party of warriors retreated from within the compound but hovered around the palisade walls, exchanging shots with the defenders.[1]

The battle must have aroused the settlers in Fort Nashborough, because the defenders of Freeland's Station heard the reassuring report of the swivel gun there. The warriors knew the signal meant reinforcements would arrive soon, and they ended the assault. Shortly thereafter, a small party from Nashborough arrived at Freeland's, bringing a little ammunition left by Robertson the day before. The warriors also received reinforcements and stayed in the area, destroying what cabins and livestock they could.[2]

Just two days later, on January 17, Continental General Daniel Morgan dealt the British a stunning defeat at the Battle of Cowpens near the South Carolina–North Carolina border. Morgan then quickly rejoined the new Continental commander, General Nathanael Greene, in North Carolina, and the whole force began withdrawing north. This led Lord Cornwallis to decide to pursue the Continentals and abandon South Carolina except for a small British force to garrison the outposts in the state. The strain of waging a two-front war now greatly diminished for the Whigs.

Stoked by the "archives" that proved Cherokee duplicity, Campbell continued to prepare for his war against the Cherokees. He instructed Major Joseph Martin, at Long Island, to construct a permanent storage facility for provisions, arms, equipment, and ammunition at Fort Patrick Henry. Obviously, Campbell intended to make further expeditions into the Cherokee Nation, and he wasted no time in making preparations.[3]

Campbell then proposed to the commissioner of the Virginia War Office the construction of a fort at the confluence of the Tennessee and Holston rivers. In his professional opinion, it should be garrisoned by regular troops, not militia, who would provide a permanent defensive force. He had three reasons for building a fortification in such a forward position, especially in relation to the most recent land cession by the Cherokees: it would "give us possession of that part of the Nation that is conquered and may be ceded to us," it would "keep the Cherokees always at our mercy," and it would enable the Whigs to prevent British agents and traders from residing among the Cherokees. It would also provide a good position from which to launch future expeditions.[4]

The apprehensions over further Cherokee attacks seemed well founded. Almost upon Campbell's return to Virginia, American Indians (thought to be Cherokees, but later proved to be Shawnees led by Captain Benjamin Logan) attacked Blackmore's Fort in Powell's Valley. They killed one and captured four militiamen besides taking a number of horses. The attack prompted Campbell to raise a company of militia, half mounted, to guard and patrol the area before warriors made the Kentucky Path impassable. Campbell strongly requested that Jefferson approve a permanent garrison in Powell's Valley and on the Tennessee River (which would require building a fort).[5]

In the midst of all the martial activity, about a dozen Cherokees voluntarily came to Joseph Martin's dwelling on Long Island to reside there. They had assisted the Whigs before, and Martin believed they would in the future. These Cherokees did not have any sympathies for the British, as some Loyalists had begun moving into their towns. Hanging Maw announced in open council his disdain for the British and supported his declaration with the statement that he would move with his entire town to live among the whites. Unfortunately, frontiersmen killed the two runners he sent to discuss the matter, but Martin believed that Hanging Maw could still be persuaded.[6]

Because of the January attack on Blackmore's Fort and other Indian activity in that sector, no frontier militia would be going to reinforce General Greene in the low country. Campbell not only raised a company of militia to patrol Powell's Valley but also more militia to safeguard travelers on the Kentucky Path and settlers in the area. Since frontier militia turned out with alacrity to meet the Indian offensive, Campbell could not understand why more militia did not turn out in the low country with an enemy in their midst. Governor Jefferson, however, argued that it would not matter what happened along the frontier if they lost the war in the east. Strategically, Jefferson made a compelling argument, but not a very practical one for a settler with a wife and children on the frontier subject to sudden and violent attack.[7]

Having done what he could to assist Greene, Jefferson pursued measures that would weaken the Cherokees and place Virginia on a firmer footing in preparation for future expeditions. He authorized Campbell to hold a peace conference with the Cherokees if he thought he could. Jefferson approved of obtaining land at the confluence of the Tennessee and Holston rivers to build a fort and the construction of a fort in Powell's Valley. Jefferson also approved the expenditure for the militia that he put on active duty. In essence, Jefferson acceded to all that Campbell had done and suggested. Then Jefferson authorized Joseph Martin, who also acted as the state's Cherokee agent, to make a peace with the Cherokees and entice as many of them onto Virginia land as possible to further weaken them.[8]

Finally, Campbell wrote to General Greene. He reasoned that since the peace conference would mediate a peace on the frontier for an "American Interest," then it fell within the purview of the Continental Congress. Therefore, the commissioners for such a conference should be chosen by the commander of the Southern Continental Army. Greene subsequently appointed Colonels Campbell, Christian, and Preston, as well as Major Martin from Virginia as commissioners. To represent North Carolina, Greene appointed Lieutenant Colonel Robert Lanier, Colonel Shelby, Williams, and Colonel Sevier. Besides working in the best interest of America, they would be guided by the laws of their respective states. The purposes of the conference, as delineated by Greene, included the suspension of hostilities, the exchange of prisoners, and "the adjustment of limits of each party"—that is, boundaries.[9]

Greene no doubt hoped for a peace along the southern frontier so that those militias could then reinforce him in the east. Unfortunately for the Revolutionary cause, peace did not prevail. Continued attacks claimed more settlers' lives and livestock, producing "daily apprehensions of attacks from the Northward and Southern Indians." Campbell still blamed British agents and traders among the Cherokees and strongly urged that if the Cherokee towns could be destroyed, "it would hardly then be worth while for our enemies to employ an Agent to reside among them, to excite them to mischief." Rather than mount an expedition, Campbell raised two companies of militia for duty in Powell's Valley. Over the next four months, they engaged warriors in several actions and guarded the Kentucky Path.[10]

Farther south in Georgia, Colonel Clarke had a fort built on the Oconee River northwest of the settlements in the Ceded Lands and ordered a militia company stationed as the garrison. In one series of attacks, Indian warriors captured two women at Scott's Fort. By the time Clarke ordered his militia to pursue the band, it had covered twenty miles. Nonetheless, the militia overtook the raiding party at the Standing Peachtree during the night. The militia achieved complete surprise and succeeded in rescuing the captives along with capturing a number of warriors.[11]

By spring 1781, the punitive expedition prevailed as the favorite tactic of the Whigs against hostile warriors. Colonel Sevier led an expedition of about 150 Watauga militiamen down into the Middle Towns in mid-March. He destroyed three major towns and several other outlying, scattered towns. Casualty estimates ranged from twenty killed and fifteen captured to thirty killed and nine captured. When they returned to the Overmountain settlements, Colonel Campbell instructed Major Martin "to drive off the Indians from their haunts near Cumberland Gap." Martin began raising about two hundred militiamen from Washington and Sullivan counties in Virginia. He planned to depart on April 1 for the Cumberland Mountains south of Cumberland Gap. They had received intelligence that warriors from various tribes relocated to that region to mount operations against the communications and settlements on either side of the mountain range. Martin hoped to eliminate this new threat to the Kentucky Road.[12]

Even as he made preparations for his expedition, Governor Jefferson charged Martin, along with Preston and Christian, with investigating the Cherokee complaint of encroachments made below the boundary established at the 1777 treaty. Though Jefferson had not heard of the complaints previously, the state legislature assured him that any settlers found south of the boundary would be removed.[13]

With Cornwallis in full pursuit of General Greene in the wake of the Battle of Cowpens, the southern Continental commander abandoned South Carolina to lure Cornwallis away from the state. Cornwallis did not catch up with the Continentals in his headlong effort to chase down Greene. The subsequent Battle of Guilford Courthouse on March 15, 1781, resulted in a Pyrrhic victory for Cornwallis and led to his decision to abandon the Carolinas for Virginia. This left

Greene free to reconquer South Carolina and Georgia, elim-
inating those states as sources of supply for the Cherokees,
Chickamaugas, and Creeks warring against the Americans.
Just a week before the Battle of Guilford Courthouse the
Spanish had finally begun their assault on the last British bastion in the Gulf of Mexico, Pensacola. The arrival of the
Spanish to besiege Pensacola meant the end of that port as a
supply point for the Cherokees and Creeks. Before long, those
Indians continuing to wage war against the Americans would
have to make the very long trek to Saint Augustine for sup-
plies and ammunition.

The Chickamaugas, Chickasaws, Choctaws, and Creeks
did not go to aid the British at Pensacola, because of their
previous treatment by the British, and they had a more immediate concern. In the spring, the Chickasaws and their allies
realized their attacks on the Cumberland settlements had
taken their toll. Settlers only remained in a few of them, and
their continued existence seemed tenuous. No doubt one final
all-out assault would spell the end to all settlements in what
is now Middle Tennessee, and it was not long in coming, in
what would be known as the Battle of the Bluffs.

The following account of the April 2, 1781, battle is based
solely on the journal of John Cotten. He wrote the description immediately after the action, and it remains the most
detailed, descriptive account of an engagement during the
American Revolution on the southern frontier. Cotten had
kept a journal since leaving North Carolina for the frontier
right after the collapse of the Regulator Movement in 1771.
Cotten does not seem prone to exaggeration or embellish-
ment in the journal. Even his biases seem mild in tone for the
age in which he lived. For these reasons, historians give much
credence to the accuracy of his account of the Battle of the
Bluffs. Cotten is candid and poignant as he describes the
absolute terror, comedy, tragedy, pathos, and even compassion
of combat in rapid succession—the far-ranging swings in
mood and perspective that individuals often experience during such episodes. The range of emotion is only accomplished
in the journal through the graphic nature of his descriptions,
and they are therefore included.

At the beginning of April 1781, the palisaded stockade of Fort Nashborough enclosed about two acres, which meant it could accommodate not only all the settlers in the area but livestock also. Unlike most frontier forts of the era, Fort Nashborough contained a large spring and therefore did not have to depend upon a water source beyond the protection of the stockade. A lookout tower with walls and a roof sat atop a large double gate. Another platform boasted a swivel gun. Walking platforms encircled the stockade at such a height that a person could stand on them and fire a weapon over the top of the wall.[14]

Sometime before about 2:00 a.m. on April 2, the sentry on duty in the watchtower discharged his rifle, arousing everyone in the fort. Five men who had been selected to guard the big double gate rushed to it with rifles in hand. James Robertson and several other militia officers rushed to the tower, whereupon the sentry pointed out where he had seen a warrior. After several minutes, and with no indication of any other activity, Robertson had everyone who had responded to the sentry's signal return to their chambers for the night. After changing the watchtower sentry, the gate guard and Robertson sat up contemplating the likelihood of an attack at daylight. John Cotten said it best when he wrote, "It has appeared, the day we have feared."

As expected, shortly after sunrise two shots rang out at some distance, and the sentry in the fort fired his rifle. At this everyone within the fort arose, and Robertson and a few others went up the sentry tower. Two warriors in full paint could be seen loading and firing at the fort from far out of range. One of the defenders returned fire, and when it fell far short, the warriors began to laugh and make gestures toward the fort. That only served to incite "Young Leiper," one of the settlers at the Bluff, into the rash act of mounting a party to go after the two. Robertson, Cotten, and some of the other more experienced men realized the foolhardiness of such action; the warriors merely wanted to lure out a mounted party into an ambush. Their wise counsel did not prevail, however, but the impetuous volunteers did allow Robertson to select the members of the pursuit party. They sallied out of the fort gate, Robertson in the lead and Cotten among them, toward the warriors, who vanished into the woods at the sight of the mounted troop.

Leiper dashed off after the fleeing warriors, and Robertson frantically called after him, to no avail. The rest of the party galloped after Leiper and through the woods until they were within a few yards of Cane Creek. At that point, some twenty warriors rose up in the cane beside the creek and fired a volley into the mounted party, which miraculously only emptied one saddle. Dismounting and firing simultaneously, the frontiersmen dropped several of the warriors. Just when Leiper imprudently "cried that victory was ours," Cotten relates that, "across the Creek such a multitude of warriors rose up out of the cane, I was hard put to keep from fleeing; at the least there were 300 of them, and they let go such a firing that the bark on both sides of my tree was cut off." The volley took its toll on the dismounted party, which returned fire as best it could. Then Cotten heard gunfire in their rear.

Crawling back to the clearing to investigate the source of the gunfire, Cotten could not believe what he saw:

> When I reached the edge of the wood I was astonished to see a vast multitude of Indians before the Fort, at the edge of the clearing, but even then advancing slowly toward the stockade. Their line ran nigh to the top of the bluff on which we had built our cabins, and down the slope nearly to the place where I lay concealed in the bushes, and the clearing was filled to overflowing with such a mass of Indians as I have never seen assembled in one place together. How many hundreds I do not know, but the sight struck terror to my heart.

The assaulting force had not only cut off the mounted party from the fort but also isolated the fort itself. Cotten crawled back to tell Robertson what he had seen, and after witnessing the situation himself, Robertson called for a general withdrawal from Cane Creek, "and at the edge of the wood we surveyed the scene with despair."

"Young Leiper, who had been so bold and eager to lead us into this foolhardy adventure, turned white as milk and said, 'Dear God.'" They were cut off from the fort in the midst of hundreds of warriors and could not help defend their families in the fort. At that point, all seemed helpless and hopeless. Just then there arose such a loud noise from the direction of the river that Cotten and company thought the several hundred warriors had crossed the creek and found them. Instead, "it was our horses that had been sent off in the brush when we dismounted, which came charging out of the cane in a herd, screaming and snorting as if possessed. Their charge carried them through the Indian's ranks, knocking a dozen of them over as if they had been corn stalks, after which the animals turned sharply to the left, striking another section of our enemy's line and knocking down another dozen or more." The animals then darted to the right and disappeared into the woods going toward the river. At least twenty warriors lay on the ground, and about a hundred took off running after the horses to secure them.

"Johny Donelson seized my arm in great excitement and pointed to the wide gap opened by their departure, and Jamie [James Robertson] told us that each man would have to try to get to the stockade on his own and with the Lord's help. We commenced running, using what shelter we could in the clearing, which was not much, and to add speed to our heels, the Indians who had been on the Creek came out of the woods directly behind us." Cotten tried to load his rifle as he ran, but he confessed that he had never become very good at it.[15]

Cotten much preferred his sword, a mark of his militia captaincy back in North Carolina, and he displayed great skill in its use. "Casper Mansker stumbled and fell on his hands and I feared he was killed, but he got his feet and found refuge behind a fallen tree, with naught worse than a ball that had pierced his lower leg. An Indian came over the rock which was my sanctuary and I spitted him on my sword, at which he screamed in such a manner I wish I had not heard."[16]

The small party suffered many wounds, and hand-to-hand struggles occurred in quick succession. Each member sought to cover the others with his rifle fire as all did their best to sprint toward the fort gate. Cotten described it as "a continuous battle all the time," and the more they fought and attempted to make their way to the fort, the more warriors would leave the main assault on the fort and attack the small party. Cotten and the others had given up all hope of reaching the safety of the fort and resigned themselves to being overwhelmed "when the Fort gate was opened and a ravening horde of dogs ran out and flew at the throats of the Indians. These were our dogs, but I had never known them to be savage."

The original settlers had brought some dogs with them, and through natural reproduction the canine population had grown so much that

> we scarce knew what to do with them, the most of them had been worthless, lazy, and not given to harm; yet they were mad now and tore the flesh of the Indians as if they had never been gentler beasts.[17] Such a sight has never been witnessed, for the confusion and noise is beyond words, men and beastes rolling together in the grass, screams of pain and cries of fear, blood flowing from torn throats, arms, and legs. One Indian nigh knocked me down in his flight from a large dog that had fastened his teeth in his buttocks; he never saw me and I had no time to strike afore both vanished in the cane, the dog hanging on in spite of the man's effort to undo him. Johny Donelson killed an Indian with the barrell of his gun who had his privates all torn out by a raging dog, yet it was an act of mercy, for the poor savage was thrashing about on the ground in mortal agony.... [T]he dog then turned on Johny and he must needs beat it to death.

In such a cacophony of noise, terror, confusion, and fear, Cotten confessed, "I was so taken by the happenings round me I had nigh forgot our purpose was to get back to the Fort, untill Peter Looney seized me by the arm and pulled me after him as our men made a run for the stockade, but the way was not easy for the Indians were not yet done with us in spite of the dogs. I cut off the heads of two with my sword and never stopt running." Cotten and several others had almost reached the fort gate and were still being attacked by warriors, who had to be shot by those inside the stockade.

Leiper had made it to within about twenty paces of the gate, running stooped over, when a shot passed through his body and made a terrible exit wound "that revealed his entrails as though a window had been opened. It was a pitiable sight to see the poor lad standing on his feet, his two hands grasping his belly to prevent his innards from falling out, and an expression of absolute astonishment on his face. He neither cried out nor fell, but stood stock still, the blood . . . gushing out betwixt his fingers." Cotten grabbed Leiper just before he collapsed and dragged him the rest of the way to the fort gate. Cotten had to stab a warrior in the breast who had attempted to take Leiper's scalp. The fort defenders fired as often as they could, but the close quarters and hand-to-hand struggles precluded a rapid fire to stem the waves of warriors attacking the small party. After several more desperate encounters with warriors, Cotten got Leiper into the fort with the help of a few men from inside.

As the warriors continued the attack, Cotten and the other survivors of the pursuit party took their places on the palisade walls. By now the defenders had devised a system that allowed almost continuous firing by having some on the palisade firing line and others reloading for them. All of the party that went out had made it back—or so Cotten thought.

"Upon looking out I saw George Aspie and Edward Swanson were yet outside the Fort." Just as Cotten saw the two men, Aspie took a bullet in his breast and fell as a warrior immediately moved to scalp him. Aspie rolled over onto his back, lifted his rifle up between his knees, and shot the fast-approaching warrior. He then arose and sprinted toward the gate, taking another shot in his shoulder just before being pulled inside the fort.

Swanson had almost reached the gate by then, "when an Indian of great sise overtook him, [and] put the mouth of his rifle against Swanson's back, but it misfired, whereupon he turned and seized the rifle, over which the twain strove mightily." Locked in a death grip, the two struggled frantically for control of the rifle. No one fired from the fort for fear of hitting Swanson, who fell on his knees and received a blow from the butt of the rifle, which the warrior now controlled. As he raised his tomahawk to finish Swanson, John Buchanan, a member of the garrison, ran out of the fort gate and fired his rifle at the warrior, wounding him in the abdomen. At that point, several shots rang out from the fort palisade and struck the warrior, who fell over dead. Buchanan then helped Swanson inside the fort.

With all the militiamen still alive now back inside the fort, some sort of commotion at the edge of the clearing to the south of the fort attracted the defenders' attention. It appeared to be a white man crawling on his stomach in the direction of the fort. Three or four warriors noticed him and ran toward him, but the crawling man reached the cover of a large rock. He managed to shoot and reload quickly enough to drop them all, the last one nearly falling on him. Finally, someone in the fort recognized the man and called out for all to hear, "It is Isaac Lucas." His blood-covered right leg explained his ability to only crawl, and his plight was obvious: either one of the garrison would rescue him, or he would die.

To the vehement protests of his wife and friends around him, Cotten told Robertson that he would go rescue Lucas. Cotten reasoned that the rescue could only be accomplished with a sword because he would probably be swarmed by warriors before he returned and a single-shot weapon would not be of much benefit. Because he was the only one with a sword and the only one trained to use it, he was the logical choice. He said a constant covering fire from the fort would ensure success for the venture. All took their places, and Cotten slipped out of the fort as stealthily as he could.

> Outside was a terrible din, what with firing and the dogs and the screams, and every where were corpses of Indians and dogs. . . . I got to Lucas without trouble and learned his thigh had been broken by a ball during the attack at Cane Creek and the poor man had crawled all that distance forgotten by his friends. Afore I got Lucas to his feet, an Indian got through the heavy firing in some manner and fired at us but missed, whereupon I seized Lucas's gun and shot him down, then with left arm supporting Lucas on his sound leg, on which he hopped, we made our way back to the Fort.

Some warriors noticed the two and apparently dashed toward them, but Cotten brandished his sword. The warriors probably had seen him in action with the weapon earlier, or what it could do in the hands of a skilled person, and did not press their attack. After getting inside the fort, Cotten took a place on the firing line on the palisade wall. The battle remained general for a short while afterward. Several of the defenders wanted to bring the swivel gun into play, but Robertson rejected the idea because it required so much gunpowder. Shortly thereafter, the entire assaulting party withdrew at about 10 o'clock in the morning.

Though the firing had ceased, the noise had been so great that Cotten's ears rang. The garrison remained in position for about a half an hour after the assault ended. Then Robertson relieved most of the defenders, who took a well deserved respite. "By what miracle we have won this engagement I know not, for the Indians surely at the least numbered a thousand, while our poor force can not be more than three hundred and a half."

Nothing happened for the remainder of the day. As evening approached, rain began to fall. About an hour after dark, a group of eight sallied forth from the fort to reclaim the dead. The instant the group emerged from the fort, warriors fired on them from the woods. The group returned fire and hastily withdrew inside the fort. The garrison suspected the attackers had not all left the area.

Around midnight a group of warriors appeared at the edge of the clearing on the south side of the fort. They fired a few shots and yelled as their numbers grew. The garrison concluded that they had received reinforcements and another large battle loomed. With ammunition running low, they concluded that another battle such as the day before would not end in their victory again. Many determined to fire the swivel gun, while Robertson and others hesitated because it required so much gunpowder and lead. The democratic process prevailed, and all contributed some powder. The piece was loaded with spare iron—and even small rocks. Although the fine mist of rain made firing the gun difficult, when it did discharge, the gathering warriors fled precipitously, leaving their casualties. No more incidents occurred that night, and the rain stopped.

Evidently the single shot from the swivel persuaded the attackers to withdraw completely, even if they had been reinforced. Scouts sent out by the garrison the next morning confirmed the entire force had left the area. They also brought back the intelligence that the force had been composed of both Chickamauga and Chickasaw warriors. After the scouts returned, the garrison retrieved the dead and prepared them for burial, which took place on April 4.

While the Cumberland settlements fought for their survival, the Overmountain leaders sought peace. Even as Joseph Martin prepared for his expedition, he met with Campbell, Shelby, and Sevier to draft a letter to the Cherokees calling for a peace conference per Greene's instructions. They also sent one to the Chickasaws, but that tribe refused to participate as long as the Whigs maintained Fort Jefferson, at the confluence of the Mississippi and Ohio rivers. All of them realized that major obstacles to peace would be the one hundred Cherokee families being supported by the British in Augusta and the continuing encroachments upon Cherokee lands. Christian believed, "The only great Inducement the Indians can have for treating are for us to do them Justice respecting their Land and to subsist their Families this Summer."[18]

Powell's Valley prepared for the anticipated onslaught of Indian attacks, but the Kentucky region of Virginia had taken measures as well. Colonel John Todd (granduncle of Mary Todd Lincoln) wrote Governor Jefferson about the fort at Lexington. Because of the attacks on Ruddle's and Martin's stations in which the combined Indian and British force utilized artillery, the fort was constructed to "make it proof against Swivels and small Artilery which so terrify our people." Constructed as a quadrangle with a bastion in each corner, the fort had one gate and a magazine. Its walls made it capable of withstanding artillery fire, being made "7 feet thick of Rammed Dirt, inclosed with good Timbers 9 feet high only, from 4 feet upwards 5 feet thick — the Top of the Wall is neatly picketed 6 feet High." The age of earthen fortifications had reached the frontiers of North America.[19]

Todd displayed foresight and wisdom in constructing the fortification at Lexington. Since the beginning of 1781,

Kentucky had experienced Indian attacks that claimed forty-seven killed and untold wounded. Garrisons, though spread out among the various forts, did not number enough to protect everyone. Colonel John Floyd, newly commissioned head of the Kentucky militia, estimated it would take fifteen days for everyone to gather in the forts and stations. Floyd's second in command, Major George Slaughter, concurred with Floyd's observations and supported his pleas for assistance in the form of reinforcements.[20]

The strategic paradigm in the southern theater shifted yet again in the spring. With the Spanish besieging Pensacola, the British decided they could not get enough land and naval forces all the way around the Florida Peninsula in time to save it. Realizing that Spain's most logical target after Pensacola would be the capital of East Florida, Saint Augustine, the British decided to bolster that city's forces. Lieutenant Colonel Alured Clarke embarked from Savannah with part of that city's garrison for Saint Augustine. After his departure, Whig militia under Colonel Williamson arrived on April 16 in the vicinity of Augusta. Learning from the previous year's abortive attempt on that city, Andrew Pickens, promoted to general, positioned about four hundred of his militiamen between Augusta and Ninety-Six so that the latter could not rescue Augusta as it had done the year before. This placed the British in a dilemma: they could not reinforce Augusta except at the expense of Saint Augustine or Savannah, the importance of which far outweighed that of the frontier outpost.

On April 20, recently promoted Lieutenant Colonel Joseph Martin returned from his expedition to the south of Cumberland Gap, after being out nineteen days. He had first discovered a large party of Indians in Powell's Valley, but part of his force stumbled into them and they withdrew. In pursuit, Martin discovered a camp that appeared to accommodate one hundred warriors, as well as other nearby trails of smaller parties. All of them seemed to have gone toward the mouth of Powell River. Martin's expedition followed one trail for some thirty miles south of Cumberland Gap but could not overtake the warriors. At one point, his column managed to fire a volley at the rear of the withdrawing warriors.

He led the expedition seventy more miles before encountering problems. The men believed Martin would lead them all the way to the Chickamauga towns, and they did not believe the expedition numbered enough; their fatigued horses and nearly depleted provisions completed the argument for heading back. His men's decision must have been difficult for Martin to accept for several reasons. He had seen fresh blood on surrounding brush, evidently from fresh hunting kills, and signs abounded that many horses had been down that trail recently. All indications were that an actual town—his true objective—lay nearby. If that were not enough, upon the expedition's return, Martin learned of an attack in Powell's Valley while they had been gone. The attack only served to fuel Martin's desire to pursue the trail to the end, so he pleaded for more men and provisions.[21]

Virginia frontier leaders needed to justify the expeditions and frontier patrol duty since they did not send any militia to Greene. They did, however, follow some of Greene's instructions. Messages had been sent to the Cherokees to stop their attacks and hold a peace conference where prisoners could be exchanged. They even invited the Chickasaws. It seemed to disconcert them that Greene believed encroachments served as the impetus for the Cherokee attacks. The Campbell-Sevier expedition in December had recovered documentary evidence that the British instigated the entire affair. With the British as the root cause, and the fact that hundreds of Cherokee families lived off the largesse of the British Crown just outside Augusta, no peace could be achieved on the frontier as long as that town remained in British hands. The implication was that no frontier militia would go to Greene unless the Southern Continental Army captured Augusta.[22]

While Virginia frontier militia leaders pleaded their case to General Greene, Campbell pleaded their case to Governor Jefferson. He reiterated his belief that the Cherokees would never sue for peace while the British maintained control of Augusta. From there, the Cherokees received supplies to wage war, and their families received provisions and goods. To make matters worse, the two-front war strained already scant Whig resources. Campbell wrote to Jefferson, "The Northward Indians have attacked three times this spring with small parties," inflicting numerous casualties and taking prisoners. They had penetrated as far south as the Holston settlements. In light of such circumstances, Campbell begged the governor to rescind his order for them to send their militias east. In fact, he had already ordered one company to patrol Powell's Valley, and he even asked for "some regular means of supplying them." Further, he strongly urged Jefferson to grant Martin's request for men and supplies to finish his expedition.[23]

In fact, not all Cherokees were hostile toward the whites. Oconostota, Hanging Maw, and Old Tassel sent a message to Martin in late April. They begged for peace because they had been forced to live in the woods, subsisting on roots they dug up day to day. They reminded Martin that they had protected him when the British trader McDonald came to Chota with the intention of making him a prisoner. Even Abraham of Chilhowee, a known combatant, hoped that Martin would consider their earnest pleas for peace and assistance. To help persuade Martin, they confessed that they "have been rogues." They also mentioned Oconostota's efforts to persuade them to move back into their old towns, as the Whigs had been pushing for, but they claimed to have no agricultural implements.[24]

Developments elsewhere in the southern theater did not improve the outlook for Britain's American Indian allies. On May 9, 1781, General Campbell surrendered his British garrison of Pensacola. Barely a week later, Colonel Elijah Clarke appeared outside Augusta. Clarke had returned for another attempt on the British post so vital for their communications with the Cherokees and Creeks. Every frontier Whig commander had long realized the importance of capturing Augusta and had let General Greene know it as well. Greene conceded the validity of their arguments and sent Colonel Harry Lee with his cavalry troopers to assist Clarke, who had been joined by General Pickens. Soon after Lee arrived, Fort Galphin fell to the besieging Whig forces, leaving them available to concentrate on British Colonel Thomas Brown, who was holding the city itself.

By the end of May, Sir James Wright, the royal governor of Georgia, could foresee the precarious state he and the capital of Savannah would be in very soon. The capitulation of Augusta seemed only a matter of time, with it being besieged by Whig forces and no troops being available for Brown's assistance. Savannah's garrison had already been weakened by sending a reinforcement to Saint Augustine, which left none to support Brown. Wright, therefore, petitioned the deputy Indian superintendant, Charles Shaw, for muskets held by his department. Wright intended to raise what militia he could from Savannah and its environs.[25] With no relief, Colonel Brown surrendered Augusta and its Fort Cornwallis on June 5 to the combined Whig forces.[26]

While the Whig assault on Augusta progressed, South Carolina militia Colonel Robert Anderson advised General Greene that he had already sent most of his troops to the frontier upon receiving information of Indian attacks. Several settlers had already been killed. But not all Cherokees had taken the offensive against the Whigs. Lieutenant Colonel Robert Lanier of North Carolina had received a message from Cherokees who wanted peace, at the same time the Chickamaugas remained on the offensive. Lanier's patience with dealing with the Cherokee attacks had reached a breaking point and he suggested to Greene that they employ one of the western tribes, from the Illinois region, in their counteroffensive. Lanier believed he could persuade one of their headmen, who had visited him recently, to attack the Cherokees. Plus, he wholeheartedly endorsed Martin's request for troops and supplies to finish his expedition from April.[27]

Colonel Arthur Campbell had not heard of Augusta's capture by the Whigs. All he knew was that by June, the frontier had seen no relief from Indian attacks, and there was very little prospect of sending Greene any troops. By then the division among the Cherokees had become plain enough even to Whig leaders. Campbell received word that British agents, Loyalists, and some Cherokee warriors had been preparing to mount new attacks against the settlements. Simultaneously, he also received information that about three hundred Cherokees had already started their journey to the peace conference.[28]

Though the Whigs had captured Augusta, which could no longer supply Indian assault parties, two groups of Indians and Loyalists (about seventy in one group and one hundred in the other) swept through the Long Canes region of the South Carolina backcountry. Unlike in prior attacks, Loyalists prevented the warriors from attacking women and children. By the time Pickens and his troops arrived in the Long Canes region, the raiding parties had left. Pickens ordered Colonels Anderson and Hammond to each select one hundred men from their regiments to patrol the region and prevent any future attacks.[29]

A month later, Virginia Colonel Isaac Shelby advised Greene he could not send any troops to his assistance for several reasons. Besides the militia needed at the peace conference, many had gone south to join Colonel Clarke in Georgia. Thinking strategically, if the British suffered a reversal in the low country, they would make reprisals in the backcountry. The most pressing reason, however, remained the continued Indian attacks on the frontier. Robert Lanier reiterated his recommendation of Martin's plan to complete his expedition, to which Greene agreed, but only on the condition that it did not detract from sending troops to him.[30]

By the end of July, hundreds of Cherokee warriors had arrived at Lieutenant Colonel Joseph Martin's house on the Long Island. For days, the headmen met with just Martin until Colonels Christian and Sevier arrived on August 1. At the meetings, Old Tassel said that trespassing and encroachments had caused the Cherokee attacks the previous year. He could understand their occurrence, however, since the Whigs failed to have the boundary line agreed upon back in 1777 marked. Settlers would meet Cherokee hunters in the woods and rob them of their possessions. Settlers even went to the towns of Toqua and Chota to steal horses. The Cherokees had protested all of these transgressions to Whig leaders, but the Whigs did nothing to catch the perpetrators or curb the crimes against the Indians. Then in August 1780, Colonel Brown invited the Cherokees to visit him in Augusta. There he supplied them and told them to settle the matter themselves and take back their lands. But the only thing the Cherokee attacks prompted was retaliatory Whig expeditions.[31]

In response to the Cherokee complaints, Sevier and Christian demanded a prisoner exchange in order for there to be any future peace. Sevier even asked the headmen to let the squatters stay until they harvested the corn they had planted. Then, in the winter, Whig leaders would meet with them and rectify all wrongs. Colonel Christian said that there were only a few squatters south of the boundary on Cherokee land and that North Carolina leaders "hate Injustice and Dishonesty," implying they would force the squatters off the land. The headmen must have been perplexed about the intolerance of "Injustice and Dishonesty" that North Carolina leaders possessed. North Carolina officials had not marked the boundary agreed upon in 1777; the goods arrived much later than they had been promised; they allowed settlers south of the boundary; and they allowed the settlers to steal and rob from the Cherokees almost at will. Yet after all these offenses, North Carolina leaders did nothing to stop them.[32]

Not much remained to be said or done. Colonel Christian invited some headmen to visit Philadelphia and meet with the Continental Congress. He spoke to the Cherokee women at the conference regarding the children of both sides growing up in friendship. On August 3, the conference ended, and everyone returned to their homes. Colonel Campbell had hoped that the Cherokees would cede enough land that its sale would pay for the recent expeditions, but it is not apparent that any cession was made, and no traditional treaty document was produced. The 1781 Treaty of Long Island appeared to be just an agreement between the Cherokees and the Whigs not to attack each other.[33] The Cherokees participated no further until the end of the Revolution, though they endured continued encroachments on their lands.[34]

In mid-August, General Pickens ordered the Hammond brothers, colonels Samuel and LeRoy, to meet each other, with their troops, by August 21, at Perkins Mill on the Saluda River. He ordered them on a seek-and-destroy mission to go after Loyalist William Cunningham and any Cherokees attacking the South Carolina frontier. Unlike previous operations, Pickens instructed them all to be "properly mounted." The nature of warfare on the frontier had changed for two primary reasons. Cunningham had mounted his Loyalist troops so that they could surprise Whig forces and be more difficult to trap. Further, surprising Cherokee towns or warriors could only be accomplished through the use of horses. A mounted force could approach with enough speed to possibly go undetected until too late. Pickens did not notify Greene that he had detached part of his brigade, but Greene realized the frontiersmen faced a two-front war. He received information that the Cherokees had attacked some of Colonel Clarke's men guarding the Georgia frontier and inflicted casualties.[35]

The frontier in Virginia seemed relatively quiet in stark contrast to that in South Carolina. The Long Island peace conference seemed to have brought a degree of peace (at least for a while) to the Overmountain region that it had not experienced in some time. Finally, Virginia militia commanders could send their troops to join other Revolutionary forces in the final push to expel the British from the southern theater. Some assisted General Washington in the allied siege of Lord Cornwallis at Yorktown, Virginia, while others joined Greene in South Carolina.[36]

But, as Washington and the general of French forces in the north, the Comte de Rochambeau, closed in upon Cornwallis in Yorktown, the tenuous Overmountain peace began to manifest problems. Though both parties had agreed to an exchange of prisoners, the Cherokees had not yet sent theirs. On September 20, Martin wrote to Campbell that he had gone all the way to Chota for the prisoners and then sent a messenger to the Chickamauga towns. The response Martin received concerning return of the prisoners was "evasive." Martin did learn that some British Chickasaw traders had moved to the Chickamauga towns, though he did not know why. A trader named Scott urged the Chickamaugas to attack the frontier, much more so than did the other traders.[37]

Oconostota discussed the matter with Martin, and surprisingly "insisted hard" that the major lead an attack on Scott. The Cherokee headman even offered to provide real assistance by leading Martin's column from his home town to Scott in such a manner that they would approach unnoticed. Oconostota assured Martin that the residents of his town would not resist Martin's expedition. To entice Martin even more, Oconostota said that thirty blacks and a few "armed white men" lived in his town. Obviously the headman was tempting Martin with the opportunity to gain some slaves while eliminating a few Loyalists.[38]

Hoping to curb Creek attacks on the Ceded Lands, Georgia governor Nathan Brownson sent a message to the Creek Nation in November. Brownson told them that Georgia desired peace such as they professed, but that it would not be possible as long as British agents and traders lived among them and persuaded them to attack Georgia settlers. He then drew an interesting comparison between Georgians and the Creeks by saying that the war had made everyone poor and life coarse, but it had also made Creeks and Georgians alike better warriors. Brownson then promised them that if they remained patient and "share our poverty" until the war's end, Georgia would share the wealth that would follow. To make his point that the war would soon be over, he informed them that General Washington had forced the surrender of Lord Cornwallis just the month before, on October 19. As a good-faith gesture, Brownson arranged for them to receive some goods from the north. The Fat King and the Tallassee King asked the governor to write to the Spanish on the Gulf Coast and persuade them to trade ammunition to the Creeks, because they currently refused. Showing his opportunism, Brownson advised the Creeks that the Spanish would not supply them with ammunition, because they still harbored British agents and traders among them. Brownson therefore left them with no other recourse than to continue their trade with the British—if they could.

In fact, both the Cherokees and the Creeks continued to be supplied by the British. That very month, about one hundred warriors and headmen from both tribes visited Savannah and received ammunition. With the winter hunt upon them, they needed to obtain ammunition from somewhere. The Spanish would not supply the Creeks, because they knew that British agents resided among them and commanded their loyalty. As a result, it was likely that any ammunition the Spanish gave the Creeks would be used against them. Besides supplying the Cherokees and Creeks with ammunition, the British engaged in a game of duplicity. They sent letters to the Spanish commandant of Pensacola, Arturo O'Neill, indicating that Georgia had made a treaty with the Creeks and won a great victory at the Battle of Eutaw Springs in South Carolina. It would therefore be all right to supply the Creeks with ammunition and whatever else they might need. Unfortunately for the British and Creeks, General O'Neill saw through the deception and wrote a letter informing Governor Brownson of the maneuver. Apprised of British machinations, Brownson ordered the east side of the Oconee River patrolled to give warning of approaching Creek warriors.[39]

THIRTEEN

Keeping Up the Pressure

January–June 1782

The war would have been almost over by January 1, 1782, but Britain did not withdraw all its troops from the southern theater. A combined American and French army had forced the surrender of Lord Cornwallis in October 1781, but British forces remained in a few coastal port cities. The two-front war for the Whigs had been practically eliminated, yet attacks continued unabated along the southern frontier. Rather than the end of the conflict, 1782 saw yet another example of what one historian has called the "time-tested strategy" of the British using American Indians to threaten the frontiers. Not so much to further their war effort at that point, but more with the principle of *uti possidetis* ("as you possess") in mind. The principle states that territory or other property remains with whoever possesses it at the end of a conflict. Therefore, whatever parts of Georgia and South Carolina the British army controlled, it could claim when it came time to negotiate a peace treaty with the United States. The fewer troops the Whigs could bring to bear against the scant British troops in the south, the more territory Britain could retain to use as a bargaining chip in peace negotiations.[1]

New Year's Day did not find Georgia Colonel Elijah Clarke celebrating the dawn of another year but sending his second in command orders to assemble half his men "Armed and Horsed and thirty days Provisions" while a packhorse for every five to six men would make up the baggage train. The Georgia assembly in Augusta had received information from a Creek informant (evidence suggests it was the Tallassee King) that Cherokee, Chickamauga, and Creek attacks on the Ceded Lands would only increase. With such news, and the recent attacks on the Georgia frontier, Clarke intended to protect the outlying settlements and planned on a February 9 rendezvous of his militia.[2]

Back in the fall, a British agent named Scott had relocated to the Chickamauga towns and begun urging them to attack all along the southern frontiers. Colonel Arthur Campbell, head of the Washington County militia in Virginia, wrote to Governor Benjamin Harrison, warning him of a Loyalist named Scott who resided among the Chickamaugas as a British agent. Campbell thought that Virginia would soon experience attacks due to Scott's agitation, and he advocated a joint North Carolina-Virginia expedition of five hundred men, to be supported by state funds. If that expedition proved successful, Campbell recommended establishing a fort on the Tennessee River to check the flow of Loyalists from the Overmountain settlements to the Chickamauga towns.[3]

The American Indian attacks on the frontiers may be explained by a letter written by North Carolina governor Alexander Martin (no relation to Joseph Martin) to Colonel Sevier. Early in February, he wrote that he had received "repeated complaints" from the Cherokees about the daily encroachments on their lands west of the French Broad River. Martin begged Colonel Sevier to prevent the encroachments because he felt the complaints were just and the Cherokees deserved the protection of the state. The squatters stood in violation of "the late act of Assembly," and the governor wanted them removed by the middle of March, "otherwise they will be drove off." Martin seemed impatient because he wanted to hold a treaty with the Cherokees "very soon" and no doubt did not want any obstacle to a peace.[4]

In an effort to appease the Cherokees and preclude any more attacks, Governor Martin wrote to the Overhill Cherokees. He told them that the goods promised to them from North Carolina during the Treaty of Long Island the summer before could not be transported beyond the mountains because of extremely severe winter weather. Delivering the goods and holding a peace conference would have to be postponed until the weather warmed, but he assured them that they had not been forgotten. He again acknowledged their complaint about the squatters on their land and advised them that he had ordered Colonels Sevier, Joseph Hardin, and Christian to "send out armed Men and pull down the Cabins and Fences of persons living on your said Lands, and drive the Trespassers off." From the capital in the far eastern part of the state, he did all he could do other than lead a force to the Overhill Towns himself. Governor Martin then asked the Cherokees to help prevent the Chickamaugas from attacking, as that would only lead to a greater conflict. He placed the blame of such aggression squarely on the three principle British agents he knew to reside among them, men named McDaniel, Campbell, and French. If the Cherokees captured them and delivered them to Lieutenant Colonel Joseph Martin, no doubt the governor would reward them.[5]

In January, General Andrew Pickens, in South Carolina, contacted General Rutherford and Colonels Clarke, Sevier, and Shelby about cooperating in yet another combined expedition against the Cherokees and Chickamaugas sometime in early February. The Georgia Assembly, however, ordered Georgia militia to Continental General Anthony Wayne, who had been dispatched from General Greene to surround the British in Savannah and contain them there. On January 5, the Georgia Assembly received depositions from frontier settlers about the severity of recent Indian attacks, and it had the militia under Major John Cunningham sent to Wilkes County. Because of a severe shortage of ammunition, the assembly directed Continental Colonel John Twiggs to provide the militia with a supply.[6] General Pickens did not know it at the time, but Rutherford was also preoccupied. After his campaign against Wilmington, North Carolina, in which the

British garrison withdrew, Rutherford turned his attention to the Loyalist units in the region.

On January 10, the assembly in Augusta entertained the Tallassee King, who brought news of pending Creek attacks. At that time, Georgia faced a shortage of manpower, provisions, salt, ammunition, and money. Realizing the desperate situation it faced, the assembly directed Georgia governor John Martin (no relation to Alexander or Joseph Martin) to send an appeal to the Creek Nation in the hopes it would forestall attacks that Georgia could not meet with force at that time. The governor informed the Creeks that the major British field army in the south had been captured at Yorktown, as had all the British posts along the Gulf Coast. Soon Charleston and Savannah would fall, not leaving an accessible British port from which they could be supplied. With the Spanish unwilling to supply them, the Creeks would be forced to secure supplies from Georgia, which might also be unwilling to trade with them if attacks continued. Governor Martin set the price for future trade as the delivery of all prisoners and livestock the Indians had taken, as well as all British agents. Evidently not as concerned as Governor Martin about the frontier, the Georgia assembly ordered another militia draft on January 19 to reinforce Wayne at Savannah. But the governor apparently made an impression on the assembly, because it then countermanded the order and redirected all militia to the frontier. That proved a wise decision, because General Wayne discovered that one hundred packhorses loaded with weapons, ammunition, and other goods had slipped through his positions and gone back into Creek territory. Resupplied, the southern Indians could then make attacks on the frontiers.[7]

In the midst of all the threats of Indian attacks on the frontiers, Pickens and other Whig leaders became distracted with Loyalist bands operating primarily in the backcountry of South Carolina. The Loyalists established bases in the mountainous region and began recruiting Indians. Further, they ranged over into Georgia. William "Bloody Bill" Cunningham, Ezekial Williams, William Bates, and others had been unleashed by the British at their evacuation of Ninety-Six in July 1781 to attack Whigs in the southern backcountry. The British hoped the Loyalists could assist the Indians in maintaining the two-front war, or at least keep enough pressure on the frontiers to occupy Whig militias that otherwise would be brought to bear on the British around Charleston and Savannah.

February proved to be a trying time for the frontiers of Georgia and South Carolina. Due to the Loyalist activity, Pickens and Clarke had to postpone their planned Cherokee expedition to address the more pressing danger of the marauding bands. On February 8, Pickens began arranging his brigade units to eliminate the Loyalist menace. Instead of being annihilated, the Loyalist units managed to disperse, with some going west to Cherokee territory as Pickens thought they might. Meanwhile, General Wayne outside Savannah lamented his inability to receive any reinforcements from Georgia: the two-front strategy was working.[8]

While the Georgia and South Carolina Whig militias pursued the Loyalist bands, Indians continued their attacks. As Clarke went to assist Pickens in South Carolina, he sent a reconnaissance party to the Georgia frontier. On March 1, 1782, Pickens received orders from South Carolina governor John Matthews to resume his Cherokee expedition. A few days later, the Georgia assembly received a petition from settlers in the Ceded Lands seeking relief from the Indian attacks. To protect the Georgia inhabitants from the Loyalists and Indians still roaming the countryside, Governor John Martin ordered Captain Patrick Carr to patrol the area between Keokee Creek and the Ogeechee River with one-half of his militia company. Because he had not eliminated the Loyalist bands, Pickens had Colonel LeRoy Hammond's regiment stay in the backcountry while he took the rest of the brigade on the Cherokee expedition. Clarke also remained in South Carolina to continue the fight and would be replaced by newly promoted Lieutenant Colonel John Cunningham from Georgia and Colonel Robert Anderson on the Cherokee expedition.[9]

Two days before their intended rendezvous with Pickens, Cunningham requested wagon transportation for the flour meant to be carried on the expedition. To preclude any further delay, Colonel Anderson advised Cunningham to send packhorses instead, as Pickens had already left and wagons could not be procured. Cunningham must have sent the horses, because he and Pickens successfully joined forces. The combined army marched up the Savannah River and crossed at the Cherokee Ford, then crossed the Broad River in Georgia, marched around Currahee Mountain, and went up to the town of Little Chota, which had been rebuilt after being razed by Williamson's expedition six years earlier. Here they buried the bones of eleven militiamen who had been taken by Loyalist Major Hezekiah Williams and given to the Cherokees, who killed them in the town. Pickens planned to meet Colonel Sevier with his column of mounted militia in what he called the "middle towns," so he pushed over the mountains toward the Little Tennessee River valley.[10]

They then marched up Chota Creek and through Chota Gap. Captain Robert Maxwell and his company of about fifty troopers charged down into the valley and entered Catoogajoy, catching the residents off-guard. The warriors fired as they fled. Pickens spent little time in the area reconnoitering because they found so little corn there. They did discover some corn stored in cribs and hollow trees, which they confiscated for their own consumption. From there they marched to Quawasee at the three forks of the Tennessee River and burned the town. While there, Colonel Anderson ordered the part of the town on the opposite side of the river to be destroyed also. After the detachment crossed the river and was about to burn the town, a body of warriors opened fire from defilade. Strong reinforcements came to the militiamen's rescue, and a hotly contested engagement ensued. Anderson withdrew the troopers to a spur, where they spent a very cold night, waking up to a heavy snowfall. Forging ahead through thigh-deep snow, they continued on to Horse Shoe town, burning several other towns along the way. Another skirmish produced casualties and a captured Loyalist among the prisoners. Through rain, snow, and lack of provisions for man or beast "many of them [horses] dropped dead on the road that day's march." Here they found no corn or cattle; the Loyalist informed them that the Cherokees took all their corn up into the mountains with them when they abandoned the towns. Pickens told the prisoners that he came to fight their warriors and he had been told the Cherokees wanted to meet him in battle. The prisoners responded that the warriors were gathering, and they expected them that night, but given the inclement weather, the warriors might not arrive until the following day.[11]

The night passed without incident, and the next day Pickens sent out foraging parties that located only thirty bushels of corn and four head of cattle. Unable to bring the warriors to battle and out of provisions, Pickens called a council of war. His officers and he agreed that they could no longer sustain themselves in hostile territory and should return before the weather precluded withdrawal. On the second day of Pickens's return march, warriors attacked his rear guard. After a successful defense, the Whig force returned to South Carolina without incident in early April 1782.[12]

Upon their return, Pickens and Cunningham complained that the expedition did not accomplish much because the North Carolina militia had not met them. The connotation was that the North Carolina militia did not even mount an expedition, but that was not the case. As Pickens and Cunningham embarked on their expedition in March, Colonel Joseph McDowell marched from Burke County, North Carolina, across the Blue Ridge to the Cherokee Middle town of Watauga on the Tennessee River. From there he made his way to Cowee, where the Whigs clashed with Cherokee warriors. McDowell and his column stayed in the area about two weeks, during which they engaged in several skirmishes with the Cherokees and captured approximately fifty prisoners, though some escaped before McDowell returned to Cathey's Fort at the head of the Catawba River. The miscommunication probably resulted from Pickens's establishing "the middle ground" as the rendezvous point, meaning the region between the Cherokees and Creeks, that is, present-day southeast Tennessee and northern Georgia. North Carolina militia leaders more than likely understood "the middle ground" to mean the Middle Towns and made them their destination.[13]

As Pickens started on his expedition, Colonel Charles Robertson gathered his militia in the Overmountain settlements with every man providing his own mount, weapons, and equipment. After passing the Long Island of the Holston, the mounted force continued to Big Creek, where it rendezvoused with the mounted force Colonel Shelby had organized. From there the combined force proceeded down the Holston River to Cloud's Creek and went into camp. A council of war comprising all unit commanders agreed that given "the impossibility of obtaining sustenance for the army and providing for the horses," the campaign should be postponed until the fall. No doubt the heavy snowstorm that bore down upon the Tennessee Valley played a large part in the decision. Once back in the settlements, Captain James Stevenson placed his mounted ranger company on patrol duty to guard the frontier along the French Broad River.[14]

As operations against British troops shifted to the low country, Whig militia from the upper parts of the Carolinas could be stationed in the forts built along the Indian border in both states. Though the British had retired to the low country of Georgia and South Carolina, Loyalist militias remained active against the Whigs. Often, they operated in conjunction with Cherokee, Chickamauga, or Creek war parties in raiding the frontier of the three southernmost states. Their activity precluded upcountry Whig militias from swelling the ranks of the Continental forces facing the British in Savannah and Charleston, precisely what British commanders had hoped for. It proved to be an effective strategy, since many settlers on the northern frontiers continued to enlist for duty on the frontiers.[15]

Farther north, aggressive military action had also become a necessity. By the middle of March, patrols ranged throughout the Kentucky settlements to at least warn of raids by Indians from north of the Ohio River, but they could not detect every threat. Early on March 19, 1782, Captain James Estill and around thirty to forty men from Estill's Station, Boonesborough, and Paint Lick left Estill's Station on a reconnoitering patrol. On their way out, they did not detect a party of about twenty-five Wyandot warriors in the area and continued on toward Scout Licks on the Kentucky River. About eight o'clock in the morning, just as Stephen Hendrick and his brother left Estill's Station to join up with the patrol, the Wyandot warriors attacked. Initially they tomahawked and killed the daughter of Captain David Gass and captured Monk, Captain Estill's slave. The Hendrick brothers, hearing the attack, returned to the fort at a gallop and prepared to defend it. The Wyandots asked Monk about the fort, and he said twenty men remained inside and therefore the place could not be taken by their small party. Actually, fewer than ten men manned the fort. As they began to fire on the Wyandots, the Indians decided to retreat with a couple of horses and Monk.[16]

Immediately upon the Wyandots' departure from the area, a messenger galloped off to inform Captain Estill of the incident. When Estill learned of the attack, five of his men returned to the fort to aid in its defense. Because it was too late in the day to pursue the war party, Estill and his men waited until the next morning to cross the Licking River and try to intercept the Wyandots. After about ten miles, they found the trail of the war party and increased the pace of their pursuit. At nightfall, Estill and his men encamped near Little Mountain (present-day Mount Sterling, Kentucky) and resumed the chase at first light.[17]

In the morning, Estill spoke to his men and expressed his intention to engage the enemy soon. He warned that anyone who felt he could not maintain the pace or be fully functional in battle should remain at the camp. Because Estill did not personally know all the men from the other settlements, he wanted to be sure he could depend on every man in battle. As a result, ten of the militiamen stayed in camp because of faulty weapons or fatigued mounts. Estill now led about twenty-five men and continued the pursuit until it became apparent from the Wyandots' tracks that contact would be imminent. Estill then halted and held a consultation on whether to continue and attack, or wait until the morning. The men finally agreed that early morning would be better, so they encamped for the night. The next morning, after going only a few miles, Estill and his men came upon some Wyandots skinning a buffalo they had killed.[18]

Estill and his men attacked the Wyandots at a place between two water branches, about three hundred yards apart, that ran west into Hinkston Creek. The militiamen occupied level ground, while the Wyandots initially occupied the lower ground around the branch directly to the north. Nothing obstructed the Indians' field of fire, as the cane had not grown very tall.[19]

Upon hearing the approach of the mounted militiamen, the Wyandots arose from their rest and readied their weapons. They urged Estill's slave, Monk, to run away; he did, but much to their surprise, he ran toward the militiamen. Estill charged Monk with the care of the horses in the rear. The militiamen advanced and caught the Wyandots in the branch, delivering the first fire. Their volley wounded the Wyandot leader, who concealed himself in the cane along the branch but continued to direct his warriors throughout the action. They began to return the fire. Estill, knowing the Wyandots would use flanking maneuvers, ordered a Lieutenant Miller to the far left, to cross the river and cover Monk with the horses. Estill then divided his men and sent an ensign to the right so that each group had about eight men.[20]

As Estill expected, the Wyandot leader sent several of his warriors to their far right near the river to outflank the militiamen. Upon reaching Lieutenant Miller's position, the warriors fired on the militiamen from their elevated position. At this, Miller told his men to withdraw or they would all be killed. Without having fired a shot, they withdrew. As they did so, Monk pleaded with them not to go, because it would leave the entire flank exposed. Indeed, the first indication Estill had of his flank being exposed came from the fire of the Wyandots coming from behind him.[21]

Realizing his flank had become exposed, Estill ordered another ensign to take a few men and cover the exposed left flank. The ensign led the small group toward the left, and they shot Wyandot warriors as they advanced. After reaching their position, they incurred casualties forcing the ensign to withdraw. In withdrawing toward a tree where he intended to take shelter, the ensign became entangled in some fallen branches and was fatally shot.[22]

During the action, a militiaman named McMillan regained his mount and rode in among the warriors, declaring adamantly that he should have already killed one of them. He fell with three wounds. In another incident, a man named Adam Caperton was wounded in the mouth and then the head. The head shot caused Caperton to become deranged, and throughout the rest of the action, before he fell dead, he attempted to make signs and talk to Estill. Because of Caperton's actions and the fact that Estill was wearing a white hunting shirt, the latter became an easy target for Wyandot warriors, and he suffered several wounds.[23]

Eventually, only a private, Joseph Proctor, remained from the ensign's detachment on the right. He called out to Estill that he intended to leave the ground because he was alone and that Estill only had a few men remaining. Estill asked Proctor to wait a moment and he would join him. At that moment, one of Proctor's brothers who was in the center called on him to shoot a pursuing warrior. Proctor did, then reloaded his rifle. Estill now began withdrawing to Proctor's position, and a Wyandot pursued him. Having suffered several wounds and being too weak from loss of blood to hold his weapon, Estill dropped it. The warrior drew his knife and stabbed him. As Estill fell to the ground, Proctor shot the warrior, and he nearly fell on the captain. After this the battle ended, seemingly by mutual consent. The four or five remaining militiamen withdrew from the battlefield only after Proctor advised them that Estill had fallen.[24]

The skirmish lasted approximately one hour and forty-five minutes, and each side had only about twenty-five men engaged. Casualty estimates for both sides vary widely, but combined they totaled approximately twenty. After leaving the battlefield, Proctor encountered a company of forty to fifty more militiamen from Boone's Station, McGee's Station, Strode's Station, and White Oak Spring. Proctor guided the company back to the battlefield, only to find that the Wyandot survivors had returned to claim their dead and had confiscated the rifles of the fallen militiamen. With no tools to dig proper graves, the relief company of militiamen could only cover their fallen comrades with brush.[25]

A food shortage in Burke County, Georgia, precluded residents from providing forage for the mounted militia there, which had proven insufficient in number to prevent Upper Creek raids from destroying what little forage existed in the region. Because the militia had been on active duty for so long, hardly any crops had been planted or harvested. The lack of food in Georgia prompted many militiamen to stay home and plant a crop in spring 1782, reducing the availability of men Martin could order into the field. Nevertheless, residents of Burke County petitioned Georgia governor John Martin for more militia in March 1782. The lack of regular recruits prompted Martin to recommend that slaves be recruited as troops, though he realized the improbability of the state assembly approving such a move. The assembly proved him correct by not even reading his motion.[26] Wilkes County militia were badly needed to deploy along the frontier in Burke County rather than going off to fight the Chickamaugas and Upper Creeks. But at least that section of the frontier could be secured with the aid of South Carolina and North Carolina.[27]

The Georgia Executive Council, the governing body of elected officials in the state, had responded in early April to a request from Continental General Anthony Wayne for two hundred riflemen. After a month, Colonel Clarke had sent only a few units to Wayne outside Savannah. In mid-May, Governor Martin advised Wayne that Clarke would soon have the full complement of two hundred riflemen and march them to Wayne. But toward the end of May, the Creeks resumed their attacks on isolated frontier settlements. Clarke had the unenviable task of trying to recruit units to march to Savannah while their homes and families suffered Creek attacks. He also needed to send others to defend the frontier.[28]

At the end of May, the Lower Creek headmen the Fat King and the Tallassee King arrived in Augusta to tell Governor Martin they had nothing to do with the ongoing Creek attacks along the frontier. Ostensibly, they desired to meet with Whig officials and assure them that the several Lower Creek towns they represented desired peace and should not be attacked. Hoboithle Mico and Neah Mico were longtime friends of the

Whigs, having frequently warned them of pending attacks on the frontier. During this visit, they warned Martin of Chickamauga and Upper Creek warriors gathering, under the direction of Loyalist and British officers, near the Oconee River with plans to attack the northern Georgia frontier all the way to Savannah. Never before had warriors combined to attempt an attack on such a grand scale in Georgia.

A week before, Martin did not seem too worried about the Creeks and wrote to Colonel Clarke that "there will be a sufficient number of the inhabitants for the protection of the settlement." Evidently Hoboithle Mico and Neah Mico explained to Martin the unprecedented scale of the pending attacks. Then, on May 21, Elijah Clarke wrote an urgent letter to Martin telling him that parties of Indians and Loyalists had attacked the settlements and forts, inflicting casualties and taking off prisoners. They seemed to be withdrawing in the direction of the middle grounds—"betwen the Cherakees and Creeks whare the Disaffected of Both Nations Resort with the outlying Torys." Things became so desperate that Clarke raised three companies of fifty men each to garrison the forts so the settlers could concentrate on their planting. He also began raising two small companies to act as rangers throughout the frontier settlements to prevent British sympathizers from harboring Loyalists, and to defend the frontier. Clarke told Martin of his "absolute necessity" of obtaining ammunition, for he had none; the settlers were entirely defenseless. Further, Clarke himself suffered from the mumps and could not even ride a horse, but he assured the governor that the corps of riflemen for Wayne would be organized and sent down as soon as possible.[29]

Martin responded quickly and sent Clarke the gunpowder and lead that he urgently requested. But he reiterated his desire for Clarke to complete the corps of riflemen and send it down to Wayne. The governor could not have foreseen how quickly priorities in Georgia would change. On May 27, the Tallassee King arrived in Augusta to once again bring the Georgia Whigs news of a pending Indian attack. He informed Martin that the British agent William McIntosh was to have assembled a large force of pro-British Creeks, including Cowetas, at Standing Peachtree by May 26. From there, he would march them to meet with a large force of Cherokees at the Big Shoals of the Oconee River. Then the combined force would advance to attack the Ceded Lands in overwhelming numbers. The Tallassee King estimated that the Georgians had about ten days to prepare. The only problem for the Whigs was that the Tallassee King and his entourage of forty other headmen and warriors arrived in Augusta the day after the planned meeting at the Big Shoals. Governor Martin wasted no time in drafting and sending an urgent plea for assistance to General Pickens that ended, "For God's sake exert yourself and come to our timely aid, as delays are dangerous." What Martin did not know was that Pickens had gone to the South Carolina low country to reinforce General Greene, then operating against Charleston. The governor then wrote to Clarke to inform him of the impending onslaught.[30]

But the onslaught had already begun. On May 23, a war party had attacked a blockhouse in the Ceded Lands. The warriors continued their attack for some time until withdrawing after killing some livestock. A company of militia garrisoning the frontier blockhouses pursued them to the South Fork of the Oconee River, but because the war party did not make a camp, and the militia's horses needed rest, the company returned two days later. Another war party attacked a station where the Broad River flows into the Savannah. The handful of defenders forced the dozen or so warriors to break off the assault. Another militia detachment from the blockhouse garrisons went after the warriors, but it, too, had to terminate pursuit before its horses gave out. On their return, they ran into the band of warriors and a skirmish developed, to no advantage for either side. By the time Clarke received Governor Martin's letter, he had already mustered a militia force and needed only a few more days before moving out to intercept McIntosh's force.[31]

Fortuitously, a pro-American trader named Jesse Spears had secretly made his way to Colonel Robert Anderson in South Carolina and told him of the pending combined Indian-Loyalist attack on the Georgia frontier. With Pickens out of easy communication, Anderson decided to reinforce

Clarke in Georgia. Anderson quickly gathered about one hundred militiamen and marched to rendezvous with Clarke at Beards Springs (just north of present-day Augusta, Georgia).[32]

About June 1, Anderson met with Clarke, and the two pushed on to the Big Shoals of the Oconee River. They arrived before McIntosh's force and positioned their troops a little further upstream. When McIntosh's combined Indian and Loyalist force of some four hundred to five hundred reached the Oconee, a sharp engagement ensued, and the Whigs forced them to withdraw. Each side suffered a few casualties, and the Whigs captured two Loyalists, Adam Luny and Daniel Murphy.[33]

At the Big Shoals, Clarke held a court-martial for Luny and Murphy. Both were found guilty (of treason to the American cause, no doubt) and hanged from a "stooping Hickory at the lower end of the big Shoals on the east side of the river." Whig leaders had always held British agents and Loyalists living among the Indians of the southeast responsible for attacks on the frontier. Intentionally, Clarke left their bodies hanging in the tree as a clear warning to any Indian or Loyalist crossing the river with hostile intentions. The Whigs carried the body of their one fatality, a Captain Holloway, from the battlefield. There they weighted it down and sunk it in the middle of the Oconee River "to prevent the Indians getting his body."[34]

Governor Martin took the opportunity afforded by the victory on the Oconee River to send a message to the Cherokees and Chickamaugas north of the Georgia frontier. He sent along an offer of peace and even some of the prisoners taken in recent engagements to indicate his sincerity. Primarily, Martin wanted the attacks to cease. Since these warriors always allied themselves with the Upper Creeks, a peace with them could weaken the Upper Creek attacks. If they did not desire peace, Martin promised to destroy their towns and any warrior who took up arms against him. The recent engagements should have served as marked examples of the truth in his message. Unfortunately for Georgia, the message did not prevent future attacks along its frontier.[35]

The Upper Creeks attacked all along the Georgia frontier, just as Hoboithle Mico and Neah Mico had said they would.

Though Anderson and Clarke met and defeated one Indian force, Wayne received intelligence that another intended to cut its way into Savannah. Wayne knew that the Upper Creek headman from Little Tallassee, Emistiseguo, and a British officer led a large contingent of pro-British Creek warriors with the intention of reinforcing the British garrison in Savannah.[36]

On June 23, Lieutenant Colonel Thomas Posey, commander of a Virginia battalion under General Wayne, had been anticipating a British sortie out of Savannah for several weeks, and therefore his men continued to sleep on the ground with their weapons rather than in a camp. As a result, the entire command suffered from exhaustion and fatigue. The men did not expect an attack from the rear. But at 1:30 a.m. on June 24, 1782, Emistiseguo and his warriors struck Posey's light infantry company, commanded by Captain Alexander Parker and guarding a battery of artillery, with such ferocity as to throw all the troops into disorder.[37]

After the Continental troops withdrew in disarray, Emistiseguo halted his attack in an attempt to fire the captured cannons at them. This pause gave Parker a chance to rally his company. Joined by Captain James Gunn with a company of dragoons, they moved to counterattack. At that moment, Posey encountered Major Samuel Findley advancing to the scene of action with a regiment. Posey led the troops that caught Emistiseguo's forces from behind. General Wayne, who had been asleep nearby, was able to join Gunn's company of dragoons and attacked the Creeks in the flank.[38]

The battleground, illuminated by a full moon, presented a scene of utter confusion: the yells of Continental troops and Creek warriors, the discharge of firearms, attacks and counterattacks from all directions. During the action, Emistiseguo was wounded by a spontoon and three bayonets, yet he continued shouting encouragement to his warriors. Before he died, the Creek headman fired his musket, killing Wayne's horse. The combined attacks overwhelmed the Creek warriors and succeeded in turning most of them back. Though British Colonel Thomas Brown claimed that the entire Creek force (minus Emistiseguo) entered Savannah where he met them, only a part of them actually succeeded.[39]

Interestingly, Emistiseguo's warriors had brought with them more than one hundred packhorses loaded with skins and pelts. After the engagement, the Continentals counted 117 captured packhorses and brought in many more over the ensuing days. Evidently, the Creeks intended to force their way through to Savannah and then exit in the same manner to avoid the circuitous route to the south by way of the Altamaha River. The acquisition of ammunition and other necessary goods, purchased with their skins and pelts, would have greatly and immediately benefitted anti-American Creek warrior attacks on the southern frontiers.[40]

As the engagements along the frontier demonstrated, British use of friendly southern Indians had proved effective in several ways. By attacking the southern frontier along its length, they effectively precluded having to fight a large Whig force in pitched battles. Linear tactics are a Western European characteristic; American Indians preferred ambushes and flanking maneuvers. Because the Indians' enemy consisted of settlers and farmers turned militiamen, their attacks necessitated the constant maintenance of a militia force in the field, taking the farmers away from their farms and crops. Without the necessary attention, fields did not yield crops to sustain even the individual families, much less the militias. Indian frontier attacks also kept Whig militias from going to the coast to join Continental forces surrounding British garrisons in Charleston and Savannah. Without the militias, the Continentals could not assault the two coastal port cities. But in the end, the militia would not be necessary as the British made what to the Royal Council in Savannah was an astonishing decision: all British forces were to evacuate Georgia.

FOURTEEN

The Beginning of the End

July–December 1782

The very day that General Wayne wrote General Greene of the British evacuation of Savannah in July 1782, Daniel McMurphy, the Whig Indian agent in the Lower Creek towns, informed the Georgia assembly that several Creek headmen wanted to meet and assure them of their continued friendly demeanor. In the wake of recent brutal attacks, the headmen wanted Georgia officials to know they had not participated in them. The Creek headmen obviously knew of the attacks but could not prevent them. They had no authority over any towns other than their own. The notoriety of the attacks and murders, whether true or fancied, had reached as far as Pennsylvania, and the *Pennsylvania Gazette* described them in brutal detail. The headmen probably warned of impending attacks on the Georgia frontier as well, since their visits usually presented an opportunity to impart intelligence directly.[1]

Noted Georgia militia leader Patrick Carr (the British and Loyalists would later call him "notorious" for his ruthlessness in hunting down both) wrote to Governor John Martin, advising him that settlers had abandoned their homes near the Ogeechee River because of Creek attacks. Those settlers had gone to an area east of there called Buckhead. Others fled south to the area known as Old Town, near the cow pens and trading store of George Galphin on the Ogeechee River. The naked aggression of the attackers intimidated the settlers to the point that they did not even plant crops for a fall harvest. After the recent food shortages, that only made a desperate situation worse.[2]

Because the British had evacuated Savannah, the Lower Creek headmen were able to meet Governor Martin there. As the governor had told them during an earlier meeting, the Whigs would be back in Savannah, which they could now see had happened. Moreover, whatever the British had said about holding Savannah and eventually bringing the Whigs to terms had clearly not happened, and the British should not be trusted. He asked them to bring in the British commissaries and traders as a genuine sign that they wanted peace. That way, the British agents also could not urge them to attack the frontier.[3]

In making his request, Martin tried to impress upon the headmen the folly of continued attacks. He stressed that another way the Creeks could show their desire for peace would be to bring in all the property they had taken from the Whigs. That also would help alleviate the desperate food and economic conditions in the state. Georgia no longer had a two-front war to wage, and Martin was attempting to bluff the Creeks into freeing the state from all fighting.[4]

While the Georgia governor pursued a diplomatic solution to frontier violence, North Carolina governor Alexander Martin took another, more aggressive approach. He authorized Colonel Joseph McDowell to raise five hundred militiamen by August 20 for an expedition against the Valley Towns and to rendezvous with Colonel Shelby and General Pickens. The North Carolina governor also told McDowell that if he could not muster the five hundred men by that date, then he should extend his recruiting until September. Martin also authorized Shelby to raise five hundred troops to attack the Chickamauga towns before the rendezvous. Though the governor obviously wanted the expedition to eliminate those Cherokees attacking the frontiers, he told McDowell to spare "those Towns you are sensible are friendly disposed." On the same day, Martin advised Shelby that his specific operating instructions would come from McDowell, but that he should apprehend the settlers who lately had murdered some Cherokees while on their way to trade with the Americans because "Such actions disgrace a Government where they pass with impunity."[5]

With Savannah evacuated, Whig militias were free to operate against the Cherokees, Chickamaugas, and Creeks that continued to attack the frontier. For the first time since 1776, the Whigs mounted several coordinated expeditions against the aggressive southern tribes. One expedition struck from the Overmountain region into the Overhill Cherokee Towns, another from North Carolina targeted the Middle Cherokee Towns, and another joint expedition from South Carolina and Georgia hit the Chickamauga and Lower Cherokee Towns.

By August 1, North Carolina had mobilized its forces and begun its expedition. Colonel McDowell raised his regiment in Burke County and marched to the head of the Catawba River. There he met with militia from neighboring Wilkes County, assuming command of the whole, being senior colonel. From there the command marched over the Blue Ridge Mountains through the Swannanoa Gap, where it met with militia from Rutherford County under Lieutenant Colonel James Miller. General Charles McDowell, brother of Colonel Joseph McDowell, then took command of the entire force and began the march west toward the Middle Cherokee Towns.[6]

General McDowell followed along the main trail down the Swannanoa River, the same route General Rutherford used in his 1776 expedition. Upon reaching the French Broad River, the expedition continued southwest until it crossed over a ford. It then crossed the ridge between the French Broad and Pigeon rivers, and crossed the Pigeon just above the present town of Waynesville. Over another ridge and down Scott's Creek, along a very treacherous foot path to the Tuckasegee River, the expedition continued to somewhere below the present town of Webster. Crossing over to the southern side, the expedition continued on for a few miles before it finally began to encounter Cherokee towns, the first being Stekoa, which

they destroyed. The destruction continued throughout present-day Macon County, along the waters of the Little
Tennessee River. The expedition went up Cartoogaja Creek
and crossed the Nantahala Mountains at Waya Gap, then
down the Nantahala River valley to its junction with the
Hiwassee River, and on to present-day Murphy. The Whig
force destroyed the rebuilt towns and destroyed corn standing
in the fields. It met with no serious resistance but did have
several skirmishes in which it killed two warriors and took a
few prisoners. After marching to the west of present-day
Murphy, the column returned across the Blue Ridge
Mountains in October.[7]

As the Whig frontier forces moved against the hostile
Cherokees and Chickamaugas, in late summer 1782, the
British commander at Fort Detroit ordered Captain William
Caldwell to take Simon Girty (an intermediary between the
British and their Indian allies), some traders, a company of
militia, and as many Indians as he could gather to attack and
destroy the American settlements south of the Ohio River.
These settlements consisted of palisaded forts with the settlers residing within the fort walls in individual cabins, and
their fields of crops located just outside the walls. The northern warriors, including Wyandot, Huron, and Miami, began
by slipping into the settlements and carrying away settlers for
the purpose of acquiring information. After gaining information regarding numbers of settlers and fortifications, the
northern warriors began their full-scale attacks, supplied by
the British in Detroit.[8]

Initially, Caldwell gathered some one thousand Hurons,
Wyandots, Delawares, Shawnees, Mingos, and others—the
largest group of warriors ever assembled in that region.
Unfortunately for the British cause, Caldwell could not keep
them assembled, and he crossed the Ohio River with a mixed
force of only three hundred Loyalist rangers, Hurons, and
Lake Indians, with a smattering of Delawares, Shawnees, and
Mingos. Caldwell intended to strike the forts in the Kentucky
region, the first being Bryan's Station (now part of Lexington,
Kentucky).[9]

The morning of August 16, 1782, dawned bright and sunny, with the residents of Bryan's Station up early as usual and attending to the morning work routine. Captain Robert Johnson commanded the militia of Bryan's Station, but he had gone to Richmond on state business. That morning his slave left the palisaded fort to cut wood for the day and started trudging up the road to Lexington on the north side of the fort. Before he had traveled far, an advance party of six warriors fired on him. He immediately turned around and ran back to the safety of the fort walls. In Captain Johnson's absence, Captain John Craig assumed command. The settlers did not give much weight to a stray party of Indians firing on them, which was not an uncommon occurrence, but Craig thought it best to prepare for a major attack.

Legend has it that in order not to convey their alarm, the men sent the women out to the spring near the south side of the fort to get water. If they did not go to get water, as they did every day, it would be a sign to the war party that the garrison knew they were about to be attacked (and therefore the settlers would not be able to surprise the Indians in the open). The advance party of warriors undoubtedly would have kept the women under surveillance, but they did not molest them. Equally certain is the fact that the armed men of the fort, upwards of forty-five, kept their rifles trained on the area. The women filled every receptacle possible in anticipation of a siege. Meanwhile, an express rider slipped out of the fort through the large cornfield on the north side to obtain assistance from Lexington, some five or six miles away. Other residents repaired downed palisades while the able-bodied men received powder and lead. Upon the return of the women from the spring, the settlers barred the gates and the fort generally readied for combat and a siege.[10]

Having heard or seen nothing since the six shots at sunrise, Lieutenant Barnett Roger proposed a mounted, armed reconnaissance to see if any warriors remained in the area. At about ten o'clock in the morning, thirteen men agreed and followed Roger out of the fort gate on the west side and down the lane toward Lexington, where the shots had been fired. It turned out to have been a wise decision to place the station in readiness because they had not ventured down the road far when a large war party fired on them. The squad of militiamen returned fire, then galloped back within the fort and closed and barred the gates.[11]

As the attempted reconnaissance transpired, the main body of warriors made a sudden charge on the east side of the palisaded fort. They presented a frightening appearance to the defenders, with tomahawks in hand and bodies painted in war colors, black and red. The defenders delivered a withering fire through the portholes in the walls, which turned back the charging warriors. For the next hour, a brisk fire between the assailants and defenders ensued, with neither side gaining a clear advantage and all knowing that exposure certainly meant being shot.[12]

At about eleven o'clock, a company of mounted and foot militiamen arrived from Lexington on the west side of Bryan's Station, as the skirmish on the east side of the fort dissipated. Accounts vary as to the strength of the company, but all agree that most of the mounted militiamen, around sixteen or twenty, entered the fort. The war party on the west side of the fort had erected an impromptu fence of sorts, but the mounted militiamen charged through it upon their arrival. They had caught the warriors preparing a meal and, though under fire for about two hundred or three hundred yards, entered the fort safely through the cornfield.[13]

The militiamen on foot, however, strayed too far to the east and encountered the main body of warriors. Many in the fort surmised that the warriors killed them all, but actually they only inflicted a few casualties. The remainder fled back to Lexington, though they were pursued for some distance.

The reinforcements brought the fighting strength of the fort to near sixty, while total occupants probably numbered upwards of two hundred. This came as a devastating blow to Caldwell's offensive at Bryan's Station. He well knew the settlers could withstand a siege until a much stronger force of militiamen arrived from Virginia and present-day Kentucky.[14]

Also around eleven o'clock, two Wyandots climbed a tall sycamore tree some distance away to fire into the fort. A settler named Stucker shot one of them, and he fell; whether the shot or the fall killed him is unclear. The other Wyandot, recognizing the marksmanship of the man who had shot his comrade, climbed down the tree, making sure to keep the trunk of the tree between him and the fort, and escaped.[15]

Toward sundown, Simon Girty called to the fort, inquiring as to who commanded the garrison. Captain Craig answered by name, saying he did. Girty must have known Craig's reputation as a tough and determined fighter, because he asked the captain to put all the women and children in one cabin and for the defenders to come outside the palisades and fight honorably like men. Craig laughingly declined, saying he knew what Girty had done at Martin's and Riddle's stations, where the residents were all killed and scalped after just such a ruse. Girty evidently became agitated at Craig's response and advised the militia commander that his artillery would arrive in the morning and he would then compel the surrender of the entire population. Whether Craig recognized Girty's bluff or not, he called it, saying that artillery would not be able to force their surrender and to bring on an attack. Girty wisely declined and settled down to sing a song that described all the food they were enjoying at the settlers' expense.

The night passed without incident. A few hours before daybreak, the warriors began a war hoop all around the fort, but no attack came. By sunrise, all the warriors had withdrawn from the area, and the settlers surmised that the war hoop in the early morning hours had been a signal to withdraw. The Wyandots suffered five killed and two wounded while inflicting four killed and three wounded on the settlers of Bryan's Station.[16]

Captain Caldwell, realizing no further efforts would effect the surrender of Bryan's Station, withdrew the war party back toward the Ohio River. Along the way, about one hundred of the warriors left Caldwell and began making their way toward the Falls of the Ohio, where they had left their possessions. Caldwell continued toward the Blue Licks, where game could be obtained and a good defensive position be assumed in case any militia pursued them. They reached the Blue Licks on August 18, 1782, and made their encampment there, in spite of objections of the warriors. They wanted to camp some distance from the licks so they would not frighten the buffalo, but Caldwell talked them into a better defensive position at the licks. Fortunately for them, the warriors listened to Caldwell.[17]

Upon receiving word about the attack on Bryan's Station, Colonels Daniel Boone, John Todd, and Stephen Trigg gathered about 180 mounted militiamen and began pursuing the large war party. After traveling some forty miles, they found the party waiting for them at the Blue Licks. A warrior advised Caldwell of the approach of the militiamen, and he placed the warriors on advantageous ground at about 7:30 on the morning of August 19. The militiamen formed their line with Boone on the left, Trigg on the right, and Major Hugh McGary in the center. A Major Harlin led the advance, and Colonel Todd had overall command.[18]

The war party fired but a single shot when the militia gave it a volley. Boone and the militia's left flank struck first and became heavily engaged. After some time, the warriors executed a flanking maneuver on their left, turning Trigg's command and forcing them to withdraw from the battleground. This left the rest of the militiamen exposed to a murderous enfilade fire, forcing their withdrawal. The war party attempted a pursuit on foot, but because the militiamen had fled on horseback, it was futile. The militiamen lost about one hundred killed and captured, and a dozen were wounded. The war party suffered only about ten killed and as many wounded.[19]

After the battle, the warriors gathered the rifles of the dead and wounded militiamen. Sensationalized accounts state that the warriors grotesquely mangled the dead. Some of the prisoners told the warriors that they expected Colonel Benjamin Logan with one hundred more militia to join them. Captain Caldwell waited on the battlefield until the second day after the Battle of Blue Licks, but Logan did not appear, so Caldwell withdrew his war party back across the Ohio River. Actually, Logan did gather a large force that would have totaled over four hundred militiamen, but he did not reach the Blue Licks before Caldwell left the area.[20]

During the battle, militia Captain John Fleming received a severe wound in the thigh, shattering the bone. Somehow he managed to mount his horse and retreat from the battlefield some eighteen miles to a large pond, where he spent the night. Daniel Boone spent that night at the base of a large tree about one mile away from Fleming. The next day, Boone came across Fleming's trail and caught up to him before they both reached Boone's Station. There Boone met with Colonel Logan's force, and he returned to the battlefield with them. They reached the ground in time to tend to the dead, who could only be covered with limbs and poles, as the men had no tools to dig graves.[21]

A month after the attack on Bryan's Station and the Battle of Blue Licks, Colonel William Christian reported that not one thousand people remained in Kentucky. The Shawnees proved their ability to strike dispersed locations simultaneously, which made the few men available for militia duty apprehensive about serving far from their families. He proposed that reinforcements make an expedition into the Shawnees' towns, noting that a punitive strike in the winter "would Distress them more vastly than at any other Season."[22]

Militia commanders to the south also believed that only offensive operations would quell Indian attacks. General Pickens wrote to Colonel Campbell on August 26 to inform him that South Carolina and Georgia would proceed with a campaign against the Chickamauga towns and asked that Virginia join the combined effort. Campbell did not feel he had authorization to proceed and did not think such a campaign would be justified. The strenuous efforts of the Cherokees to make peace with the Americans alone "renders it still more improper," Colonel Christian wrote to Virginia governor Benjamin Harrison on September 28. Campbell had heard of the recent interception of the Cherokees' ammunition pack train and of Colonel Clarke's defeat of a large party on the Georgia frontier. Between the two events, Campbell did not consider the Cherokees much of a threat. His greatest apprehension about the proposed campaign against the Cherokees lay in the inability, or unwillingness, of the South Carolina and Georgia Whigs to discriminate between hostile and peaceful Cherokees.[23]

On September 1, Pickens received a letter from General McDowell that his North Carolina militia would embark on an expedition into the Cherokee nation about the middle of the month. Pickens immediately wrote Colonel Clarke in Georgia, conveying the information and requesting his participation in a simultaneous expedition. The Georgia and South Carolina militias would rendezvous on the sixteenth at the Cherokee Ford on the Savannah River and proceed from there. In preparation for the expedition, Pickens ordered a Captain Butler, stationed along the Edisto River to the south, to gather twenty-five to thirty head of cattle and deliver them by September 16 to the Cherokee Ford.[24]

Pickens crossed the Savannah River at Cherokee Ford on September 16 with the militia regiments of Colonels John White and Robert Anderson. Though each man had only about five or six rounds of ammunition, Pickens provided over fifty of his men with broadswords made by Carolina blacksmiths. For some unknown reason, Clarke did not rendezvous with Pickens at the Cherokee Ford, and after two days, Pickens moved to the Buffalo Fork of Long Creek in the Ceded Lands. There he met Colonel Clarke with his nearly one hundred Georgia militia. The total Whig force numbered about four hundred.[25]

As Pickens forged ahead with his campaign, Colonel Joseph Martin returned from the Overhill Cherokee and Chickamauga towns. Martin had given the towns the preliminary conditions for a lasting peace, which included the cessation of all attacks, the return of all captives, and the delivery of all those pro-British (whether Cherokee or Loyalist) as prisoners—the most important issues to the militia leaders on the frontier. Colonel Martin had returned from his meeting with the headmen on September 18 with all of their captives but three and seemed assured the Chickamaugas would bring them in very soon. Several weeks earlier, Colonel Martin had written to the North Carolina governor informing him of his efforts and the progress made, hoping to deter a punitive expedition. When he arrived back at the Long Island, he became alarmed for the peace negotiations after hearing that Sevier had been mustering men for an expedition, and he hurried off to see him.[26]

Campbell supported Joseph Martin's efforts at postponing any military expedition into the Cherokee or Chickamauga territory at this stage. The British had all but withdrawn from the southern theater, which meant the Cherokees could receive no goods or ammunition from them. Fortunately, the goods from North Carolina promised to the Cherokees during the 1781 peace conference had finally arrived to Campbell's care. All of Colonel Martin's efforts at securing a lasting peace were about "to be brought to a point." Campbell learned that orders had recently been reissued by the North Carolina governor to proceed with the expeditions. By Campbell's assessment, "several arguments have been sent to embrace the present very submissive overtures for peace from the Indians, as the best means to secure the prosperity of the States."[27]

By then, however, North Carolina governor Alexander Martin's position toward militant Chickamauga warriors had become intensely aggressive. In mid-September, he instructed the North Carolina peace commissioners for the Cherokees to send out offerings of peace, but only after the Georgia, South Carolina, North Carolina, and Virginia militias formed a junction of their forces in the Chickamauga towns and destroyed every town from which warriors had recently attacked the frontiers. The price of peace for the Chickamaugas would be for them to return to the Cherokee nation, to the towns they had left in 1777, and to cede "all the Western lands contained within the chartered bounds of North Carolina to the Ohio and Mississippi." Additionally, they had to surrender all Loyalists, British, captured or runaway slaves, livestock, and other property taken from the settlements. McDowell and Sevier would agree upon a boundary and proscribe the Cherokees within it so that they would eventually be surrounded by settlers "and their power reduced to the harmless and inoffensive situation of the Catawbas." To allay any qualms the Cherokees might have, the commissioners should guarantee them the boundaries will be "most inviolably and sacredly observed on the part of this State." As in the past, undoubtedly, the Cherokees must have felt that assurance was hollow.[28]

The Pickens-Clarke expedition had as its primary objective the capture of Loyalist Colonel Thomas Waters and all Loyalists who lived among the Cherokees in what Pickens termed the "middle ground": the territory between the

Cherokees and the Creeks. Because Pickens knew Waters used Long Swamp Town as his base of operations, he steered the column up the Hightower Trail heading directly for the town. Upon reaching the Chattahoochee River, the Whigs captured a couple of warriors, who informed Pickens that earlier, a Loyalist had been among his Carolina militia but had slipped away at the Cherokee Ford to warn the Cherokees of his expedition. Expecting Pickens to move north as he had in previous expeditions, the Cherokees sent scouts into the area between the Chattahoochee and Tugaloo rivers. The column did go that way, but farther to the west. It still had an opportunity to surprise Waters if it moved quickly. The expedition crossed the Chattahoochee that day, September 24, and the two Cherokees guided the Whigs along a little-used path straight to Long Swamp Town.[29]

The column pushed on throughout the night and arrived just outside the town in the dark. Everyone was quiet in the dark early morning hours. They dismounted, and no man or horse was allowed to stray, lest they encounter a Cherokee and betray their presence. At daybreak, Pickens ordered his force mounted and gave one last warning to spare women and children; all warriors, however, were to be killed. Pickens conveyed his vision of a sudden, heavy cavalry strike with swords as the primary weapon to his troopers, who were so armed. Pickens then divided his command, with Clarke taking one-half around to the north end of the town. Attacking simultaneously, the Whigs achieved complete surprise. The fighting was quick and brutal. A William Greene rode through the town and, with his quite large frame, wielded his sword like a scythe, beheading fleeing Cherokees.[30]

Quite a few Cherokees escaped via the creek that divided the town in half, but many others did not fare well. One militiaman chased a warrior into the creek and bludgeoned him to death with the barrel of his musket while shouting obscenities. Upon observing the scene, Pickens spoke derisively of the militiaman. Pickens apparently had no emotional feelings for his Loyalist cousin, David Pickens, who was captured in the town. The general did not even speak to him when he was brought to the commander, and he was herded among the other prisoners. Given the attitude toward Loyalists living among the Cherokees at the time, David Pickens is fortunate his cousin did not hang him on the spot. Disappointingly for the Whigs, Waters fled from the town before the attack.[31]

Pickens drafted messages to the Cherokee headmen of the "middle ground" and the Valley Towns, offering his terms for peace. He conveyed the fact that the Whigs had recaptured practically all of South Carolina and Georgia. Peace with Great Britain seemed imminent, and the states wanted to be at peace with the Cherokees. In order for that peace to be achieved, however, the Cherokees had to bring in all the Loyalists and British agents who lived among them. The Whigs did not blame the Cherokees, he told them, but those Loyalists and others who seemed to encourage the Cherokees to attack the frontier settlements. A prisoner exchange would be most acceptable, because Pickens did not wish to hold any Cherokees. If the Cherokees decided not to surrender the Loyalists, he would continue his campaign of death and destruction. If the Cherokees wished to face the Whigs in battle, they would not be difficult to find: he did not intend to withdraw until he had destroyed every town he could find. He gave them four days to comply with his demands.[32]

After gathering the Loyalist prisoners, Pickens realized they had not captured Waters, so he ordered Colonel Robert Anderson up the Chattahoochee River and Colonel Clarke downstream. Pickens charged both with capturing Waters and destroying every town they encountered. Going upriver, Anderson first came upon the town of Hightower and then Blue Savannah. Heading downriver, Clarke attacked Selacoa, where his force discovered a quantity of scalps. After learning of another Cherokee town called Pine Log to the west, they attacked and destroyed it. Encamping there for a few days, Clarke sent out a detachment to Vann's Town and Coosa Town, but it did not capture Waters.[33]

After a few days, Witch Killer and another Cherokee headman arrived at Long Swamp Town to meet with Pickens. They told him that some of the headmen had gathered to hear his message, but they needed more time to comply with all his demands. More time would be required just to finish gathering the headmen, so Pickens allowed them three more days. On September 30, Terrapin, Wolf, and other headmen arrived at Long Swamp Town, bringing with them six Loyalists and some horses taken from the settlements. Pickens advised the headmen to make haste because the corn his men had confiscated in Long Swamp Town would soon be gone, and they would have to relocate in the hopes of obtaining more provisions. Terrapin requested five more days to bring in the rest of the Loyalists.[34]

On October 17, a dozen headmen and about two hundred warriors converged on Long Swamp Town. If they had been there to attack Pickens, it would have been the most serious engagement between the two sides since 1776. Fortunately for the Whigs, the Cherokees came to make peace. Pickens recounted all the expeditions that had been made against them in the past few years and noted that the Whigs stood ready to drive the British from the continent. The Whigs did not blame them for their warfare, but rather the Loyalists and British agents. That is why the Cherokees had to bring them all in as prisoners, as well as all their property. Pickens would leave two men in Frog Town, about halfway between Long Swamp and South Carolina, to collect all the Loyalists and the property, which was to take no longer than twenty days.[35]

Pickens tried to make the process as easy and profitable for the Indians as possible. They would be paid for their time and effort, and reimbursed for any expenses they had, in bringing in the Loyalists and their property. If a few headmen also came down to meet with him, Pickens would accompany them to the governors of South Carolina and Georgia so that new trade associations could be arranged. Of course, they would enjoy the hospitality of the states throughout their trip. Finally, Pickens delineated a new southern boundary for Cherokee territory, running from the North Carolina line down the Tennessee Valley Divide to the Chattahoochee. Everything would be formalized at Augusta some time the next year, to which the headmen agreed. The conference took several days, and at its adjournment, Pickens and Clarke returned to their homes after being on the expedition for over a month.[36]

While Pickens and Clarke were sweeping through the Chickamauga towns in the "middle ground" of present-day northern Georgia, Old Tassel sent a message to North

Carolina governor Alexander Martin, saying that the Overmountain territory seemed to be in a perpetual state of turmoil. His chief complaint stemmed from the daily encroachments by the Nolichucky settlers to the point that the Cherokees did not have any place to hunt. In fact, squatter-settlers had already built their cabins within a day's walk of the Overhill Towns. Because Old Tassel spoke for those Cherokees who had not attacked the settlers, he stressed, "We don't want to quarrel with our Elder Brother." Quite the contrary, he reminded the governor that they had agreed to a peace treaty. But the boundary line agreed on had not yet been marked, a clear failing of the states. He then asked the governor to send Colonel Sevier to remove the settlers squatting on Cherokee land.[37]

In response, Governor Martin told Old Tassel how much he regretted that North Carolina had not been able to prevent the encroachments, and how much he appreciated the Overhill Towns' not resorting to aggression. He, too, blamed the British and Loyalists for inciting the warriors who attacked the frontiers and understood it had been the Chickamaugas who made the attacks. Martin told Old Tassel that he would send Sevier to mark the boundary and that the squatters "shall be ordered to comply with your request." In the meantime, he asked that the Overhill Towns assist in apprehending the Chickamaugas, whom he regarded as enemies of both the Cherokees and the North Carolinians—otherwise there would be bloodshed.[38]

Soon after Old Tassel sent his message to Martin, the Overmountain militia also went on the offensive as a part of the coordinated effort. It had already experienced the effects of numerous small raids by the Lower Cherokees with the Chickamaugas and decided to coordinate a punitive expedition with its neighboring frontiers. Colonel Sevier gathered some militiamen and met with others on October 3 at a place known locally as "the bend of the Nolichucky" River. There they met other volunteers from Washington County. The total force numbered about two hundred, and Sevier led them south to the French Broad at the Big Island, crossed, and marched to the Tennessee River. Sevier then steered the column for the venerable Cherokee town of Chota, the established capital of peace for the Cherokees. There, Cherokee headmen gave Sevier a guide, John Watts, a future headman of the Cherokees.[39]

From the Overhill Towns on the Little Tennessee River, the column marched south to the Tellico River, where it attacked several towns. After skirmishing with the towns' warriors and fruitlessly pursuing them over the flat country, the militiamen destroyed the towns. Continuing its progress, the column reached the Hiwassee River, where Hanging Maw met with Sevier and impressed on him the peaceful nature of the towns along that river. Sevier spared all but one.[40]

Watts then led the column to the west, toward the Chickamauga towns on Chickamauga Creek, crossing the Hiwassee River about eight miles south of present-day Calhoun, Tennessee. The column first reached the town of Chickamauga at the confluence of Chickamauga Creek and the Tennessee River. The town was deserted, and the troops burned it and destroyed its crops. Then Sevier divided the column into several units that attacked and destroyed the towns along the creek, except Roger's town. John Rogers, a British trader who lived among the Chickamaugas, communicated his desire to join the Whigs, which he did, bringing along a man who had been a slave captured in the Cumberland settlements.[41]

The column then made its way toward the junction of the Coosa and Hightower rivers. Before reaching it, Captain Isaac Thomas created a scout company as an advance guard. Stealthily entering a town, the advance guard surprised a white man named Clemens. Thomas shot and killed Clemens as he attempted to flee. Papers on Clemens indicated he had been a sergeant in the British army. Once past the Facing Mountain (now Rocky Face Mountain, Georgia), which divided the waters of the Tennessee and Coosa rivers, Sevier's column crossed over into the Coosa River valley.[42]

As the Whigs made their way north up the river, they engaged in skirmishes and destroyed all towns and crop fields as they crossed and recrossed the river many times. The towns included Coosa, Big Shumate, Little Shumate, and Ustanali. The towns and crops along the Conasauga and Coosawattee rivers were burned next, and all the livestock killed. They went as far as Talking Rock, at present-day Carter's Lake, and Sevier sent word to the Cherokee headmen that he would meet them at Chota to make peace. Marching back to Chota, Sevier divided his troops, with one division going through the Chilhowee Mountains and temporarily losing its way, while the other retraced its route back to Chota.[43]

At Chota, Hanging Maw, Old Tassel, and the aged Oconostota met with Sevier, marking an end to the expedition. The Cherokees and Sevier agreed to a peaceful future, and both sides exchanged prisoners. The two prisoners the Cherokees turned over were Jane Ireland, taken from the Overmountain settlements, and Samuel Martin, taken from the Cumberland settlements.[44]

The Whig expedition fought many skirmishes and inflicted about twenty to thirty casualties, while capturing fifty Cherokees. There are no accurate casualty figures for Sevier's troops, but given the frequency of combat and ambush, he no doubt suffered a number of casualties. The Whig expedition destroyed a number of outlying Cherokee towns, their livestock, and much of their corn crop. It also destroyed a cache of goods in what one observer described as a British storehouse.[45]

Even though he had written to Pickens that he could mount an expedition in the middle of September, Colonel Joseph McDowell did not muster his militia force until sometime in October, about the time "when the corn began to harden." He did, however, muster a much larger force than he had in August. Several hundred militiamen rendezvoused on Hominy Creek, a tributary of the French Broad River. From there they followed Rutherford's Trace again back into the Middle Towns. The Cherokees skirmished with the militiamen at several major towns but ultimately withdrew into the mountains. McDowell's column destroyed practically every town and all the crops in the Little Tennessee Valley.[46]

While Clarke, Pickens, and Sevier spread the torch throughout the Chickamauga towns and effectively ended their attacks for some time, the Shawnees and their allies remained unsubdued. In addition to their siege of Bryan's Station and their tremendous victory at the Battle of Blue Licks, the

Shawnees captured thirty-seven settlers from another station in western Kentucky, and forty more from the Lexington settlements. Colonel Christian confessed to Virginia's governor Harrison, "These successes will surely encourage the Shawnees to new Enterprises." He conservatively estimated that not more than one thousand settlers could be counted in all of Kentucky. The scant population was so scattered that it would take a week to collect a number sufficient to defend any one point. The dispersed layout of the settlements also meant there would be a problem getting men to leave the defense of their families. To make matters worse, Christian had received intelligence that the Wabash Indians might go on the offensive in Kentucky. Christian pleaded for Governor Harrison to send Continental troops, particularly dragoons, who "would be of essential service against Indians." If that could not be done, Christian felt that the situation was so desperate that he volunteered himself to raise five hundred mounted men, go to Kentucky, where he hoped to raise five hundred more, and then lead them on an expedition into the Shawnee territory.[47]

By the end of September 1782, Lieutenant Colonel Thomas Brown, British superintendant of Indian affairs in the Southern Department, had advised the Cherokees and Creeks who had been active against the frontier to cease their attacks. Without knowing about the coordinated Whig expeditions, Brown had wisely given the American Indians of the south the best advice to preclude any further devastating attacks by the Whigs: go hunting and do not attack the frontiers. Brown had actually been ordered by his commander, General Alexander Leslie in Charleston, to end all relations with the American Indians as preparatory to the British withdrawal from the southern theater. Brown believed in the moral force of his opinion when he wrote to Lord Cornwallis that the Cherokees had suffered a great deal by participating in the war on behalf of the British and should not be abandoned.[48]

The Chickasaws had not attacked the Cumberland settlements with any degree of severity since the Battle of the Bluffs on April 2, 1781. After the abandonment of Colonel George Rogers Clark's Fort Jefferson on the Ohio River in

June 1781, the Chickasaws sought a peace with Virginia. Finally, on October 24, 1782, Chickasaw headmen signed a peace treaty with Virginia. Once the Chickasaws realized that not only the British but the Americans would provide them with trade, their enmity seemed to diminish. Curiously, neither side mentioned the Cumberland settlements. The Chickasaw headmen did object to settlements on the Mississippi River, where a few settlers had ventured. Though the document the headmen signed was just a preliminary agreement, the Chickasaws did not again materially interfere with the Cumberland settlements, and they signed a formal treaty agreement a year later.[49]

In early November 1782, George Rogers Clark mounted an expedition with 1,050 men against the Shawnee towns north of the Ohio River. Clark reached Chillicothe on the tenth and achieved complete surprise. Over the course of that and the next four days, his troops fanned out and destroyed some two-thirds of the towns and crops. He then withdrew back across the Ohio, and for the remainder of the war, the Shawnees did not make any significant attacks on the Kentucky or Overmountain settlements.[50]

Colonel Christian reported to Virginia's governor Harrison in mid-December that a large group of Cherokees wanted to visit Richmond, ostensibly so they could have the state of Virginia sustain them, but he and Colonel Martin had dissuaded them. Their desire stemmed from the Cherokees' absolute destitution. Many had only old bear skins to cover themselves, which made the winter unbearable. Also, their crops had failed and their food would run out before winter ended. Worse still, they could not provide for themselves because they lacked ammunition. Sending goods without sending ammunition would be useless, because the Cherokees could not pay for anything without being able to hunt and acquire skins for trade. Christian advised that Colonel Martin had already provided for about fifty Cherokees out of his own provisions. In the name of humanity, Christian asked the governor to authorize the purchase of a few hundred bushels of corn, at least, to keep them from starving to death. The problem was that years of continued warfare had left practically everyone destitute: Indians, settlers—and state governments.[51]

FIFTEEN

1783 & Beyond

Early in 1783, some Cherokee headmen who refused to have any interaction with the Americans ventured to Saint Augustine in East Florida to meet with Lieutenant Colonel Thomas Brown, the British superintendant of Indian affairs. While there, they discovered that the British government, their supporter throughout the American Revolution, had already essentially abandoned them. Brown told them to simply return to their hunting. When the Indians brought up the problem of continued encroachment by American settlers, Brown suggested they move to where the Tennessee River flowed into the Ohio River; at least from there they could still be useful to British interests by interrupting American and Spanish shipping.[1]

Other Cherokee headmen realized the support and supply of the British had come to an end, and they faced the inevitable, at least for the time being. Kenitah wrote to Colonel Joseph Martin, confessing his previous friendship with the British but saying he no longer was their ally. Accepting Martin's promise that the Cherokees would have plenty of trade goods and ammunition for their fall hunting, Kenitah sent Martin the commission and medal the British had bestowed on him years earlier. To signify the end of his relationship with the British, he told Martin in a letter that he grasped some ashes in his hands and scattered them to the wind.[2]

Then, in a letter from Old Tassel, Martin learned about the wretched condition of the Cherokees. They walked around naked, and game passed all around yet they starved for lack of ammunition. The ammunition Martin had sent them earlier did not arrive, and Old Tassel pleaded with Martin to send more in the care of someone who would see it delivered safely to them. If not, he said, they would surely starve, for they had no other way to get food.[3]

Martin received some other alarming news from Old Tassel: delegations from four tribes around Detroit were going to meet with the southern Indians and then go to Saint Augustine to gather as many warriors as possible for a proposed campaign. In the spring, all the mobilized warriors would meet around Detroit and campaign against the Americans from Fort Pitt all the way to the Illinois country. The northern delegates had promised the Cherokees they would be well supplied with everything they needed if they joined their proposed offensive.[4]

Within a couple of months, attacks began on the frontier in Powell's Valley and Clinch Valley. But, they were not the widespread attacks of earlier years. The northern tribes no longer had the support of the southern tribes. Ravaged by years of harsh warfare, failing crops, and dwindling sources of supply goods, many of the pro-British Indians in the southern theater had grown weary of a conflict that brought them only more devastation and hardship. In spite of the promise of lavish goods and supplies, the northern delegation that Martin had so feared was unable to recruit many warriors in the south—certainly not enough to continue a general war against the frontiers. As a result, Martin no longer anticipated problems of any real substance in the summer.[5]

It is uncertain whether it happened through usurpation or not, but Alexander McGillivray assumed leadership of the anti-American coalition of Creeks after Emistiseguo died in July 1782. With the defeat of the British and their expulsion from the southern theater, McGillivray's faction had to secure a means of supply. In April, McGillivray even appealed to Georgia for ammunition, implying that the Upper and Lower

Creeks would not oppose a cession of land. As further entice-ment, he suggested that the garrison at Pensacola was weak enough to be recaptured with Creek assistance. At the same time, the British agent to the anti-American Creeks wrote to Superintendant Brown in Saint Augustine, requesting ammu-nition. He affirmed the continued loyalty of the Creeks and also mentioned the weak state of the garrison at Pensacola. There is no evidence to suggest that Georgia ever sent its recent enemies supplies of any kind, much less ammunition. Neither did Brown, because the British had already decided to abandon their former loyal Creek allies. British officials did, however, want Brown "to take every measure possible to preserve Indian friendship and secure the country." Unfortunately for Brown and the southern Indians, they did not authorize any material support.6

By June 1, Brown had ordered all the British agents and Indian Department officers to withdraw from the Indian nations to Saint Augustine. Brown genuinely understood what the future held for the southern Indians and did all he could to persuade them not to further provoke the Americans. "I dread the effect of abandoning the Creeks," he said, and lamented that a war with Georgia and South Carolina loomed on the horizon for them. That summer, the British had no plans for the southern Indians and really did not know what to do with them. From Detroit, Major Arant S. DePeyster bemoaned the fact that "seventy Cherokees and other southern Indians are coming here . . . what to do with them I know not."7

As the summer progressed, the North Carolina assembly authorized Governor Alexander Martin to make a peace treaty with the Cherokees—the one promised the summer before at the Great Island peace conference. Martin would have held it earlier, but he had no goods or supplies to host the conference. He even contacted Governor Harrison of Virginia about that state's policy for trading with the British, since several of their trading ships sat in North Carolina waters. In fact, unknown to Governor Martin, the availability of goods was not a problem. Colonel Joseph Martin still had most of the goods North Carolina had sent him the year before, because the Cherokees did not have the ammunition they needed to hunt with and obtain the skins necessary to buy goods.[8]

Throughout early fall, Colonel Martin worked diligently out of a genuine concern for the welfare of the Cherokees. On September 25, he returned from the Overhill Cherokee towns, which all desired peace, except a few at the head of the Hiwassee River. In fact, the Chickamaugas conveyed their displeasure with those towns and told Colonel Martin they wanted to put the towns' leaders to death. Martin learned that a Colonel Logan had raised a force to go against the Chickamaugas for the recent attacks actually perpetrated by the Creeks. Apparently the Creeks had gone to Augusta for a peace treaty, yet they sent all their force against the Kentucky frontiers. As if that were not enough to complicate matters, Colonel Martin had reliable reports that the Spanish, their erstwhile allies, had been encouraging the Indians to continue their war against the United States.[9]

The Creek headmen who had always assisted the Whigs in Georgia during the Revolution met with Georgia officials on November 1 and signed a peace treaty. The treaty included a large cession of land. A new boundary as far north as Curahee Mountain and as far west as the Oconee River had been established. The lands between the Oconee and Ogeechee rivers included in the cession had been marked and squatted on by Georgia settlers for years during the Revolution and had been the source of countless Creek complaints. By the time of the treaty, it is uncertain exactly who could claim authority over the lands. Alexander McGillivray, ostensibly leader of the anti-American coalition of Creeks, did not recognize the validity of the treaty and became the source of violence for years to come in Georgia.[10]

On November 5, the Americans signed a peace treaty with the Chickasaws at the French Licks in the Cumberland settlements. No sooner had the treaty been concluded than the Spanish began establishing trade connections with the Chickasaws and other Indians east of the Mississippi River. By the middle of December, the Spanish had established trading posts on the Tennessee River and "were endeavoring by every means to gain the Indians to their favor, to the detriment of the United States." Previously, the Americans learned that the Shawnees could not attend their proposed peace conference because they had gone to a conference with the British in Niagara. Further, the Creeks had maintained their open hostility even to the chagrin of the Chickamaugas.[11]

The peace treaties with some of the Indians only meant a lull in the violence on the southern frontiers. Spain had been an ally of France during the American Revolution, but only a *de facto* ally to the United States. In the postwar years, however, Spain gained the Floridas through the Anglo-Spanish peace agreement of September 1783 and shared a border with the United States. Immediately, the interests of the two countries made them antagonists. With the British still ensconced in Canada supporting American Indians against the United States, and the Spanish replacing the British below the Ohio River, not much was different for the southern frontiers at the end of the Revolution. It would be only a few years before open warfare erupted again.

Notes

Introduction

1. John Filson, *The Discovery, Settlement, and Present State of Kentucky* (London: John Stockdale, 1793), 36–37.

Chapter One: Early Interrelations

1. John Richard Alden, *John Stuart and the Southern Colonial Frontier: A Study of Indian Relations, War, Trade, and Land Problems in the Southern Wilderness, 1754-1775* (Ann Arbor: University of Michigan Press, 1944), 135–136.

2. For encroachment, see Colin Calloway, *The Scratch of a Pen: 1763 and the Transformation of North America* (New York: Oxford University Press, 2006), 92–100. For trade, see J. Russell Snapp, *John Stuart and the Struggle for Empire on the Southern Frontier* (Baton Rouge: Louisiana State University Press, 1996), especially chapters 2, 3, and 4.

3. James William Hagy and Stanley J. Folmsbee, eds., "The Lost Archives of the Cherokee Nation, Part I: 1763–1772," *East Tennessee Historical Society Publications* 43 (1971): 114–117; John Richard Alden, "The Eighteenth Century Cherokee Archives," *American Archivist* 5, no. 4 (October 1942): 240–244; Calloway, *Scratch of a Pen*, 102.

4. Henry Mouzon, et al., "An accurate map of North and South Carolina, with their Indian frontier, shewing in a distinct manner all the mountains, rivers, swamps, marshes, bays, creeks, harbours, sandbanks and soundings on the coasts; with the roads and Indian paths; as well as the boundary or provincial lines, the several townships, and other divisions of the land in both the provinces; the whole from actual surveys by Henry Mouzon and others," http://memory.loc.gov/cgi-bin/query/h?ammem/gmd:@field (NUMBER+@band(g3900+ar139404)); map of Northeast Georgia, C. L. Williams, 1874, Draper MSS, 3VV85; Gerald F. Schroedl, "Cherokee Ethnohistory and Archaeology from 1540 to 1838," in *Powhattan's Mantle: Indians in the Colonial Southeast*, edited with an introduction by Gregory A. Waselkov, Peter H. Wood, and Tom Hatley (Lincoln: University of Nebraska Press, 2006), 205; Gary C. Goodwin, *Cherokees in Transition: A Study of Changing Culture and Environment Prior to 1775* (Chicago: University of Chicago Press, 1977), 121–123.

5. Calloway, *Scratch of a Pen*, 98.

6. *Journal of the Congress of the Four Southern Governors and the Superintendent of that District with the Five Nations of Indians at Augusta, 1763* (Charleston, SC: n.p., 1764).

7. John Stuart to General Gage, May 20, 1764, Gage Papers.

8. John P. Brown, *Old Frontiers: The Story of the Cherokee Indians from Earliest Times to the Date of Their Removal to the West, 1838* (Kingsport, TN: Southern Publishers, 1938), 124.

9. Louis De Vorsey Jr., *The Indian Boundary in the Southern Colonies, 1763–1775* (Chapel Hill: University of North Carolina Press, 1966), 125–129; John Stuart to General Gage, May 20, 1764, Gage Papers.

10. South Carolina Council, *The Journal of the Council of the Assembly*, 778–781; William Stevens Powell, ed., *The Correspondence of William Tryon and Other Selected Papers* (Raleigh, NC: Division of Archives and History, 1980–1981), I: 298–302.

11. Powell, *Tryon*, I: 301–302.

12. Powell, *Tryon*, I: 349; Talk from Cherokee Chiefs to John Stuart, September 22, 1766, CO 5/67: 240–243.

13. Powell, *Tryon*, I: 496–500; *NCCR*, 7: 468–470.

14. Powell, *Tryon*, I: 503–505.

15. Commissioners for the Boundary Line to Judd's Friend and Saluy, June 13, 1767, CO 5/310: 270–270d.

16. John Stuart to General Gage, August 13, 1768, Gage Papers.

17. De Vorsey, *Indian Boundary*, 157–161.

18. Treaty of Hard Labor, Gage Papers, vol. 137, no. 8, 1–14.

19. Ibid.

20. Ibid.

21. Ibid.; De Vorsey, *Indian Boundary*, 104.

22. Brown, *Old Frontiers*, 128–132. Brown states that the settlements grew because the Cherokees were distracted by their "war" with the Chickasaws.

23. John William Gerard de Brahm, "De Brahm's Account," in *Early Travels in the Tennessee Country: 1540–1800*, ed. Samuel Cole Williams (Johnson City, TN: 1928), 193.

24. "Virginia and the Cherokees, &c.: The Treaties of 1768 and 1770," *Virginia Magazine of History and Biography* 13, no. 1 (July, 1905): 20–23.

25. J. P. Kennedy and H. R. McIlwaine, eds., *Journals of the House of Burgesses of Virginia, 1619–1776*, 13 vols. (Richmond: E. Waddey, 1905–1915), 11: xxx–xxxiv; H. R. McIlwaine, et al., eds., *Executive Journals of the Council of Colonial Virginia*, 6 vols. (Richmond, VA: Virginia State Library, 1925–1966), 6: 308–309; *VMHB* 13: 28–36.

26. Kennedy and McIlwaine, *Journals*, 11: x–xii, 334–336.

27. Congress with the Cherokee Indians, April 1770, Gage Papers, vol. 137, no. 11, 1–16.

28. Kennedy and McIlwaine, *Journals*, 12: 74; McIlwaine, *Executive Journals*, 6: 353–357.

29. Report of the General Meeting of the Principle Chiefs and Warriors of the Cherokee Nation with John Stuart, October 18–20, 1770, CO 5/72: 29–53.

30. Memorial from the Principle Traders to the Creek and Cherokee Nations to Governor Wright, 1771, CO 5/661: 213; Memorial from Merchants Trading with Georgia to Board of Trade, March 25, 1772, CO 5/661: 219–220.

31. *DAR*, 3: 70–73.

Chapter Two: Mounting Tensions

1. *EAID*, 14: 323–325.

2. De Vorsey, *Indian Boundary*, 79–83.

3. Governor Dunmore to Earl of Hillsborough, March 1772, CO 5/1350: 19, 27.

4. Louis De Vorsey Jr., "The Virginia-Cherokee Boundary of 1771," *East Tennessee Historical Society Publications* 33 (1961): 17–31.

5. De Vorsey, *Indian Boundary*, 165.

6. *EAID*, 14: 323–325.

7. John Stuart to Earl of Dartmouth, January 8, 1772, CO 5/74: 35; *NCCR*, 9: 632–633; *DAR*, 6: 45–47.

8. *NCCR*, 9: 632–633.

9. William Bartram, *William Bartram Travels* (New Haven, CT: Yale University Press, 1958), repr., Salt Lake City: Peregrine Smith, 1980, 26.

10. Some Indian names, such as the War Woman, were also titles.

11. Alden, *John Stuart*, 306, 307, 309; *CRG*, 38(1): 172–175; Lord Germain to Lieutenant Governor Bull, Governor Tryon, Governor Chester, July 6, 1774, CO 5/75: 137–139; Extract from the Journal of Alexander McKee, 1774, CO 5/75: 145–146; Affidavits of Isaac Thomas and Thomas Sharp, August 20, 1774, CO 5/75: 168–169; Copy of a Letter from the Earl of Dunmore, April 5, 1774, CO 5/75: 170–171d; Charles Stuart to John Stuart, May 19, 1774, CO 5/75: 172–173d; *NCCR*, 9: 825–826.

12. John Stuart to Earl of Dartmouth, August 2, 1774, CO 5/75: 165.

13. Lord Dunmore to John Stuart, April 5, 1774, CO 5/75: 169–172. Wampum were pieces of the quahog shell (purple) and whelk shell (white), cut and bored into beads.

14. Ibid. Some confusion may stem from the terms "beloved woman" and "beloved man." "Beloved Woman" represented both the title of a particular woman and of several women. It referred to women who were respected and known as peacemakers, such as Nancy Ward, the Beloved Woman of Chota. "Beloved Man" referred to Cherokee leaders, often retired warriors, who were known for their caution and calm deliberation. Attakullakulla would often be called a "beloved man." For more on these positions in Cherokee society, see Susan Abram, "'Souls in the Treetops': Cherokee War, Masculinity, and Community, 1760–1820" (PhD diss., Auburn University, 2009), ch. 1, "The Beloved Occupation: Warfare, Gender, and Community."

15. Charles Stuart to John Stuart, May 19, 1774, CO 5/75: 173–174.

16. *DAR*, 8: 56–58.

17. *EAID*, 14: 355.

18. Ibid., 356–358. The Creeks called most settlers "Virginians" and used the word "English" to refer to British officials and British army troops.

19. *CRG*, 38(I): 246–261.

20. Alden, *John Stuart*, 308.

21. *DAR*, 7: 189, 193.

22. Letter to the Governor about Henderson, 1775, Draper MSS, 4QQ1.

23. Ibid.

24. Otis K. Rice, *Frontier Kentucky* (Lexington: University Press of Kentucky, 1975), 20.

25. The sources for the description of the Henderson Purchase are found in the Draper Manuscripts, Depositions of Samuel Wilson (1CC160), Nathanael Henderson (1CC164–167), Isaac Shelby (1CC169), James Robertson (1CC174–177), Charles Robertson (1CC181–183), John Lowry (1CC183), and John Reid (1CC187).

26. Captain Russell to Lord Dunmore, March 10, 1775, Draper MSS, 4QQ7.

27. William Stewart Lester, *The Transylvania Colony* (Spencer, IN: Samuel R. Guard, 1935), 38.

28. Theodore Roosevelt, *The Winning of the West*, 4 vols. (New York: G. P. Putnam's Sons, 1889–1896), 1: 296.

29. South Carolina Committee of Intelligence to John Stuart, June 29, 1775, CO 5/76: 158–160; Hamer, *Laurens Papers*, 10: 188–190.

30. John Stuart to Earl of Dartmouth, January 8, 1776, CO 5/77: 74–75; Hamer, *Laurens Papers*, 10: 214, 223–224.

31. John Stuart to William Drayton, July 18, 1775, CO 5/76: 163–165.

32. Hamer, *Laurens Papers*, 10: 244–246.

33. John Stuart to Earl of Dartmouth, September 17, 1775, CO 5/76: 172–181; Hamer, *Laurens Papers*, 10: 243–244.

34. Extract of Letter from David Taitt to John Stuart, April 14, 1775, and Governor Wright to John Stuart, July 6, 1775, CO 5/76: 164–168; Hamer, *Laurens Papers*, 10: 188–190.

35. Hamer, *Laurens Papers*, 10: 243.

36. *DAR*, 10: 83, 131.

37. John Drayton, *Memoirs of the American Revolution as Relating to the State of South Carolina*, 2 vols. (Charleston, SC: A. E. Miller, 1821), 1: 374, 412.

38. Ibid., 407, 419–427.

39. Ibid., 424–425.

40. Ibid., 425–427. An Osnaburg split shirt was a garment worn in the backcountry that was made not to button and to be worn open in the front during warmer months.

41. John Stuart to Earl of Dartmouth, January 6, 1776, CO 5/77: 40–49; John Stuart to Earl of Dartmouth, January 8, 1776, CO 5/77: 67–88.

CHAPTER THREE: THE BREAKING POINT

1. John Stuart to Earl of Dartmouth, January 6, 1776, CO 5/77: 48–49; Talk to John Stuart from Upper Creeks, August 15, 1775, CO 5/77: 55–62; Hamer, *Laurens Papers*, 10: 437, 467–469, 491.

2. John Stuart to Earl of Dartmouth, September 17, 1775, CO 5/76: 172–189; John Stuart to Earl of Dartmouth, January 6, 1776, CO 5/77: 45–46.

3. John Stuart to Earl of Dartmouth, December 17, 1775, CO 5/77: 22–31; John Stuart to Earl of Dartmouth, January 6, 1776, CO 5/77: 40–41; Secoffee to Continental Commissioners, n.d., CO 5/77: 195–199.

4. Hamer, *Laurens Papers*, 10: 558–559, 572–573; John Stuart to General Gage, October 24, 1775, CO 5/77: 50–64.

5. General Gage to John Stuart, September 12, 1775, CO 5/76: 188–189; John Stuart to Earl of Dartmouth, December 17, 1775, CO 5/77: 30–31; Philip M. Hamer, "John Stuart's Indian Policy during the Early Months of the American Revolution," *Mississippi Valley Historical Review* 17, no. 3 (December 1930), 360–361.

6. John Stuart to Earl of Dartmouth, December 17, 1775, CO 5/77: 28–31, John Stuart to General Henry Clinton, March 15, 1776, CO 5/77: 107–111.

7. John Stuart to Earl of Dartmouth, December 17, 1775, CO 5/77: 22–31.

8. *DAR*, 10: 170; Hamer, *Laurens Papers*, 10: 601.

9. John Stuart to Earl of Dartmouth, January 19, 1776, CO 5/77: 38–41; John Stuart to Earl of Dartmouth, January 8, 1776, CO 5/77: 67–68.

10. Hamer, *Laurens Papers*, 11: 93–97.

11. Ibid., 102.

12. Talk from Lower Creeks to John Stuart, March 23, 1776, CO 5/77: 130–131.

13. North Carolina State Archives, Secretary of State Records, *Continental Congress, 1774–1779* (S.S.317).

14. Ibid.

15. Ibid.

16. Robert Rae to Samuel Thomas, May 3, 1776, CO 5/77: 139–141.

17. John Stuart to Lord George Germain, August 23, 1776, CO 5/77: 126–130; M. F. Stephenson to Lyman C. Draper, September 18, 1873, Draper MSS, 3VV107.

18. Hugh Hamilton to Alexander Cameron, July 5, 1776, CO 5/77: 163–167; Secoffee to Continental Commissioners, n.d., CO 5/77: 195–197; *NCCR*, 22: 744.

19. Ibid.; *NCCR*, 22: 742–743

20. Robert Rae to Samuel Thomas, May 3, 1776, CO 5/77: 139–141.

21. Ibid., 281; Hamer, "John Stuart," 352–353.

22. John Carter to Henry Stuart and Alexander Cameron, May 13, 1776, CO 5/77: 149–150; Hamer, "John Stuart," 353–355.

23. Hamer, "John Stuart," 355–356.

24. Henry Stuart's Account of His Proceedings with the Indians, August 25, 1776, CO 5/77: 169; *NCCR*, 10: 769; *DAR*, 12: 196. "Raven" was a military-like title as well as a name. Generally, each town had an individual with this title, but when Cherokees refer simply to "the Raven," they usually mean the Raven of Chota, which was the principle Cherokee town.

25. Henry Stuart and Alexander Cameron to Nolichucky Settlers, May 23, 1776, CO 5/77: 152; Hamer, "John Stuart," 356–358.

26. *DAR,* 12: 197.

27. Ibid.

28. Ibid., 198; *NCCR*, 10: 657.

29. John Stuart to Lord George Germain, May 20, 1776, CO 5/77: 93–94, unknown to unknown, May 9, 1776, 111–113.

30. *NCCR*, 10: 773; Colin G. Calloway, *The American Revolution in Indian Country: Crisis and Diversity in Native American Communities* (Cambridge: Cambridge University Press, 1995), 194.

31. *NCCR*, 10: 773; *DAR,* 12: 197.

32. *NCCR*, 10: 774; Henry Stuart and Alexander Cameron to Nolichucky Settlers, May 23, 1776, CO 5/77: 150–153.

33. Henry Stuart and Alexander Cameron to John Carter, May 23, 1776, CO 5/77: 153–155.

34. *NCCR*, 10: 774; Henry Stuart to Edward Wilkinson, June 28, 1776, CO 5/77: 155–158.

35. *NCCR*, 10: 774–775; *DAR*, 12: 200.

36. *NCCR*, 10: 775.
37. *NCCR*, 10: 776; *DAR*, 12: 201; Calloway, *American Revolution*, 194.
38. *NCCR*, 10: 777; *DAR*, 12: 202. The meaning of the belts lies in the colors and the material (beads or wampum). White is the color of peace, and purple is the color indicating war or suffering. Beads can be obtained through simple trade, but wampum carries a much higher price—it is the most expensive material that can be used for this purpose.
39. Calloway, *American Revolution*, 195; Gregory Evans Dowd, *A Spirited Resistance: The North American Indian Struggle for Unity, 1745–1815* (Baltimore: Johns Hopkins University Press, 1992), 47.
40. Dowd, *Spirited Resistance*, 49.
41. *NCCR*, 10: 779; *DAR*, 12: 203.
42. *NCCR*, 10: 779; John Carter for the People at Watauga to Henry Stuart and Alexander Cameron, May 13, 1776, CO 5/77: 142–187.
43. *NCCR*, 10: 779–780; *DAR*, 12: 203–204.
44. *NCCR*, 10: 781; *DAR*, 12: 204–205.
45. *NCCR*, 10: 781–782; *DAR*, 12: 205.

CHAPTER FOUR: CHEROKEE OFFENSIVE

1. *NCCR*, 11: 301, 303.
2. Draper MSS, Adventures of Andrew Pickens, 3VV149–151.
3. Draper MSS, Interview notes of John Spelts, 1841–1843, 28S25–27.
4. Vicki Rozema, *Footsteps of the Cherokees: A Guide to the Eastern Homelands of the Cherokee Nation* (Winston-Salem, NC: John F. Blair, 1995), 270. Local legend states that a Cherokee named Skiuka came to Captain Howard, whom he knew previously, and warned him of the pending attack. Skiuka then led the militiamen to a position whence they forced the retreat of the Cherokees. No primary material could be located as a source for the legend.
5. David Taitt to John Stuart, July 7, 1776, CO 5/77: 163–167, Henry Stuart's Account of His Proceedings with the Indians, August 25, 1776, CO 5/77: 169; Hamer, *Laurens Papers*, 10: 572.
6. Samuel A. Ashe, *The History of North Carolina*, 2 vols. (Greensboro, NC: Charles L. Van Noppen, 1908), 1: 11.
7. *NCCR*, 10: 651–652.
8. *NCCR*, 10: 657.
9. Ibid., 658.
10. William Campbell to Lord George Germain, July 8, 1776, CO 5/396: 304–307; J. G. M. Ramsey, *The Annals of Tennessee to the End of the Eighteenth Century* (Charleston, SC: John Russell, 1853), 148–149.
11. Ramsey, *Annals*, 148–149.
12. Ibid., 150.
13. Interview notes of General Thomas Love, 1841–1844, Draper MSS, 30S67; *NCCR*, 10: 665–666.
14. *NCCR*, 10: 665–666; *NCCR*, 11: 315–316, 320.
15. *NCCR*, 10: 662.
16. Ibid., 669.

17. Williamson's Cherokee Campaign, 1776, by William Gilmore Simms, Draper MSS, 3VV178–179.

18. William Stewart Lester, *The Transylvania Colony* (Spencer, IN: Samuel R. Guard, 1935), 169.

19. Interview notes of Mrs. David Musick, 1868, Draper MSS, 22S183–184; "Life of Boone," Draper MSS, 4B76–77, 80; Notes of Historical Collections, Draper MSS, 12CC204–206; John Floyd to William Preston, July 21, 1776, Draper MSS, 17CC172; Lester, *Transylvania*, 163.

20. Notes of Historical Collections, Draper MSS, 12CC205; "Life of Boone," Draper MSS, 4B81; Interview notes of Mrs. Susan Howell, 1868, Draper MSS, 23S228–229; John Floyd to William Preston, July 21, 1776, Draper MSS, 17CC172.

21. "Life of Boone," Draper MSS, 4B87–89; John Floyd to William Preston, July 21, 1776, Draper MSS, 17CC172.

22. John Floyd to William Preston, July 21, 1776, Draper MSS, 17CC172; "Life of Boone," Draper MSS, 4B89.

23. Interview notes of Mrs. Susan Howell, 1868, Draper MSS, 23S240; Lester, *Transylvania*, 167.

24. Interview notes of Mrs. Susan Howell, 1868, Draper MSS, 23S230; "Life of Boone," Draper MSS, 4B81; Notes on Historical Collections, Draper MSS, 12CC173; John Floyd to William Preston, July 21, 1776, Draper MSS, 17CC173.

25. "Life of Boone," Draper MSS, 4B91–92; Lester, *Transylvania*, 167.

26. Interview notes of Mrs. David Musick, 1868, Draper MSS, 22S184–5; Interview notes of Mrs. Susan Howell, 1868, Draper MSS, 23S229–230, 241; John Floyd to William Preston, July 21, 1776, Draper MSS, 17CC172.

27. Interview notes of Mrs. David Musick, 1868, Draper MSS, 22S185.

28. Drayton, *Memoirs*, 342; RWPA, Jonathan Downs (W21000).

29. Lindley S. Butler, ed., *The Narrative of David Fanning* (Davidson, NC: Briarpatch Press, 1981), 4.

30. Rachel Klein, *Unification of a Slave State: The Rise of the Planter Class in the South Carolina Backcountry, 1760–1808* (Chapel Hill: University of North Carolina Press, 1990), 95–96.

31. Drayton, *Memoirs*, 341–343.

32. *NCCR*, 11: 318–319.

33. Ibid., 303, 328, 338.

34. *NCCR*, 10: 671–672, 680; *NCCR*, 11: 333.

35. Drayton, *Memoirs*, 344.

36. Drayton, *Memoirs*, 345.

37. *NCCR*, 11: 338–339.

38. Ibid., 10: 726–727.

39. *Virginia Gazette* (Dixon and Hunter), September 27, 1776; *South Carolina and American Gazette*, August 14, 1776.

40. *Virginia Gazette* (Dixon and Hunter), September 27, 1776; *South Carolina and American Gazette*, August 14, 1776; Bartram, *Travels*, 209.

41. *Virginia Gazette* (Dixon and Hunter), September 27, 1776; Williamson's Campaign of 1776, by Andrew Pickens, Draper MSS, 3VV 137; *South Carolina and American Gazette*, August 14, 1776.
42. *Virginia Gazette* (Dixon and Hunter), September 27, 1776; Williamson's Campaign of 1776, by Andrew Pickens, Draper MSS, 3VV 137–138; *South Carolina and American Gazette*, August 14, 1776; Drayton, *Memoirs*, 345–347, 370.
43. *Virginia Gazette* (Dixon and Hunter), September 27, 1776; Williamson's Campaign of 1776, by Andrew Pickens, Draper MSS, 3VV 137–138; *South Carolina and American Gazette*, August 14, 1776; Drayton, *Memoirs*, 345–347, 370.
44. Williamson's Campaign of 1776, by Andrew Pickens, Draper MSS, 3VV 137–138.
45. Drayton, *Memoirs*, 346–347, 370; Draper MSS, 3VV137–139.
46. *Virginia Gazette* (Dixon and Hunter), September 27, 1776; Williamson's Campaign of 1776, by Andrew Pickens, Draper MSS, 3VV 137–138; *South Carolina and American Gazette*, August 14, 1776; Drayton, *Memoirs*, 349–350.
47. Maurice Moore, *Reminiscences of York,* Elmore Oris Parker, ed. (Greeneville, SC: A Press, 1981), 19.
48. Ibid., 19–20.
49. Ibid., 20; Draper MSS, Williamson's Cherokee Campaign of 1776 Journal, 3VV179–180.
50. Drayton, *Memoirs*, 351; *NCCR* 10: 746; *Philadelphia Evening Post*, October 15, 1776.
51. *Philadelphia Evening Post*, October 15, 1776; *NCCR* 10: 746; *South Carolina and American Gazette*, August 14–21, 1776.
52. Williamson's Campaign of 1776, by Andrew Pickens, Draper MSS, 3VV140.
53. Williamson's Cherokee Campaign, 1776, by William Gilmore Simms, Draper MSS, 3VV180; Memoir of Major Joseph McJunkin, Draper MSS, 23VV7; Moore, *Reminiscences*, 21; RWPA, Samuel Otterson (S25344).
54. Drayton, *Memoirs*, 351; *Philadelphia Evening Post*, October 15, 1776; *NCCR*, 10: 746–747.
55. *Pennsylvania Evening Post*, October 15, 1776; *NCCR*, 10: 747; Drayton, *Memoirs*, 351.
56. *Philadelphia Evening Post*, October 15, 1776; *NCCR*, 10: 747–748; Drayton, *Memoirs*, 351–352. Estimates vary as to how many men were with Pickens, but somewhere between fifty and sixty seems proper, given the amount of action the army had encountered thus far in the expedition. Some accounts name Pickens's brother, Joseph, as leading the relief column, while others name Hammond, and still others Williamson himself. Casualty estimates stated in the eighteenth century are patriotically low for the South Carolinians and high for the Cherokees. Such disparate casualty rates seem unlikely given the close proximity of the action, the time required to load an eighteenth-century rifle, and the numbers involved.

57. Drayton, *Memoirs*, 352.
58. Williamson's Cherokee Campaign, 1776, by William Gilmore Simms, Draper MSS, 3VV181–182; Drayton, *Memoirs*, 352.
59. Williamson's Cherokee Expedition–1776, Draper MSS, 3VV152–153.
60. Ibid., 3VV154–155; Williamson's Cherokee Campaign, 1776, by William Gilmore Simms, Draper MSS, 182.
61. Williamson's Cherokee Expedition–1776, Draper MSS, 3VV155–156.
62. Ibid., 3VV156–157; Williamson's Cherokee Campaign, 1776, by William Gilmore Simms, Draper MSS, 182–183.
63. Hamer, *Laurens Papers*, 10: 572.
64. Alexander Cameron to John Stuart, August 31, 1776, CO 5/78, 22–25.

Chapter Five: Whig Expeditions

1. J. G. de Roulhac Hamilton, "Revolutionary War Diary of William Lenoir," *Journal of Southern History* 6, no. 2 (May 1940), 254; Rutherford's Campaign of 1776, Draper MSS, 28S14–15; RWPA, William Williamson (R11628).
2. Rutherford's Campaign of 1776, Draper MSS, 30S72, 28S15.
3. Williamson's Cherokee Campaign–1776, Draper MSS, 3VV157.
4. Ibid., 3VV157–159; Drayton, *Memoirs*, 351.
5. Drayton, *Memoirs*, 353–354.
6. Hamilton, "Revolutionary War Diary," 254–255; Rutherford's Campaign of 1776, Draper MSS, 30S72–73.
7. Hamilton, "Revolutionary War Diary," 255; RWPA, William Alexander (S361); RWPA, Arthur McFalls (W9187).
8. Hamilton, "Revolutionary War Diary," 255.
9. Silas McDowell to L. F. Miles, July 9, 1850, "Miscellaneous Papers, Series 1, vol. 3, 1831–1861," 87–88, North Carolina Department of Archives and History; David L. Swain, "Historical Sketch of the Indian War of 1776," *North Carolina University Magazine* 1, no. 4 (May 1852): 274; Hamilton, "Revolutionary War Diary," 255.
10. Williamson's Cherokee Campaign–1776, Draper MSS, 3VV159.
11. Hamilton, "Revolutionary War Diary," 255; Samuel A. Ashe, *Rutherford's Expedition against the Indians, 1776* (Raleigh, NC: E. M. Uzzel, 1904), 17; C. L. Hunter, *Sketches of Western North Carolina, Historical and Biographical* (Raleigh, NC: Raleigh News Steam Job Print, 1877), 91, 196, 198; RWPA, William Williams (R11628); J. R. Bryson to Lyman C. Draper, June 14, 1870, Draper MSS, 3VV81.
12. Williamson's Cherokee Campaign–1776, Draper MSS, 3VV160.
13. Ibid., 3VV160–161; Drayton, *Memoirs*, 355.
14. Hamilton, "Revolutionary War Diary," 255; Hunter, *Sketches*, 198; RWPA, William Lenoir (S7137); Mary Elinor Lazenby, comp., *Catawba Frontier, 1775–1781: Memories of Pensioners* (Washington, DC: Mary Elinor Lazenby, 1950), 73–74.
15. Williamson's Cherokee Campaign–1776, Draper MSS, 3VV161.

16. Hamilton, "Revolutionary War Diary," 255–256; Hunter, *Sketches*, 198.
17. Hamilton, "Revolutionary War Diary," 256–257.
18. Drayton, *Memoirs*, 355.
19. Drayton, *Memoirs*, 356–357.
20. John McDowell to Lyman C. Draper, June 23, 1874, Draper MSS, 1KK85–85(2); Drayton, *Memoirs*, 356–357. A wall gun was shaped like a regular musket but was larger because the ball it fired could weigh almost one pound.
21. Swain, "Historical Sketch," 275; Drayton, *Memoirs*, 356–357.
22. John McDowell to Lyman C. Draper, June 23, 1874, Draper MSS, 1KK85–85(2), Williamson's Cherokee Campaign, 1776–Col. Samuel Hammond, Draper MSS, 3VV126(1).
23. Williamson's Cherokee Campaign, 1776–Col. Samuel Hammond, Draper MSS, 3VV126; Lazenby, *Catawba Frontier*, 73–74.
24. Drayton, *Memoirs*, 360. Anyone who has hiked the southern Appalachian Mountains knows of laurel thickets, locally known as "hells" for a reason. They grow close together, and their limbs, though small in diameter, are wire-like and can fuse with one another, becoming impenetrable. Whitewater enthusiasts will recognize Drayton's description of the gorge when they run the stretch between "The Ledges" and "Surfing Rapid."
25. Drayton, *Memoirs*, 357; Williamson's Cherokee Campaign, 1776, William Gilmore Simms, Draper MSS, 3VV191.
26. Rutherford's Campaign of 1776, Draper MSS, 28S16–17.
27. Ibid., 28S18–19.
28. Williamson's Cherokee Campaign, 1776, William Gilmore Simms, Draper MSS, 3VV192. In the Draper manuscript, the diarist has "Tomassee," but undoubtedly meant "Tomatley," as the former was a Lower Town.
29. Williamson's Cherokee Campaign, 1776, William Gilmore Simms, Draper MSS, 3VV192–193.
30. Hamilton, "Revolutionary War Diary," 256–257.
31. Williamson's Cherokee Campaign, 1776, William Gilmore Simms, Draper MSS, 3VV193–194; Rozema, *Footsteps*, 181. Rutherford no doubt turned over the prisoners to Williamson because of a few incidents in which individuals murdered helpless Cherokees. See Rutherford's Campaign of 1776, Draper MSS, 28S17–18, 20–21.
32. Williamson's Cherokee Campaign, 1776, William Gilmore Simms, Draper MSS, 3VV195–196.
33. Ibid., 3VV197–199.
34. Ibid., 3VV199–200.
35. Hamilton, "Revolutionary War Diary," 257.
36. *NCCR*, 11: 350.
37. Williamson's Cherokee Campaign, 1776, William Gilmore Simms, Draper MSS, 3VV201–203.
38. John Stuart to Lord George Germain, October 26, 1776, CO 5/78: 15–54.

39. *NCCR*, 10: 658.
40. Wayne E. Lee, "Fortify, Fight, or Flee: Tuscarora and Cherokee Defensive Warfare and Military Culture Adaptation," *Journal of Military History* 68, no. 3 (July 2004), 739–744, 751.
41. Ibid., 763.
42. Ibid., 769.
43. Ian K. Steele, *Warpaths: Invasions of North America* (New York: Oxford University Press, 1994), 135.
44. Ibid.
45. Colin G. Calloway, *New Worlds for All: Indians, Europeans, and the Remaking of Early America* (Baltimore: Johns Hopkins University Press, 1997), 103.
46. RWPA, William Lenoir (S7137).
47. Calloway, *New Worlds*, 97, 109; Lee, "Fortify," 766.
48. *NCCR*, 10: 652.

CHAPTER SIX: THE END OF A VERY VIOLENT YEAR

1. *VMHB*, 16: 170–172.
2. *NCCR*, 10: 837–839.
3. Notes of John Tanner, August 1844, Draper MSS, 32S234; *VMHB*, 17: 55–56; "Wm. Christian to Capt. Isaac Shelbey, September 30, 1776," Reuben T. Durrett Collection on Kentucky and the Ohio River Valley, Special Collections Research Center, University of Chicago; and "Day Book of Isaac Shelby, Aug-Dec, 1776," Reuben T. Durrett Collection, University of Chicago; Lest, *Transylvania*, 171. In outdoor parlance, traveling a few miles and pitching camp would come to be known as a "pioneer's start." This forced a night and a day in the field, and anything found to be lacking could be obtained easily from the starting point.
4. *NCCR*, 10: 838.
5. *VMHB*, 17: 56; *NCCR*, 10: 842; Notes of John Tanner, August 1844, Draper MSS, 32S234.
6. *VMHB*, 17: 57.
7. *Pennsylvania Evening Post*, November 12, 1776; http://aa.usno.navy.mil/data/docs/RS_OneDay.php; Notes of John Tanner, August 1844, Draper MSS, 32S235.
8. *VMHB*, 17: 57–58.
9. Hugh McCall, *The History of Georgia: Containing Brief Sketches of the Most Remarkable Events up to the Present Day* (Savannah, GA: Seymour & Williams, 1811), 78–81; *NCCR*, 10: 846; *Virginia Gazette* (Purdie), November 1, 1776.
10. *VMHB*, 17: 59–60.
11. *NCCR*, 10: 846.
12. *VMHB*, 17: 61.
13. Ibid., 60; *Virginia Gazette* (Purdie), November 1, 1776.
14. *VMHB*, 17: 58.
15. Ibid., 61; Notes of John Tanner, August 1844, 32S235.
16. Ibid., 61, 62.

17. Ibid.; John Stuart to Lord George Germain, January 23, 1777, CO 5/78: 76–80.

18. *VMHB*, 17: 62–63; Samuel Cole Williams, *Tennessee during the Revolutionary War* (Nashville: Tennessee Historical Commission, 1944; repr., Knoxville: University of Tennessee Press, 1974), 45–46.

19. *NCCR*, 10: 845.

20. William Christian to unknown, January 19, 1777, CO 5/78: 147.

21. Ibid., 148.

22. *NCCR*, 11: 895.

23. Ibid.

24. Ibid.

25. Ibid.

26. *NCCR*, 11: 895–896

27. Ibid.; http://aa.usno.navy.mil /data/docs/RS_OneDay.php.

28. *NCCR*, 11: 897; D. J. Reinbold and A. C. Johnston, "Historical Seismicity in the Southern Appalachian Seismic Zone," Department of the Interior, US Geological Survey, Open-File Report 87–433, 1987, p. 4.

29. *NCCR*, 22: 995–1005.

30. John Stuart to Lord George Germain, October 26, 1776, CO 5/78: 15–19.

31. Lord George Germain to John Stuart, November 6, 1776, CO 5/77: 121–123; *DAR*, 10: 400, 401; 13: 74.

32. Document No. 677, 63rd Cong., 3rd sess., *Indians of North America: Letter from the Secretary of the Interior transmitting, in response to a senate resolution of June 30, 1914, a report on the condition and tribal rights of Robeson and adjoining counties of North Carolina* (Washington: Government Printing Office, 1915), 167; Calloway, *American Revolution*, 200.

33. The Cherokee War of 1776, Draper MSS, 30S70.

34. Colonel Cleveland, by Major Thurmond, n.d., Draper MSS, 30S19, 23(2), 26, 29; John Stuart to Lord George Germain, October 26, 1776, CO5/78: 21.

CHAPTER SEVEN: AN UNEASY PEACE

1. William Christian to unknown, January 19, 1777, CO5/78: 147–148.

2. Ibid., 148–150.

3. Rutherford's Campaign of 1776, Draper MSS, 30S70–71.

4. Lord George Germain to John Stuart, February 7, 1777, CO 5/78: 3–7, John Stuart to Lord George Germain, January 23, 1777, CO 5/78: 76–85, 111; *DAR*, vol. 13: 53.

5. *NCSR*, 11: 372, 392–393.

6. Drayton, *Memoirs*, 2: 361.

7. Ibid.

8. Ibid., 2: 362.

9. Captain James Thompson to Captain Joseph Martin, March 1, 1777, Draper MSS, 1XX15, 25; *EAID*, 18: 215.

10. *NCSR*, 11: 428–429.

11. Ibid.

12. Proceedings of April 1777, Draper MSS, 4QQ120–122; James H. O'Donnell, *The Southern Indians in the American Revolution* (Knoxville: University of Tennessee Press, 1973), 55.

13. "Life of Boone," Lyman C. Draper, Draper MSS, 4B106, 115, 117; General Levy Todd's Narrative, Draper MSS, 48J10; Memorandum of George R. Clark, Draper MSS, 48J12; John Cowan's Journal, Draper MSS, 4CC30; Shane Notes, n.d., Draper MSS, 26CC55.

14. Patrick Henry to Oconostota, March 5, 1777, CO 5/78: 160–161.

15. Ibid.

16. Ibid.

17. Proceedings of April 1777, Draper MSS, 4QQ108–119.

18. Brown, *Old Frontiers*, 162; *NCSR*, 11: 446, 458; Ramsey, *Annals*, 171; Lester, *Transylvania*, 183, 191.

19. Proceedings of April 1777, Draper MSS, 4QQ122–123.

20. Ibid., 4QQ123–128.

21. Ibid., 4QQ128–131.

22. Ibid., 4QQ131–134.

23. Ibid., 4QQ135–138.

24. Ibid.

25. *NCSR*, 11: 459.

26. Proceedings of April 1777, Draper MSS, 4QQ140.

27. Ibid., 4QQ95–97, 140–141; italics added by the author.

28. Ibid., 4QQ97.

29. Ibid., 4QQ98.

30. Ibid., 4QQ99.

31. Ibid., 4QQ99–102, 105; O'Donnell, *Southern Indians*, 56.

32. *NCSR*, 11: 460; Ramsey, *Annals*, 172.

33. "Life of Boone," Lyman C. Draper, Draper MSS, 4B119–123; General Levy Todd's Narrative, Draper MSS, 48J10; John Cowan's Journal, Draper MSS, 4CC30; Lewis Collins, *Historical Sketches of Kentucky . . . Divines, etc.* (Maysville, KY: Lewis Collins, 1848; repr., New York: Arno Press, 1971), 445–446.

34. General Levy Todd's Narrative, Draper MSS, 48J10; Draper's copy of *The Pioneer to the Kentucky Emigrant (1832),*1872, Draper MSS, 25CC55; Notes of Judge Moses Boone, Fall of 1846, Draper MSS, 19C6–7; Mann Butler, *A History of the Commonwealth of Kentucky* (Louisville: Wilcox, Dickerman, 1834), 43–44.

35. Lester, *Transylvania*, 191.

36. *DAR*, 13: 110–111.

37. *EAID*, 18: 218–220.

38. *Virginia Gazette* (Dixon and Hunter), May 30, 1777; *EAID*, 18: 220–221.

39. David Taitt to John Stuart, June 5, 1777, CO 5/78: 157–159; David Taitt to John Stuart, May 23, 1777, CO 5/593: 395–398.

40. David Taitt to John Stuart, June 5, 1777, CO 5/78: 157–159.

41. Ibid.

42. Ibid.

43. Collins, *Historical Sketches*, 528; "Life of Boone," Lyman C. Draper, Draper MSS, 4B127; Boone Hays, February 1846, Draper MSS, 23C36.

44. Collins, *Historical Sketches*, 469; "Life of Boone," Lyman C. Draper, Draper MSS, 4B129–130; Jesse Green to Lyman C. Draper, July 15, 1884, Draper MSS, 9C21–23.

45. *DAR*, 13: 119, 121.

46. *RRG*, 1: 311.

47. George Galphin to Henry Laurens, July 20, 1777, Laurens Papers, South Carolina Historical Society.

48. David H. Corkran, *The Creek Frontier, 1540–1783*, Civilization of the American Indian Series, no. 86 (Norman: University of Oklahoma Press, 1967), 304–305; John McKay Sheftall, "George Galphin and Indian-White Relations in the Georgia Backcountry during the American Revolution," master's thesis, University of Virginia, May 1983, 33.

49. For American Indians, horse stealing had its foundations in tribal warfare because it utilized two of the attributes of a warrior and hunter: stealth and courage. Because American Indians did not personally possess land, stealing horses became a means of attaining private wealth. For frontier settlers, Daniel Trabue summed it up best when he said, "It was much better to Do that [steal horses from American Indians] than to give my Mony for a horse." See George Galphin to Henry Laurens, July 20, 1777, Henry Laurens Papers, SCHS; Peter C. Mancall and James Hart Merrell, *American Encounters: Natives and Newcomers from European Contact to Indian Removal, 1500–1850* (New York: Routledge, 2000), 470–471.

50. "Speech delivered to the Head men and warriors of the Creek nation," North Carolina State Archives, Treasurer's and Comptroller's Records, Indian Affairs (Box 1), Cherokee Nation, 1739–1791.

51. "Copy of Speech delivered to the head men and Warriors of the Creek Nation, 17th Day of June 1777," Henry Laurens Papers, SCHS; George Galphin to Henry Laurens, July 20, 1777, Henry Laurens Papers, SCHS.

52. "Copy of Speech delivered to the head Men and Warriors of the Creek Nation at the Treaty held on the River Ogeechee on the 17th Day of June 1777," Henry Laurens Papers, SCHS. Pallachuitas was probably a town associated with the Lower Town of Apalachicola, if not one in the same.

53. "A Talk Delivered by the old Tallassee King's Son at Ogeechee the 18 June 1777," Henry Laurens Papers, SCHS.

54. John Stuart to George Germain, October 6, 1777, CO 5/78, folio 57; John Rutledge to Henry Laurens, August 8, 1777, Henry Laurens Papers, SCHS; John Lewis Gervais to Henry Laurens, August 16, 1777, Henry Laurens Papers, SCHS; *Gazette of the State of South Carolina*, July 14, 1777; "Talk to the Handsome Man 1777 Aug. 13/S Elbert; 1777 Aug. 14, Augusta, to Capt Porter/S Elbert; 1777 Aug. 13/S Elbert," in Keith Read Collection.

55. Lord George Germain to Sir Henry Clinton, March 12, 1778, CO 5/79: 56–56d.

56. John Rutledge to Henry Laurens, August 8, 1777, Laurens Papers, SCHS.

57. Ibid.

Chapter Eight: Peace and War

1. Robert Derry to Captain Joseph Martin, March 3 1777, Draper MSS, 1XX16.
2. The source for this discussion of the 1777 Treaty of Long Island is Archibald Henderson, ed., "The Treaty of Long Island of Holston, July 1777," *North Carolina Historical Review* 8 (January 1931): 62–116.
3. Lester, *Transylvania*, 191.
4. John Stuart to Alexander Cameron, July 11, 1777, CO 5/78: 195–196d.
5. David Taitt to John Stuart, CO 5/78: 197–197d.
6. Alexander Cameron to John Stuart, July 13, 1777, CO 5/78: 198–200.
7. *DAR*, 13: 147, 174.
8. John Stuart to David Taitt, July 14, 1777, CO 5/78: 203; John Stuart to General Augustine Prévost, July 24, 1777, CO 5/78: 205–208d.
9. *DAR*, 13: 160; David Taitt to John Stuart, August 3, 1777, CO 5/78: 209–210, 211–213.
10. *DAR*, 13: 160; David Taitt to John Stuart, August 13, 1777, CO 5/78: 211–213.
11. *DAR*, 13: 159; William Grant to unknown, n.d., CO 5/78: 184–185; John Stuart to Lord George Germain, August 22, 1777, CO 5/78: 186–189.
12. *NCSR* 11: 566–567.
13. Ibid., 608–610.
14. Ibid., 654–655.

Chapter Nine: The Calm Before the Storm

1. Robert Morgan, *Boone: A Biography* (Chapel Hill, NC: Algonquin Books of Chapel Hill, 2007), 226–233.
2. John Mack Faragher, *Daniel Boone: The Life and Legend of an American Pioneer* (New York: Henry Holt, 1992), 162–174.
3. Morgan, *Boone*, 251–252, 271–272.
4. Lyman C. Draper, unpublished manuscript on the life of Daniel Boone, Wisconsin Historical Society, 497; "Life of Boone," Lyman C. Draper, Draper MSS, 4B205.
5. Chester Raymond Young, ed., *Westward into Kentucky: The Narrative of Daniel Trabue* (Lexington: University Press of Kentucky, 1981), 57.
6. Faragher, *Daniel Boone*, 182.
7. Young, *Westward*, 57.
8. It is not known whether these Cherokees were actually Chickamaugas.
9. Stephen Aron, *How the West Was Lost: The Transformation of Kentucky from Daniel Boone to Henry Clay* (Baltimore: Johns Hopkins University Press, 1996), 45; Young, *Westward*, 58, 170.
10. Notes of Historical Collections, Lyman C. Draper, Draper MSS, 22C14(13).
11. Notes on Historical Collections, n.d., Draper MSS, 11CC12–14.
12. Ibid., Notes of Nathaniel Hart, Jr., n.d., 17CC198.
13. John Wilson Townsend, ed., *John Bradford's Historical Notes &c. on Kentucky* (San Francisco: Grabhorn Press, 1932), 41.

14. John Bakeless, *Daniel Boone* (Harrisburg, PA: Stackpole, 1939), 204; Morgan, *Boone*, 259.

15. Notes on Historical Collections, n.d., Draper MSS, 11CC12–14.

16. Notes of Gen. Simon Kenton, n.d., Draper MSS, 11C77–78; Notes of Judge Moses Boone, fall 1846, Draper MSS, 19C11–13.

17. Daniel Vanderslice to Lyman C. Draper, Feb. 1843, Draper MSS, 22C5(15); Notes of Historical Collections, Lyman C. Draper, Draper MSS, 22C14(13).

18. Young, *Westward*, 58; Notes of Judge Moses Boone, fall 1846, Draper MSS, 19C11–13; Notes on Historical Collections, n.d., Draper MSS, 11CC13.

19. Notes of Judge Moses Boone, fall 1846, Draper MSS, 19C15; Notes on Historical Collections, n.d., Draper MSS, 11CC81–83; Notes on Historical Collections, n.d., Draper MSS, 12CC205.

20. Morgan, *Boone*, 268.

21. Punk is pinewood that naturally contains a large amount of resin and is highly flammable, burning quickly and intensely. It is also commonly known as "lighter" or "fat pine" and is used for starting a fire or making a quick, hot fire.

22. Notes on Historical Collections, n.d., Draper MSS, 11CC13; Neal O. Hammon, ed., *My Father, Daniel Boone: The Draper Interviews with Nathan Boone* (Lexington: University Press of Kentucky, 1999), 68.

23. Young, *Westward*, 58–59, 170–171; Morgan, *Boone*, 272.

24. Moses Boone's Account of the Siege of Boonesborough–1778, Draper MSS, 19CC21–22.

25. Notes of General Simon Kenton, n.d., Draper MSS, 11C77–78; Draper, unpublished manuscript, 519; Young, *Westward*, 59.

26. Young, *Westward*, 59.

27. Young, *Westward*, 59.

28. RWPA, John Harris (S21808), John Webb (S32055); *PCC*, M247, r86, i72, p469–470; John Houston to Henry Laurens, October 1, 1778, Henry Laurens Papers, SCHS.

29. Hamer, *Laurens Papers*, 14: 375–376; Corkran, *Creek Frontier*, 315; Samuel Elbert, "Order Book of Samuel Elbert, Colonel and Brigadier-General in the Continental Army, October 1776, to November 1778," *Collections of the Georgia Historical Society*, vol. 5, part 2 (Savannah, GA: Wimberly Jones DeRenne, 1902), 181–183.

30. O'Donnell, *Southern Indians*, 76; Hamer, *Laurens Papers*, 14: 192, 213; *PCC* M247, r87, i73, p218; *DAR*, 13: 338.

31. "Talk delivered to Col. LeRoy Hammond and Edward Wilkinson Esq at Fort Rutledge September 26, 1778," Henry Laurens Papers, SCHS; O'Donnell, *Southern Indians*, 77.

32. "A Talk sent down from the nation by the Tallassee King in answer to talk sent up by George Galphin Esq. Commissioner of Indian Affairs demanding satisfaction for the several murders committed on the frontiers Oct. 10th 1778"; and, Patrick Carr to George Galphin, November 4,

1778; and, "A Talk from the Patuey Mico to George Galphin Esq. Commissioner of Indian Affairs", November 4, 1778, all in Henry Laurens Papers, SCHS. By this time, the Old Tallassee King, father of the Young Tallassee King, had died, and the son was now known simply as the Tallassee King.

33. CO 5/80: 51–53; Patrick Carr to George Galphin, November 4, 1778, Henry Laurens Papers, SCHS; Hamer, *Laurens Papers*, 14: 425, 452–454.

34. Patrick Carr to George Galphin, November 4, 1778, Henry Laurens Papers, SCHS; RWPA, John Webb (S32055).

35. Henry Laurens to Patrick Henry, November 16, 1778, Henry Laurens Papers, SCHS.

36. Patrick Carr to George Galphin, November 4, 1778; "A Talk from the Patuey Mico to George Galphin Esq. Commissioner of Indian Affairs", November 4, 1778, Henry Laurens Papers, SCHS.

37. Patrick Carr to George Galphin, November 4, 1778; "A Talk from the Patuey Mico to George Galphin Esq. Commissioner of Indian Affairs", November 4, 1778, Henry Laurens Papers, SCHS; John Stuart to Lord George Germain, October 9, 1778, CO 5/80: 3–13.

38. *DAR*, 16: 21; David Wilson, *The Southern Strategy: Britain's Conquest of South Carolina and Georgia, 1775–1780* (Columbia: University of South Carolina Press, 2005), 76–80.

CHAPTER TEN: THE TWO-FRONT WAR

1. *NCSR*, 13: 282; *NCSR*, 14: 343; *CVSP*, 1: 13; Colonel William Snodgrass to General David Campbell, August 1845, Draper MSS, 16DD62; Williams, *Tennessee*, 94.

2. A. W. Putnam, *History of Middle Tennessee, or, Life and Times of Gen. James Robertson* (Nashville: n.p., 1859), 64; Roosevelt, *Winning of the West*, 3: 5–6.

3. David Taitt to Lord George Germain, August 6, 1779, CO 5/80: 235–239.

4. C. F. W. Coker, ed., "Journal of John Graham, South Carolina Militia, 1779,"*Military Collector & Historian* (Summer 1967), 39; Edward Wilkinson to James Ramsay, March 2, 1779, CO 5/80: 217–217d.

5. Colin Campbell, ed. *Journal of an Expedition against the Rebels of Georgia in North America under the Orders of Archibald Campbell Esquire, Lieut. Colol. of His Majesty's 71st Regimt. 1778* (Darien, GA: Ashantilly Press, 1981), 58–60.

6. Andrew Pickens to Major General H. Lee, August 28, 1811, Draper MSS, 1VV107–114.

7. Ibid.

8. *DAR* 16: 156; David Taitt to Lord George Germain, August 6, 1779, CO 5/80: 234–251; Edward J. Cashin Jr., *The King's Ranger: Thomas Brown and the American Revolution on the Southern Frontier* (Athens: University of Georgia Press, 1989), 91.

9. Andrew Pickens to Major General H. Lee, August 28, 1811, Draper MSS, 1VV107–114.

10. Walter Scott to Alexander Cameron, March 27, 1779, CO 5/80: 210–212; Robert Dewes to Alexander Cameron, April 9, 1779, CO 5/80: 213–214d.

11. *DAR*, 16: 156.

12. James Keeff to David Holmes, April 27, 1779, CO 5/80: 204–205; Jacob Monroe to Commissioners, May 1, 1779, CO 5/80: 207; Walter Scott to Alexander Cameron, March 27, 1779, CO 5/80: 210–212; David Taitt to Lord George Germain, August 6, 1779, CO 5/80: 235–239.

13. Robert Dewes to Alexander Cameron, April 9, 1779, CO 5/80: 213–214d.

14. Cowee Warrior to John Stuart, n.d., CO 5/80: 215–216.

15. Robert Dewes to Alexander Cameron, April 9, 1779, CO 5/80: 213–214.

16. Thomas Jefferson, *The Papers of Thomas Jefferson*, 36 vols., ed. Julian P. Boyd, L. H. Butterfield, Charles T. Cullen, John Catanzariti, and Barbara Oberg (Princeton, NJ: Princeton University Press, 1950–1980), 3: 6; James Paul Pate, "The Chickamauga: A Forgotten Segment of Indian Resistance on the Southern Frontier" (PhD diss., Mississippi State University, 1969), 94–95.

17. Jacob Monroe to Commissioners, May 1, 1779, CO 5/80: 207–208.

18. *PCC*, m247, r85, i71, v1, p259.

19. Ibid., p265; m247, r65, i51, v2, p61.

20. Jefferson, *Papers*, 3: 125, 160.

21. *PCC*, m247, r85, i71, v1, p263.

22. Craig Thompson Friend, *Kentucke's Frontiers* (Bloomington: Indiana University Press, 2010), 87.

23. Notes from *The Southern Home*, May 10, 1876, Draper MSS, 1HH111–114.

24. Louise Phelps Kellogg, ed., *Frontier Advance on the Upper Ohio, 1778–1779* (Madison: State Historical Society of Wisconsin, 1916), 392–400.

25. Calloway, *American Revolution*, 203.

26. Kellogg, *Frontier Advance*, 392–400.

27. Notes from *The Southern Home*, May 10, 1876, Draper MSS, 1HH111–114.

28. *South Carolina and American Gazette*, September 24, 1779.

29. Clyde Ferguson, "General Andrew Pickens" (PhD diss., Duke University, 1960), 84.

30. *South Carolina and American Gazette*, September 24, 1779.

31. Louise F. Hays, *Indian Depredations, 1787–1825*, typescript, vol. 2, parts 2 and 3 (Morrow: Georgia Department of Archives and History, 1939), 452, 684, 686, 813, 939, 969–970.

32. Putnam, *History of Middle Tennessee*, 66.

CHAPTER ELEVEN: THE CHANGING TIDES OF WAR

1. Arbuthnut to unknown, May 26, 1780, CO 5/81: 134; Thomas Brown to Lord George Germain, April 11, 1780, CO 5/81: 165–170; Charles

Stuart to Alexander Cameron, February 12, 1780, CO 5/81: 181–183; Thomas Brown to Lord George Germain, May 25, 1780, CO 5/81: 188–191.

2. Kenneth Coleman, *The American Revolution in Georgia, 1763–1789* (Athens: University of Georgia Press, 1958), 131; *DAR*, 16: 286; Roosevelt, *Winning of the West*, 3: 27–29; Putnam, *Middle Tennessee*, 107–120.

3. Putnam, *Middle Tennessee*, 83, 93–94, 104–108, 112.

4. Ibid., 86.

5. *DAR* 16: 333; Heard Robertson, "The Second British Occupation of Augusta, 1780–1781," *Georgia Historical Quarterly* 58 (Winter 1974), no. 4, 425.

6. Thomas Brown to unknown, June 18, 1780, Cornwallis Papers, 30/11/2: 166; Nisbet Balfour to Lord Cornwallis, June 24, 1780, Cornwallis Papers, 30/11/2: 191; Thomas Brown to Lord Cornwallis, June 28, 1780, Cornwallis Papers, 30/11/2: 208.

7. Thomas Brown to Lord Cornwallis, June 28, 1780, Cornwallis Papers, 30/11/2: 208.

8. Lord Cornwallis to Nisbet Balfour, July 3, 1780, Cornwallis Papers, 30/11/78: 3; Lord Cornwallis to Thomas Brown, July 17, 1780, Cornwallis Papers, 30/11/78: 22; Lord Cornwallis to Thomas Brown, July 21, 1780, Cornwallis Papers, 30/11/78: 36.

9. Edward J. Cashin Jr., *The King's Ranger: Thomas Brown and the American Revolution on the Southern Frontier* (Athens: University of Georgia Press, 1989), 110; Thomas Brown to Lord Cornwallis, June 28, 1780, Cornwallis Papers, 30/11/2: 208; John Cruger to Lord Cornwallis, August 11, 1780, Cornwallis Papers, 30/11/63: 30; Lord Cornwallis to Thomas Brown, July 17, 1780, Cornwallis Papers, 30/11/78: 22; List of military stores from Fort Seneca, August 1, 1780, Cornwallis Papers, 30/11/103: 1.

10. Putnam, *Middle Tennessee*, 109, 121.

11. Jefferson, *Papers*, 3: 421–422, 447–449, 517–518; Robert Wilson Gibbes, ed., *Documentary History of the American Revolution*, 3 vols. (New York: Appleton, 1853–1857), 2: 135.

12. Jefferson, *Papers*, 3: 517–518, 544–545.

13. Cashin, *King's Ranger*, 108.

14. Ibid., 113.

15. John Cruger to Lord Cornwallis, September 13, 1780, Cornwallis Papers, 30/11/64: 52; John Cruger to officer commanding at Camden, August 4, 1780, Cornwallis Papers, 30/1163: 13; RWPA, Joshua Burnett (S32154). Estimates vary for Clarke's troop strength, ranging from 450 to 600.

16. Unidentified newspaper article, CO 5/82: 329; Thomas Brown to John Cruger, September 14, 1780, Cornwallis Papers, 30/11/64: 65; John Cruger to Lord Cornwallis, September 15–16, 1780, Cornwallis Papers, 30/11/64: 67; John Cruger to Lord Cornwallis, September 19, 1780, Cornwallis Papers, 30/11/64: 77.

17. Unknown newspaper article, CO 5/82: 329; Thomas Brown to John Cruger, September 14, 1780, Cornwallis Papers, 30/11/64: 65; John Cruger to Lord Cornwallis, September 15–16, 1780, Cornwallis Papers,

30/11/64: 67; John Cruger to Lord Cornwallis, September 19, 1780, Cornwallis Papers, 30/11/64: 77.
18. Unidentified newspaper article, CO 5/82: 329.
19. Ibid.
20. Ibid.
21. Ibid.
22. John Cruger to Lord Cornwallis, September 19, 1780, Cornwallis Papers, 30/11/64: 77; John Cruger to Lord Cornwallis, September 23, 1780, Cornwallis Papers, 30/11/64: 104; John Cruger to Lord Cornwallis, September 28, 1780, Cornwallis Papers, 30/11/64: 116.
23. John Cruger to Lord Cornwallis, September 23, 1780, Cornwallis Papers, 30/11/64: 104; John Cruger to Lord Cornwallis, September 28, 1780, Cornwallis Papers, 30/11/64: 116.
24. Charles Ross, ed., *Correspondence of Charles, First Marquis Cornwallis*, 3 vols. (London: John Murray, 1859), 1: 76.
25. *CVSP* 1: 447.
26. Joseph Martin to unknown recipient, December 12, 1780, Draper MSS, 1XX41; *VMHB* 27: 314–315; John R. Finger, *Tennessee Frontiers: Three Regions in Transition* (Bloomington: Indiana University Press, 2001), 89.
27. *VMHB* 27: 314–315; Jefferson, *Papers*, 4: 200–201, 217; Colonel Arthur Campbell to Major Joseph Martin, December 9, 1780, Draper MSS, 1XX40.
28. RWPA, Samuel Riggs (S4095).
29. Roosevelt, *Winning of the West*, 2: 360–361.
30. Ibid.
31. Jefferson, *Papers*, 4: 360, 362–363.
32. Ibid., 360.
33. Ibid.
34. Ibid., 360–361.
35. Ibid., 361.
36. Ibid.
37. Ibid.; RWPA, Samuel Riggs (S4095).
38. Jefferson, *Papers*, 4: 362; Pension Statement of Jacob Beeles, August 22, 1832, Draper MSS, 2DD439–443.
39. Jefferson, *Papers*, 4: 362; *CVSP* 1: 414–415.
40. Jefferson, *Papers*, 4: 362; Pension Statement of Isaac Taylor, November 20, 1838, Draper MSS, 2DD184.
41. Jefferson, *Papers*, 4: 363.
42. *CVSP*, 1: 447.

CHAPTER TWELVE: WINNING BATTLES
1. Putnam, *Middle Tennessee*, 123–124.
2. Ibid., 124–125.
3. Colonel Campbell to Major Joseph Martin, January 9, 1781, Draper MSS, 1XX42; Jefferson, *Papers*, 4: 407–408.
4. *PCC*, M247, r85, i71, v2, p43.

5. Jefferson, *Papers*, 4: 457, 499–500, 546; *CVSP*, 1: 457–458.

6. Jefferson, *Papers*, 4: 551–552.

7. Ibid., 587, 613–614.

8. Ibid., 634–635, 657–658.

9. Conrad, *Greene Papers*, 7: 258, 351–352.

10. Jefferson, *Papers*, 5: 20; Pension Statement of Josiah Culbertson, September 1832, Draper MSS, 2DD408.

11. RWPA, William C. Smith (S3924).

12. *CVSP*, 1: 602–603, 613; Jefferson, *Papers*, 5: 267–268, 304–305, 552; Calloway, *American Revolution*, 205.

13. Jefferson, *Papers*, 5: 236.

14. J. W. L. Matlock, ed., "The Battle of the Bluffs: From the Journal of John Cotten," *Tennessee Historical Quarterly* 18, no. 3 (September, 1959), 252–265. This part of the chapter is based on the John Cotten journal in this source.

15. Matlock states in a footnote, "John Rains had such a reputation as a huntsman that it was said when on a bear hunt, if his first shot missed, he could turn and run with the bear clawing at his heels, reloading his rifle as he raced away, then turn and shoot the bear when it was almost at his muzzle tip." "Battle of the Bluffs," 258, n15.

16. Traditionally, when soldiers are trained in bayonet practice, they are taught to yell as loudly as they can when lunging. This is in the hopes of drowning out the screams of the victim, or at least minimizing their psychological impact.

17. Putnam says, "These dogs were trained to hostility," but evidently that was not the case. See Putnam, *Middle Tennessee*, 130.

18. Jefferson, *Papers*, 5: 395–396.

19. Ibid., 462–463.

20. Ibid., 467, 493. James John Floyd was better known as John Floyd. He had been appointed the county lieutenant of Jefferson County and therefore colonel of the militia in that county.

21. Ibid., 535.

22. *CVSP* 1: 446–447; Conrad, *Greene Papers*, 8: 136–7.

23. Jefferson, *Papers*, 5: 552–553.

24. A Talk Delivered by Clanosee or the Horse Leach and Aucoo Messengers Sent by Oconostota & Some Other Chiefs of the Cherokee Nation on the 28th of April 1781, Draper MSS 1XX43–43(2).

25. "1781 May 29, Savannah Sir James Wright [to Charles Shaw]," Telamon Cuyler Collection.

26. Conrad, *Greene Papers*, 8: 291–292; Lee, *Memoirs*, 354.

27. Conrad, *Greene Papers*, 8: 307–308, 317.

28. Jefferson, *Papers*, 6: 80, 94.

29. Conrad, *Greene Papers*, 9: 49.

30. Ibid., *Greene Papers*, 8: 482, 9: 7–8, 73.

31. Ibid., 266.

32. Ibid., 268–269.

33. Ibid., 269–270; Calloway, *Indian Country*, 205 and n110.

34. *EAID*, 18: 265–267.
35. Colonel Samuel Hammond's Services, Draper MSS, 1DD20; Judge J. B. O'Neal, "Random Recollections of Revolutionary Characters and Incidents," *Southern Literary Journal and Magazine of Arts* 4 (July 1838): 40–45; Conrad, *Greene Papers*, 9: 261.
36. RWPA, Avery Mustain (W7488) and Zachariah Prewit (S5952).
37. *PCC*, M247, r93, i78, v6, p59–60; Isaac Shelby to Arthur Campbell, December 31, 1781, Draper MSS, 11S71–73.
38. *PCC*, M247, r93, i78, v6, p59–60; Isaac Shelby to Arthur Campbell, December 31, 1781, Draper MSS, 11S71–73.
39. "Deposition of Deserters Mark King and William Henson, 1782" and "Arturo O'Neill to Nathan Brownson, November 18, 1781," Telamon Cuyler Collection; Conrad, *Greene Papers*, 9: 644–645.

Chapter Thirteen: Keeping Up the Pressure

1. Cashin, *King's Ranger*, 144–145; Conrad, *Greene Papers*, 10:107.
2. *RRG*, 2: 290; RWPA, John Cunningham (W6752).
3. *CVSP*, 3: 4.
4. Ramsey, *Annals of Tennessee*, 270–271.
5. *NCSR*, 19: 941–942.
6. Ferguson, "General Andrew Pickens," 259; *RRG*, 2: 297.
7. *RRG*, 2: 299, 307, 312; Joseph Martin, "Official Letters of Governor Joseph Martin, 1782–1783," *Georgia Historical Quarterly* 1, no. 4 (December 1917): 282–285; Conrad, *Greene Papers*, 10: 303.
8. Colonel Samuel Hammond's Services, Draper MSS, 1DD20, 20–21; Conrad, *Greene Papers*, 10:343.
9. Colonel Samuel Hammond's Services, Draper MSS, 1DD20; TCC269; Gibbes, *Documentary History*, 3: 277.
10. Colonel Samuel Hammond's Services, Draper MSS, 1DD21; RWPA, John Cunningham (W6752) and William Eddins (S32230).
11. RWPA, John Cunningham (W6752) and William Eddins (S32230); Reverend William Bacon Stevens, *A History of Georgia, from Its First Discovery by Europeans to the Adoption of the Present Constitution in MDC-CXCVIII*, vol. 2 (Philadelphia: E. H. Butler, 1859), 284.
12. RWPA, William Eddins (S32230) and Joseph McCluskey (W1449); Stevens, *History of Georgia*, 2: 283–284.
13. RWPA, George Hodge (W4234), John Davidson (S1758), and James Withrow (S6403).
14. RWPA, Bowling Baker (S12950), James Sevier (S45889), and John Asher (R280).
15. Pension Statement of Samuel Palton, June 18, 1833, Draper MSS, 2DD26–27, Pension Statement of James Alexander, October 9, 1832, Draper MSS, 162—170.
16. Draper's notes on Estill's Defeat, 1845, Draper MSS, 13C40–41; Dillard W. Hazelrigg to Lyman C. Draper, April 29, 1842, Draper MSS, 51(2)–51(4); Wallace Estill to Lyman C. Draper, September 13, 1845, Draper MSS, 53(1); Estill's Defeat–1782, Draper MSS, 56.

17. Estill's Defeat–1782, Draper MSS, 13C56–57.
18. Dillard W. Hazelrigg to Lyman C. Draper, April 29, 1842, Draper MSS, 50(1), 51(2)–51(4); Wallace Estill to Lyman C. Draper, September 13, 1845, Draper MSS, 53(1).
19. Draper's notes on Estill's Defeat, 1845, Draper MSS, 42–44, 47.
20. Ibid., 44; Dillard W. Hazelrigg to Lyman C. Draper, April 29, 1842, Draper MSS, 51(2); Wallace Estill to Lyman C. Draper, September 13, 1845, Draper MSS, 53(1), 53–54(2).
21. Draper's notes on Estill's Defeat, 1845, Draper MSS, 44; Dillard W. Hazelrigg to Lyman C. Draper, April 29, 1842, Draper MSS, 51(2), 54; Estill's Defeat–1782, Draper MSS, 56.
22. Estill's Defeat–1782, Draper MSS, 56.
23. Dillard W. Hazelrigg to Lyman C. Draper, April 29, 1842, Draper MSS, 51(3).
24. Wallace Estill to Lyman C. Draper, May 25, 1845, Draper MSS, 54.
25. Draper's notes on Estill's Defeat, 1845, Draper MSS, 40, 43–44; Dillard W. Hazelrigg to Lyman C. Draper, April 29, 1842, Draper MSS, 51(3); Wallace Estill to Lyman C. Draper, September 13, 1845, Draper MSS, 54; Estill's Defeat–1782, Draper MSS, 57.
26. Petition of the inhabitants of Burke County, Georgia, to John Martin, March 2, 1782, Telamon Cuyler Collection; Harden, "Official Letters," 297–299.
27. Petition of the inhabitants of Burke County, Georgia, to John Martin, March 2, 1782, Telamon Cuyler Collection; *RRG*, 2: 312; Harden, "Official Letters," 297–298.
28. *RRG*, 2: 326; Harden, "Official Letters," 308–309, 310, 311; Conrad, *Greene Papers*, 11: 156.
29. Louise F. Hays, *The Hero of Hornet's Nest: A Biography of Elijah Clarke, 1733–1799* (New York: Stratford House, 1946), 329–330.
30. Harden, "Official Letters," 310.
31. Hays, *Hero of Hornet's Nest*, 156–157.
32. Walter Lowrie and Matthew St. Clair Clarke, eds., *American State Papers, Documents, Legislative and Executive, of the Congress of the United States (1789–1815)*, class 2, Indian Affairs (Washington, DC: Gales & Seaton, 1832), 4(I): 317.
33. RWPA, James Lochridge (W472), Moses Perkins (S3677), Alexander Smith (S16530), John Smith (R9769), John Smith (S31967), and David H. Thurmond (S32010).
34. RWPA, Moses Perkins (S3677), Alexander Smith (S16530), and John Smith (S31967).
35. A Talk Del[ivere]d to Kaakee, 1782 June 8, by Governor Martin of the State of Georgia, Telamon Cuyler Collection.
36. Conrad, *Greene Papers*, 11: 338, 342, 385.
37. Ibid., 365; Lee, *Memoirs*, 558.
38. Conrad, *Greene Papers*, 11: 365–366; Lee, *Memoirs*, 558–559.
39. Lee, *Memoirs*, 558; Conrad, *Greene Papers*, 11: 366.
40. Lee, *Memoirs*, 559; Conrad, *Greene Papers*, 11: 366.

CHAPTER FOURTEEN: THE BEGINNING OF THE END

1. *RRG*, 3:157; *Pennsylvania Gazette*, August 28, 1782.
2. "1782 Aug. 11, Silver Bluff, Georgia, Patrick Carr to Governor John Martin," Telamon Cuyler Collection.
3. "friends and brothers of the uper and lower Creek Nation," Telamon Cuyler Collection.
4. Ibid.
5. *NCSR*, 16: 697–698.
6. Pension Statement of Abraham Forney, October 31, 1832, Draper MSS, 2DD78–79, 416.
7. Ibid., 2DD78–79.
8. *Pennsylvania Gazette*, May 8, 1782.
9. Roosevelt, *Winning of the West*, 2: 393.
10. Draper's notes, n.d., Draper MSS, 13C71; Joseph Ficklin to Lyman C. Draper, June 26, 1845, Draper MSS, 74; Elizabeth Payne to Lyman C. Draper, January 14, 1846, Draper MSS, 116.
11. Elizabeth Payne to Lyman C. Draper, January 14, 1846, Draper MSS, 117.
12. Ibid.
13. Draper's notes, n.d., Draper MSS, 70, 71; Elizabeth Payne to Lyman C. Draper, January 14, 1846, Draper MSS, 116–117.
14. Draper's notes, n.d., Draper MSS, 70, 71.
15. Draper's notes, n.d., Draper MSS, 71; Elizabeth Payne to Lyman C. Draper, January 14, 1846, Draper MSS, 117.
16. Draper's notes, n.d., Draper MSS, 69; Elizabeth Payne to Lyman C. Draper, January 14, 1846, Draper MSS, 116–117.
17. Notes from *Annals of the West,* n.d., Draper MSS, 114; Roosevelt, *Winning of the West*, 2: 393–394.
18. Notes from *Annals of the West,* n.d., Draper MSS, 13C114; Roosevelt, *Winning of the West*, 2: 394.
19. *CVSP*, 3:275–276; Roosevelt, *Winning of the West*, 2: 394.
20. Roosevelt, *Winning of the West*, 2: 390; *CVSP*, 3: 275–276; Notes from *Annals of the West,* n.d., Draper MSS, 13C114; *Pennsylvania Gazette*, October 16, 1782.
21. *CVSP*, 3: 275–276; Notes of Honorable V. B. Young, Aug. 21, 1883, Draper MSS, 13C36. Of the four contemporary accounts of the siege of Bryan's Station and the Battle of Blue Licks, two (Boone's and Todd's) give the dates of August 16 for the former and August 19 for the latter. Caldwell gives the fifteenth and eighteenth, while McKee gives the eighteenth and twenty-first.
22. *CVSP*, 3: 331.
23. Ibid., 271–272, 292.
24. Andrew Pickens to Colonel Elijah Clarke, September 2, 1782, Draper MSS, 1VV69; Gibbes, *Documentary History*, 2: 220–221.
25. Andrew Pickens to John Martin, October 26, 1782, Miscellaneous Letters, Pierpont Morgan Library, New York; RWPA, Robert Hobbs (W5300) and Beckman May (R7049).

26. *CVSP*, 3: 316–318.
27. Ibid.
28. *NCSR*, 19: 905–906.
29. Pickens to Martin, October 26, 1782, Pierpont Morgan Library; RWPA, Moses Perkins (S3677) and Beckman May (R7049).
30. Pickens to Martin, October 26, 1782, Pierpont Morgan Library; Andrew Pickens to Major General H. Lee, August 28, 1811, Draper MSS, 1VV107(7); Pickens' Campaign of 1781, Draper MSS, 3VV142–144.
31. Ferguson, "General Andrew Pickens," 273–274.
32. Pickens to Martin, October 26, 1782, Pierpont Morgan Library.
33. RWPA, William Eddins (S32230), Beckman May (R7049), Joseph McClaskey (W1449), and Moses Perkins (S3677).
34. Pickens to Martin, October 26, 1782, Pierpont Morgan Library.
35. Ibid.
36. Ibid.; Ferguson, "General Andrew Pickens," 275–276; RWPA, Jeremiah Files (S13025) and Beckman May (R7049).
37. *NCSR*, 19: 939–940.
38. Ibid.
39. Pension Statement of Bowling Baker, October 22, 1832, Draper MSS, 2DD382; RWPA, Walter Billingsly (R840).
40. RWPA, Tidence Lane (W377).
41. RWPA, Jesse Byrd (R1574) and Tidence Lane (W377).
42. RWPA, Jesse Byrd (R1574) and William Robertson (S4790).
43. RWPA, James Smith (S21489), John Crabb (R2417), Jesse Byrd (R1574), James Boyd (S32127), and William Robertson (S4790).
44. Brown, *Old Frontiers*, 202; RWPA, William Smith (S1723) and William Robertson (S4790).
45. RWPA, Bowling Baker (S12950), Joel Callahan (S21110), John Crabb (R2417), and William Robertson (S4790).
46. RWPA, George Hofstaler (S15176) and George Musick (R16988).
47. *CVSP*, 3: 331–334.
48. Thomas Brown to Earl of Shelburne, September 25, 1782, CO 5/82: 343–346.
49. *CVSP*, 3: 356–358.
50. Ibid., 381.
51. Ibid., 398.

Chapter Fifteen: 1783 and Beyond

1. Royal Commission on Historical Manuscripts, 4 vol., *Report on American Manuscripts in the Royal Institution* (London: Mackie, 1904), 3: 325.
2. *CVSP*, 3: 420.
3. Ibid., 421.
4. Ibid., 426–427.
5. Thomas Brown to Lord North, July 30, 1783, CO 5/82: 392–394; *CVSP*, 3: 464, 479.

6. Thomas Brown to Thomas Townshend, June 1, 1783, CO 5/82: 367–379.

7. Ibid.; Original Correspondence: Canada: 1760–1823, CO 42/44: 241–277, British Public Record Office, Kew, Richmond, Surrey.

8. *CVSP*, 3: 509, 511.

9. Ibid., 532, 533.

10. Articles of a convention held at Augusta, in the County of Richmond, 1783 Nov. 1, Keith Read Collection.

11. *CVSP*, 3: 536, 539, 548.

Bibliography

PRIMARY SOURCES

Manuscripts

Belcher, James, Papers, 1782. David M. Rubenstein Rare Book and Manuscript Library, Duke University, Durham, NC.

Bevan, Joseph Vallence, Papers, 1733–1826. Georgia Historical Society, Savannah.

Colonial Office Records. America and the West Indies. Class 5. Great Britain, Public Record Office, Kew, Richmond, Surrey.

Colonial Office Records. Original Correspondence: Canada: 1760–1823. Great Britain, Public Record Office, Kew, Richmond, Surrey.

Cornwallis Papers. Class 30. Great Britain, Public Record Office, Kew, Richmond, Surrey.

Cuyler, Telamon, Collection. Hargrett Rare Book and Manuscript Library, University of Georgia, Athens.

Dibble, Samuel, Papers, 1779–1910. David M. Rubenstein Rare Book and Manuscript Library, Duke University, Durham, NC.

Draper, Lyman Copeland, Manuscripts. State Historical Society of Wisconsin. On microfilm.

Durrett, Reuben T., Collection on Kentucky and the Ohio River Valley. Special Collections Research Center, University of Chicago.

Executive Department, Governor's Subject Files, 1781–2008. Georgia Department of Archives and History, Morrow.

Gage, Thomas, Papers. American Series. William L. Clements Library, University of Michigan, Ann Arbor.

Georgia Executive Council Papers, 1777–1788. Georgia Historical Society, Savannah.

Greene, Nathanael, Papers, 1742–1786. David M. Rubenstein Rare Book and Manuscript Library, Duke University, Durham, NC.

Habersham, John, Letters, 1780–1789. Georgia Historical Society, Savannah.

Hargrett, Felix, Collection. Hargrett Rare Book and Manuscript Library, University of Georgia, Athens.

Houstoun, John, Letters, 1775–1784. Georgia Historical Society, Savannah.

Indian Claims, Treaties, and Spoliations, 1783–1829. Georgia Department of Archives and History, Morrow.

Jackson, James, Papers, 1781–1796. Georgia Historical Society, Savannah.

Jones, John, Papers, 1778–1870. David M. Rubenstein Rare Book and Manuscript Library, Duke University, Durham, NC.

Laurens, Henry, Collection. South Carolina Historical Society, Charleston.

Martin, John, Papers, 1782. David M. Rubenstein Rare Book and Manuscript Library, Duke University, Durham, NC.

McIntosh, Lachlan, Papers, 1742–1799. Georgia Historical Society, Savannah.

Miscellaneous American, Literary, and Historical Manuscripts. Pierpont Morgan Library, New York.

Papers of the Continental Congress, 1774–1789. National Archives Microfilm, No. M247.

Pickens, Andrew, Papers, 1779–1838. David M. Rubenstein Rare Book and Manuscript Library, Duke University, Durham, NC.

Read, Keith, Collection. Hargrett Rare Book and Manuscript Library, University of Georgia, Athens.

Revolutionary War Pension and Bounty-Land-Warrant Application Files. National Archives, Microfilm, No. M804.

State Library Cherokee Collection. Tennessee State Library and Archives, Nashville.

Tennessee Historical Society Collection. Tennessee State Library and Archives, Nashville.

Thompson, C. Mildred, Collection. Hargrett Rare Book and Manuscript Library, University of Georgia, Athens.

William R. Perkins Library, including the David M. Rubenstein Rare Book and Manuscript Library, Duke University, Durham, NC.

Wright, James, Papers, 1772–1784. Georgia Historical Society, Savannah.

Articles

Barnwell, Joseph W., ed. "Letters of John Rutledge." *South Carolina Historical and Genealogical Magazine* 17 (1916): 131–146; 18 (1917): 43–49, 59–69, 131–142, 155–167.

Coker, C. F. W., ed. "Journal of John Graham, South Carolina Militia, 1779." *Military Collector and Historian* (Summer 1967): 35–47.

"Deposition of William Springstone, December 11, 1780." *Virginia Magazine of History and Biography* 27 (1919): 313–314.

Hamer, Philip M., ed. "Correspondence of Henry Stuart and Alexander Cameron with the Wataugans." *Mississippi Valley Historical Review* 17 (December 1930): 451–459.

Hamilton, J. G. de Roulhac, ed. "Revolutionary War Diary of William Lenoir." *Journal of Southern History* 6, no. 2 (May 1940): 247–259.

Henderson, Archibald, ed. "The Treaty of Long Island of Holston, July 1777." *North Carolina Historical Review* 8 (January 1931): 55–116.

Lamb, Martha J. ed., "Original Documents: memorandum of the Route pursued by Colonel Campbell and his column of invasion, in 1779... ." *Magazine of American History with Notes and Queries, Illustrated* 18 (July–December 1887): 256–288, 342–348.

Martin, Joseph, "Official Letters of Governor Joseph Martin, 1782–1783." *Georgia Historical Quarterly* 1, no. 4 (December 1917): 281–335.

Matlock, J. W. L., ed. "The Battle of the Bluffs: From the Journal of John Cotten." *Tennessee Historical Quarterly* 18, no. 3 (September 1959): 252–265.

"A Memoir of John Sevier." *American Historical Magazine* 6 (1901): 40–45.

O'Neal, Judge J. B. "Random Recollections of Revolutionary Characters and Incidents." *Southern Literary Journal and Magazine of Arts* 4 (July 1838), 40–45.

Redd, John. "Reminiscences of Western Virginia, 1770–1790." *Virginia Magazine of History and Biography* 7, no. 1 (July 1899): 1–16.

"Virginia Legislative Papers." *Virginia Magazine of History and Biography* 16, no. 2 (October 1908): 148–173; 17, no. 1 (January 1909): 52–64.

Books

Butler, Lindley S., ed. *The Narrative of David Fanning*. Davidson, NC: Briarpatch Press, 1981.

Campbell, Colin, ed. *Journal of an Expedition against the Rebels of Georgia in North America under the Orders of Archibald Campbell Esquire, Lieut. Colol. Of His Majesty's 71st Regimt. 1778*. Darien, GA: Ashantilly Press, 1981.

Candler, Allen D., comp. *The Colonial Records of the State of Georgia*. 25 vols. (1–19, 21–26). Atlanta: Franklin, 1904–1916; 20, 27–39, Athens: University of Georgia Press, 1976–1989.

———. *The Revolutionary Records of the State of Georgia*. 3 vols. Atlanta: Franklin-Turner, 1908.

Davies, K. G., ed. *Documents of the American Revolution, 1770–1783.* Colonial Office Series. Shannon: Irish University Press, 1972–1981.

Draper, Lyman C. Unpublished manuscript on the life of Daniel Boone. Wisconsin Historical Society.

Drayton, John. *Memoirs of the American Revolution.* Charleston, SC: A. E. Miller, 1821.

Elbert, Samuel. "Order Book of Samuel Elbert, Colonel and Brigadier-General in the Continental Army, October 1776, to November 1778." *Collections of the Georgia Historical Society,* vol. 5, part 2. Savannah, GA: Wimberly Jones DeRenne, 1902.

Filson, John. *The Discovery, Settlement, and Present State of Kentucky.* London: John Stockdale, 1793.

Fitzpatrick, John C., ed. *The Writings of George Washington from the Original Manuscript Sources, 1745–1799.* 39 vols. Washington, DC: Government Printing Office, 1931–1944.

Gibbes, Robert Wilson, ed. *Documentary History of the American Revolution.* 3 vols. New York: Appleton, 1853–1857.

Hamer, Philip M., ed. *The Papers of Henry Laurens,* 16 vols. Columbia: University of South Carolina Press, 1968–2003.

Hammon, Neal O. *My Father, Daniel Boone: The Draper Interviews with Nathan Boone.* Lexington: University Press of Kentucky, 1999.

Hays, Louise F. *Indian Depredations, 1787-1825.* 2 vols. Morrow: Georgia Department of Archives and History, 1939. Transcript.

Heckewelder, John Gottlieb Ernestus. *A Narrative of the Missions of the United Brethren among the Delaware and Mohegan Indians from Its Commencement in the Year 1740 to the Close of the Year 1808.* Philadelphia: McCarty and Davis, 1820. Reprint, New York: Arno Press, 1971.

Higginbotham, Don, ed. *The Papers of James Iredell, 1751–1799.* 3 vols. Raleigh: North Carolina Division of Archives and History, 1976.

Jefferson, Thomas. *The Papers of Thomas Jefferson.* 36 vols. Edited by Julian P. Boyd, L. H. Butterfield, Charles T. Cullen, John Catanzariti, and Barbara Oberg. Princeton, NJ: Princeton University Press, 1950–1980.

Journal of the Congress of the Four Southern Governors and the Superintendent of that District with the Five Nations of Indians at Augusta, 1763. Charleston, SC: n.p., 1764.

Kellogg, Louise Phelps, ed. *Frontier Advance on the Upper Ohio, 1778–1779.* Madison: State Historical Society of Wisconsin, 1916.

Kennedy, J. P., and H. R. McIlwaine, eds. *Journals of the House of Burgesses of Virginia, 1619–1776.* 13 vols. Richmond, VA: E. Waddey, 1905–1915.

Lazenby, Mary Elinor, comp. *Catawba Frontier, 1775–1781: Memories of Pensioners.* Washington, DC: Mary Elinor Lazenby, 1950.

Lee, Henry. *Memoirs of the War in the Southern Department of the United States.* New York: University Publishing, 1869.

Lowrie, Walter, and Matthew St. Clair Clarke, eds. *American State Papers, Documents, Legislative and Executive, of the Congress of the United States (1789–1815).* Class 2, Indian Affairs. Washington, DC: Gales and Seaton, 1832.

McIlwaine, H. R., ed. *Official Letters of the Governor of the State of Virginia.* 3 vols. Richmond: Virginia State Library, 1926.

McIlwaine, H. R., Wilmer Lee Hall, and Benjamin J. Hillman, eds. *Executive Journals of the Council of Colonial Virginia.* 6 vols. Richmond: Virginia State Library, 1925–1966.

Moore, Maurice. *Reminiscences of York.* Elmer Oris Parker, ed. Greenville, SC: A Press, 1981.

Palmer, William P., Sherwin McRae, Raleigh Edward Colston, and Henry W. Flournoy, eds. *Calendar of Virginia State Papers and other Manuscripts Preserved in the Capitol at Richmond.* 11 vols. Richmond: James E. Goode, 1875–1883.

Powell, William Stevens, ed. *The Correspondence of William Tryon and other Selected Papers.* 2 vols. Raleigh: North Carolina Division of Archives and History, 1980–1981.

Ross, Charles, ed. *Correspondence of Charles, First Marquis Cornwallis.* 3 vols. London: John Murray, 1859.

Royal Commission on Historical Manuscripts. 4 vols. *Report on American Manuscripts in the Royal Institution.* London: Mackie, 1904.

Saunders, William L., and Walter Clark, eds. *The Colonial Records of North Carolina.* 10 vols. Raleigh: Secretary of State, 1886–1890.

———. *The State Records of North Carolina.* 12 vols. Raleigh: Secretary of State, 1895–1907.

Showman, Richard K., Dennis Michael Conrad, and Roger N. Parks, eds. *The Papers of Nathanael Greene.* 13 vols. Chapel Hill: University of North Carolina Press, 1976–2005.

Townsend, John Wilson, ed. *John Bradford's Historical Notes &c. on Kentucky.* San Francisco: Grabhorn Press, 1932.

Vaughan, Alden T., general ed. *Early American Indian Documents.* 19 vols. Washington, DC: University Publications of America, 1979–2003.

Warren, Mary Bondurant, ed. *Revolutionary Memoirs and Muster Rolls*. Athens, GA: Heritage Papers, 1994.

Williams, Samuel Cole, ed. *Early Travels in the Tennessee Country*. Johnson City, TN: Watauga Press, 1925.

SECONDARY SOURCES

Articles

Alden, John R. "The Eighteenth Century Cherokee Archives." *American Archivist* 5 (1942): 240–244.

Ashe, S. A. "Rutherford's Expedition against the Indians." *North Carolina Booklet* 4 (December 1904): 3–24.

Ashmore, Otis. "Wilkes County, Its Place in Georgia History." *Georgia Historical Quarterly* 1 (1917): 59–69.

Bast, Homer. "Creek Indian Affairs, 1775–1778." *Georgia Historical Quarterly* 33 (1949): 1–25.

Connelly, Thomas L. "Indian Warfare on the Tennessee Frontier, 1776–1794." *East Tennessee Historical Society Publications* 36 (1964): 3–22.

Corkran, David H. "The Virginia-Chickasaw Treaty of 1783." *Journal of Southern History* 8 (1942): 482–496.

Davis, Andrew M. "The Employment of Indian Auxiliaries in the American War." *English Historical Review* 2 (1887): 709–728.

Davis, Robert Scott, Jr. "George Galphin and the Creek Congress of 1777." *Proceedings and Papers of the Georgia Association of Historians* (1982), 13–29.

De Vorsey, Louis, Jr. "The Virginia-Cherokee Boundary of 1771." *East Tennessee Historical Society Publications* 33 (1961): 17–31.

Dickens, Roy S., Jr. "A Note on Cherokee House Construction of 1776." *Southern Indian Studies* 19 (1967), 35.

———. "The Route of Rutherford's Expedition against the North Carolina Cherokees." *Southern Indian Studies* 19 (1967): 3–24.

Downes, Randolph C. "Cherokee-American Relations in the Upper Tennessee Valley, 1776–1791." *East Tennessee Historical Society Publications* 8 (1936): 35–53.

———. "Creek-American Relations, 1782–1790." *Georgia Historical Quarterly* 21 (1937): 142–184.

Foster, William O. "James Jackson in the American Revolution." *Georgia Historical Quarterly* 31 (1947): 249–281.

Ganyard, Robert L. "Threat from the West: North Carolina and the Cherokee, 1776–1778." *North Carolina Historical Review* 45 (January 1968): 47–66.

Goodpasture, Albert V. "Indian Wars and Warriors of the Old Southwest, 1730–1807." *Tennessee Historical Magazine* 4 (1918): 3–49, 106–145, 161–210, 252–289.

Hagy, James William, and Stanley J. Folmsbee, eds. "The Lost Archives of the Cherokee Nation: Part 1, 1763–1772." *East Tennessee Historical Society Publications* 43 (1971): 112–122; "Part 2, 1772–1775." 44 (1972): 114–125; "Part 3, 1777." 45 (1973): 88–99.

Hamer, Philip M. "Correspondence of Henry Stuart and Alexander Cameron with the Wataugans." *Mississippi Valley Historical Review* 17, no. 3 (December 1930): 451–459.

———. "John Stuart's Indian Policy during the Early Months of the American Revolution." *Mississippi Valley Historical Review* 17 (1930): 351–366.

———. "The Wataugans and the Cherokee Indians in 1776." *East Tennessee Historical Society Publications* 3 (1931): 108–126.

Hatley, Thomas. "The Three Lives of Keowee: Loss and Recovery in Eighteenth-Century Cherokee Villages." In Peter H. Wood, Gregory A. Waselkov, and M. Thomas Hatley, eds. *Powhatan's Mantle: Indians in the Colonial Southeast.* Lincoln: University of Nebraska Press, 1980, 223–248.

Jackson, George B. "John Stuart: Superintendent of Indian Affairs for the Southern District." *Tennessee Historical Magazine* 3 (September 1917): 165–191.

Jacobs, Wilbur R. "Wampum: The Protocol of Indian Diplomacy." *The William and Mary Quarterly*, 3rd series, vol. 6, no. 4 (Oct. 1949): 596–604.

Keel, Bennie C., Brian J. Egloff, and Keith T. Egloff. "Reflections on the Cherokee Project and the Coweeta Creek Mound." *Southeastern Archaeology* 21, no. 1 (Summer 2002): 49–53.

Kelly, A. R., and Clemens de Baillou. "Excavation of the Presumptive Site of Estatoe." *Southern Indian Studies* 12 (1960): 3–29.

Lafferty, Maude Ward. "Destruction of Ruddle's and Martin's Forts in the Revolutionary War." *The Register of the Kentucky Historical Society* 54, no. 189 (October 1956): 297–338.

Lambert, Patricia M. "Bioarchaeology at Coweeta Creek: Continuity and Change in Native Health and Lifeways in Protohistoric Western North Carolina." *Southeastern Archaeology* 21, no. 1 (Summer 2002): 36–48.

Lee, Wayne E. "Fortify, Fight, or Flee: Tuscarora and Cherokee Defensive Warfare and Military Culture Adaptation." *Journal of Military History* 68, no. 3 (July 2004): 713–770.

Mahon, John K. "Anglo-American Methods of Indian Warfare, 1676–1794." *Mississippi Valley Historical Review* 45 (September 1958): 254–275.

Martin, William. "A Biographical Sketch of General Joseph Martin." *Virginia Magazine of History and Biography* 8 (1901): 347–359.

Meriwether, Colyer, ed. "General Joseph Martin and the Cherokees," *Publications of the Southern History Association* 8 (November 1904): 441–450.

Montgomery, James R. "The Nomenclature of the Upper Tennessee River." *East Tennessee Historical Society Publications* 38 (1965): 46–57.

Myer, William E. "Indian Trails of the Southeast." Bureau of American Ethnology, *Seventh Annual Report* (1885–1886): 301–397.

O'Donnell, James A., III. "The Virginia Expedition against the Overhill Cherokee, 1776." *East Tennessee Historical Society Publications* 39 (1967): 13–25.

Peña, Elizabeth S. "The Role of Wampum Production at the Albany Almshouse." *International Journal of Historical Archaeology* 5, no. 2 (2001): 155–174.

Quaife, Milo M. "When Detroit Invaded Kentucky." *Filson Club Historical Quarterly* 1, no. 2 (January 1927): 53–67.

Radford, P. M. "Block Houses." *American Historical Magazine* 1 (July 1896): 247–252.

Robertson, Heard. "The Second British Occupation of Augusta, 1780–1781." *Georgia Historical Quarterly* 58, no. 4 (Winter 1974): 422–446.

Rockwell, E. F. "Parallel and Combined Expeditions against the Cherokee Indians in South and in North Carolina, in 1776." *Historical Magazine* 1 (October 1867): 212–220.

Rodning, Christopher B. "The Townhouse at Coweeta Creek." *Southeastern Archaeology* 21, no. 1 (Summer 2002): 10–20.

Rodning, Christopher B., and Amber M. VanDerwarker. "Revisiting Coweeta Creek: Reconstructing Ancient Cherokee Lifeways in Southwestern North Carolina." *Southeastern Archaeology* 21, no. 1 (Summer 2002): 1–9.

Royce, Charles C. "The Cherokee Nation of Indians: A Narrative of their Official Relations with the Colonial and Federal Governments." Bureau of American Ethnology, *Fifth Annual Report* (1883–1884): 121–378.

———. "Indian Land Cessions in the United States." Bureau of American Ethnology, *Eighth Annual Report* (1896–1897): part 2, 527–997.

Sullivan, Martin. "Return of the Sacred Wampum Belts of the Iroquois." *History Teacher* 26, no. 1 (November 1992): 7–14.

Swain, David L. "Historical Sketch of the Indian War of 1776." *North Carolina University Magazine* 1, no. 4 (May 1852): 132–136.

VanDerwarker, Amber M., and Kandace R. Detwiler. "Gendered Practice in Cherokee Foodways: A Spatial Analysis of Plant Remains from the Coweeta Creek Site." *Southeastern Archaeology* 21, no. 1 (Summer 2002): 21–28.

Weeks, Stephen B. "General Joseph Martin and the War of the Revolution in the West." *American Historical Association Annual Report for the Year 1893.* Washington, DC: American Historical Association, 1894.

Williams, Samuel C. "Colonel Elijah Clarke in the Tennessee Country." *Georgia Historical Quarterly* 25, no. 2 (June 1941): 151–158.

Wilson, Gregory D., and Christopher B. Rodning. "Boiling, Baking, and Pottery Breaking: A Functional Analysis of Ceramic Vessels from Coweeta Creek." *Southeastern Archaeology* 21, no. 1 (Summer 2002): 29–35.

Books

Albright, Edward. *Early History of Middle Tennessee.* Nashville: Brandon Printing, 1909.

Alden, John Richard. *John Stuart and the Southern Colonial Frontier: A Study of Indian Relations, War, Trade, and Land Problems in the Southern Wilderness, 1754–1775.* Ann Arbor: University of Michigan Press, 1944.

Aron, Stephen. *How the West Was Lost: The Transformation of Kentucky from Daniel Boone to Henry Clay.* Baltimore: Johns Hopkins University Press, 1996.

Ashe, Samuel A. *The History of North Carolina.* 2 vols. Greensboro, NC: Charles L. Van Noppen, 1908.

———. *Rutherford's Expedition against the Indians, 1776.* Raleigh, NC: E. M. Uzzel, 1904.

Bakeless, John. *Daniel Boone.* Harrisburg, PA: Stackpole, 1939.

Bartram, William. *William Bartram Travels.* New Haven, CT: Yale University Press, 1958. Reprint. Salt Lake City: Peregrine Smith, 1980.

Bass, Robert D. *Ninety-Six: The Struggle for the South Carolina Back Country.* Lexington, KY: Sandlapper Store, 1978.

Brown, Douglas S. *The Catawba Indians: The People of the River.* Columbia: University of South Carolina Press, 1966.

Brown, John P. *Old Frontiers: The Story of the Cherokee Indians from Earliest Times to the Date of their Removal to the West, 1838.* Kingsport, TN: Southern Publishers, 1938.

Butler, Mann. *A History of the Commonwealth of Kentucky*. Louisville: Wilcox, Dickerman, 1834.

Calloway, Colin G. *The American Revolution in Indian Country: Crisis and Diversity in Native American Communities*. Cambridge: Cambridge University Press, 1995.

———. *New Worlds for All: Indians, Europeans, and the Remaking of Early America*. Baltimore: Johns Hopkins University Press, 1997.

———. *The Scratch of a Pen: 1763 and the Transformation of North America*. New York: Oxford University Press, 2006.

Caruso, John A. *The Appalachian Frontier: America's First Surge Westward*. Indianapolis: Bobbs-Merrill, 1959.

Cashin, Edward J., Jr. *The King's Ranger: Thomas Brown and the American Revolution on the Southern Frontier*. Athens: University of Georgia Press, 1989.

Cashin, Edward J., Jr., and Heard Robertson. *Augusta and the American Revolution: Events in the Georgia Backcountry, 1773–1783*. Darien, GA: Ashantilly Press, 1975.

Champagne, Duane. *Social Order and Political Change: Constitutional Governments among the Cherokee, the Choctaw, the Chickasaw, and the Creek*. Stanford: Stanford University Press, 1992.

Chapman, John A. *History of Edgefield County, From the Earliest Settlements to 1897*. Newberry, SC: Elbert H. Aull, 1897.

Charleton, Thomas U. P. *The Life of Major General James Jackson*. Augusta, GA: G. F. Randolph, 1809.

Coleman, J. Winston, Jr. *The British Invasion of Kentucky: With an Account of the Capture of Ruddell's and Martin's Stations, June 1780*. Lexington, KY: Winburn Press, 1951.

Coleman, Kenneth. *The American Revolution in Georgia, 1763–1789*. Athens: University of Georgia Press, 1958.

Collins, Lewis. *Historical Sketches of Kentucky . . . Divines, etc.* Maysville, KY: Lewis Collins, 1848. Reprint. New York: Arno Press, 1971.

Corkran, David H. *The Cherokee Frontier: Conflict and Survival, 1740–1762*. Norman: University of Oklahoma Press, 1962.

———. *The Creek Frontier, 1540–1783*. Civilization of the American Indian Series, no. 86. Norman: University of Oklahoma Press, 1967.

Cotterill, Robert S. *The Southern Indians: The Story of the Civilized Tribes before Removal*. Norman: University of Oklahoma Press, 1954.

Crane, Verner W. *The Southern Frontier, 1670–1732*. Ann Arbor: University of Michigan Press, 1929.

Crow, Jeffrey J., and Larry E. Tise, eds. *The Southern Experience in the American Revolution*. Chapel Hill: University of North Carolina Press, 1978.

De Vorsey, Louis, Jr. *The Indian Boundary in the Southern Colonies, 1763–1775*. Chapel Hill: University of North Carolina Press, 1966.

Dowd, Gregory Evans. *A Spirited Resistance: The North American Indian Struggle for Unity, 1745–1815*. Baltimore: Johns Hopkins University Press, 1992.

Elliott, Lawrence. *The Long Hunter: A New Life of Daniel Boone*. New York: Reader's Digest Press, 1976.

Faragher, John Mack. *Daniel Boone: The Life and Legend of an American Pioneer*. New York: Henry Holt, 1992.

Finger, John R. *Tennessee Frontiers: Three Regions in Transition*. Bloomington: Indiana University Press, 2001.

Foster, H. Thomas, II. *Archaeology of the Lower Muskogee Creek Indians, 1715–1836*. Tuscaloosa: University of Alabama Press, 2007.

Freeze, Gary R. *The Catawbans: Crafters of a North Carolina County, 1747–1900*. Newton, NC: Catawba County Historical Association, 1995.

Friend, Craig Thompson. *Kentucke's Frontiers*. Bloomington: Indiana University Press, 2010.

Goodwin, Gary C. *Cherokees in Transition: A Study of Changing Culture and Environment Prior to 1775*. Chicago: University of Chicago, Department of Geography, Research Paper 181, 1977.

Gordon, John W. *South Carolina and the American Revolution: A Battlfield History*. Columbia: University of South Carolina Press, 2003.

Grenier, John. *The First Way of War: American War Making on the Frontier, 1607–1814*. Cambridge: Cambridge University Press, 2005.

Hatley, M. Thomas. *The Dividing Paths: Cherokees and South Carolinians through the Era of Revolution*. New York: Oxford University Press, 1995.

Hays, Louise F. *The Hero of Hornet's Nest: A Biography of Elijah Clark, 1733–1799*. New York: Stratford House, 1946.

Haywood, John. *The Civil and Political History of the State of Tennessee, from Its Earliest Settlement up to the Year 1796, Including the Boundaries of the State*. Knoxville: Heiskell and Brown, 1823.

Hoffman, Ronald, and Peter J. Albert, eds. *An Uncivil War: The Southern Backcountry during the American Revolution*. Charlottesville: University Press of Virginia, 1985.

Hunt, Caroline C. *Oconee: Temporary Boundary*. University of Georgia, Laboratory of Archeology Series, Report no. 10. Athens: Department of Anthropology, Laboratory of Archeology, 1973.

Hunter, C. L. *Sketches of Western North Carolina, Historical and Biographical*. Raleigh, NC: Raleigh News Steam Job Print, 1877.

Klein, Rachel. *Unification of a Slave State: The Rise of the Planter Class in the South Carolina Backcountry, 1760-1808*. Chapel Hill: University of North Carolina Press, 1990.

Klinck, Carl F., and James J. Talman, eds. *The Journal of John Norton 1816*. Toronto: Champlain Society, 1970.

Lambert, Robert Stansbury. *South Carolina Loyalists in the American Revolution*. 2nd ed. Clemson, SC: Clemson University, 2010.

Lester, William Stewart. *The Transylvania Colony*. Spencer, IN: Samuel R. Guard, 1935.

Malone, Henry T. *Cherokees of the Old South*. Athens: University of Georgia Press, 1956.

Mancall, Peter C., and James Hart Merrell. *American Encounters: Natives and Newcomers from European Contact to Indian Removal, 1500–1850*. New York: Routledge, 2000.

Mason, Kathryn Harrod. *James Harrod of Kentucky*. Baton Rouge: Louisiana State University Press, 1951.

McCall, Hugh. *The History of Georgia: Containing Brief Sketches of the Most Remarkable Events up to the Present Day*. Savannah, GA: Seymour & Williams, 1811.

McClain, G. Lee. *Military History of Kentucky*. Frankfort, KY: State Journal, 1939.

Merrell, James H. *The Indians' New World: Catawbas and Their Neighbors from European Contact through the Era of Removal*. Chapel Hill: University of North Carolina Press, 1989.

Mohr, Walter H. *Federal Indian Relations, 1774–1788*. Philadelphia: University of Pennsylvania Press, 1933.

Mooney, James. *James Mooney's History, Myths, and Sacred Formulas of the Cherokees*. Asheville, NC: Historical Images, 1992.

Morgan, Robert. *Boone: A Biography*. Chapel Hill, NC: Algonquin Books of Chapel Hill, 2007.

O'Donnell, James H., III. *The Cherokees of North Carolina in the American Revolution*. Raleigh: North Carolina State University Graphics, 1976.

———. *The Southern Indians in the American Revolution*. Knoxville: University of Tennessee Press, 1973.

Piecuch, Jim. *Three Peoples, One King: Loyalists, Indians, and Slaves in the Revolutionary South, 1775–1782*. Columbia: University of South Carolina Press, 2008.

Piker, Joshua. *Okfuskee: A Creek Indian Town in Colonial America.* Cambridge, MA: Harvard University Press, 2004.

Putnam, A. W. *History of Middle Tennessee, or, Life and Times of Gen. James Robertson.* Nashville: n.p., 1859. Reprint, Knoxville: University of Tennessee Press, 1971.

Ramsey, J. G. M. *The Annals of Tennessee to the End of the Eighteenth Century.* Charleston, SC: John Russell, 1853.

Ranck, George W. *Boonesborough: Its Founding, Pioneer Struggles, Indian Experiences, Transylvania Days, and Revolutionary Annals.* Filson Club Publication no. 16. Louisville, KY: John P. Morton, 1901.

Rand, James H. *The North Carolina Indians and Their Relations with the Settlers.* Chapel Hill: University of North Carolina Press, 1913.

Reid, John Phillip. *A Law of Blood: The Primitive Law of the Cherokee Nation.* New York: New York University Press, 1970.

Reinbold, D. J., and A. C. Johnston. *Historical Seismicity in the Southern Appalachian Seismic Zone.* Open-File Report 87–433, US Geological Survey, Department of the Interior, 1987.

Rice, Otis K. *Frontier Kentucky.* Lexington: University Press of Kentucky, 1975.

Roosevelt, Theodore. *The Winning of the West.* 4 vols. New York: G. P. Putnam's Sons, 1889.

Rozema, Vicki. *Footsteps of the Cherokees: A Guide to the Eastern Homelands of the Cherokee Nation.* Winston-Salem, NC: John F. Blair, 1995.

Schroedl, Gerald F. "Cherokee Ethnohistory and Archaeology from 1540 to 1838." In *Powhattan's Mantle: Indians in the Colonial Southeast,* edited with an introduction by Gregory A. Waselkov, Peter H. Wood, and Tom Hatley. Lincoln: University of Nebraska Press, 2006.

Shaw, Helen L. *British Administration of the Southern Indians, 1756–1783.* Lancaster, PA: Lancaster Press, 1931.

Smith, Marvin T. *Historic Period Indian Archaeology of Northern Georgia.* University of Georgia, Laboratory of Archaeology Series, Report no. 30. Georgia Archaeological Research Design Paper no. 7. Athens: University of Georgia, Department of Anthropology, 1992.

Smith, Marvin T., Mark Williams, Chester B. DePratter, Marshall Williams, and Mike Harmon. *Archaeological Investigations at Tomassee (38OC186) A Lower Cherokee Town.* Research Manuscript Series 206. Box Springs, GA: LAMAR Institute, 1988.

Sosin, Jack M. *The Revolutionary Frontier, 1763–1783*. New York: Holt, Rinehart and Winston, 1967.

Steele, Ian K. *Warpaths: Invasions of North America*. New York: Oxford University Press, 1994.

Stevens, Reverend William Bacon. *A History of Georgia, from Its First Discovery by Europeans to the Adoption of the Present Constitution in MDCCXCVIII*. 2 vols. Philadelphia: E. H. Butler, 1859.

Summers, Lewis Preston. *History of Southwest Virginia, 1746–1786, Washington County, 1777–1870*. Richmond, VA: J. L. Hill Printing, 1903.

Swanton, John R. *Early History of the Creek Indians and Their Neighbors*. Bureau of American Ethnology Bulletin no. 73. Washington, DC: Government Printing Office, 1922. Reprint, Gainesville: University Press of Florida, 1998.

———. *The Indians of the Southeastern United States*. Bureau of American Ethnology Bulletin no. 137. Washington, DC: Government Printing Office, 1946. Reprint, Washington, DC: Smithsonian Institution Press, 1979.

Whitaker, Arthur P. *The Spanish-American Frontier, 1783–1795*. New York: Houghton Mifflin, 1927.

Williams, Mark. *Shovel Testing of the Estatoe Site 9St3*. LAMAR Institute Report 70. Box Springs, GA: LAMAR Institute, 2004.

Williams, Marshall W. *The Estatoe Towns*. LAMAR Institute Publication 142. Box Springs, GA: LAMAR Institute, 2009.

Williams, Samuel Cole. *Tennessee during the Revolutionary War*. Nashville: Tennessee Historical Commission, 1944. Reprint, Knoxville: University of Tennessee Press, 1974.

Wilson, David. *The Southern Strategy: Britain's Conquest of South Carolina and Georgia, 1775-1780*. Columbia: University of South Carolina Press, 2005.

Wilson, Samuel M. *Battle of the Blue Licks, August 19, 1782*. Lexington, KY: n.p., 1927.

Young, Chester Raymond, ed. *Westward into Kentucky: The Narrative of Daniel Trabue*. Lexington: University Press of Kentucky, 1981.

Theses and Dissertations

Abram, Susan. "'Souls in the Treetops': Cherokee War, Masculinity, and Community, 1760–1820." PhD diss., Auburn University, 2009.

Ferguson, Clyde A. "General Andrew Pickens." PhD diss., Duke University, 1960.

MacDonald, James M. "Politics of the Personal in the Old North State: Griffith Rutherford in Revolutionary North Carolina." PhD diss., Louisiana State University, 2006.

Pate, James Paul. "The Chickamauga: A Forgotten Segment of Indian Resistance on the Southern Frontier." PhD diss., Mississippi State University, 1969.

Sheftall, John McKay. "George Galphin and Indian-White Relations in the Georgia Backcountry during the American Revolution." Master's thesis, University of Virginia, May 1983.

Index

Acknowledgments

There are always those who provide invaluable assistance to a project of this magnitude. The specialized knowledge of the staffs at the Georgia Historical Society, the Georgia Department of Archives and History, the South Caroliniana Library at the University of South Carolina, the Perkins Library at Duke University, the Tennessee State Library and Archives, the Pierpont Morgan Library, the Cooper Library of Clemson University, and the Hargrett Rare Book and Manuscript Library at the University of Georgia proved indispensable. Special mention must be made of the staff at the Ralph B. Draughon Library, Auburn University, particularly Marilyn Floyd, Joyce Ledbetter, Kitty Siu, and Liza Weisbrod, without whose gracious assistance and knowledge this work would not have been possible.

I would also like thank my publisher Bruce H. Franklin, my copy editor Ron Silverman, Trudi Gershenov for the beautiful cover design, and Paul Dangel for his maps. A special thank you must also be given to Beth Topping, whose extensive and probing knowledge of English grammar has improved my writing abilities. She was always at the ready with a humorous and calming, "Their, they're," and an encouraging pat on the back. The acknowledgment of family and friends would be too extensive, but mention must be made of Shirley and Al for always believing.

CHEROKEE LANDS

Lower Towns

Cherokee

A MAP OF
the LANDS Ceded by the CHERO-
KEE INDIANS to the STATE of
SOUTH — CAROLINA
At a Congress held in May A.D 1777
Containing about 1,697,700 Acres

STATE OF GEORGIA

Tugulo River

KEOWEE RIVER

West Lon. from Charleston.

"A map of the lands ceded by the Cherokee Indians to the state of South Carolina at a congress held in May AD 1777, containing about 1,697,700 acres." The Savannah River is shown at the bottom center and extends to the "Fork of the Savanna River" where the Tugulo [Tugaloo] and Keewohee [Keowee] rivers meet. Moving north along the Keowee River, the important Cherokee town of Seneca is shown along with Fort Rutledge, followed by the principal Cherokee Lower Town of Keewohee [Keowee]. To the west along the Tugaloo, is the Lower Town of Tugulo [Tugaloo]. Note that the map illustrates that Cherokee towns along rivers occupied both banks. (*Library of Congress*)

The Abduction of Daniel Boone's Daughter by the Indians by Carl Wimar (1853). See page 57. (Amon Carter Museum)